EUROPE'S NETWORK INDUSTRIES: CONFLICTING PRIORITIES

Telecommunications

Monitoring European Deregulation 1

Lars Bergman
Stockholm School of Economics

Chris Doyle
London Business School

Jordi Gual
IESE, Universidad de Navarra, and CEPR

Lars Hultkrantz
Dalarna University, Borlänge

Damien Neven
Université de Lausanne, and CEPR

Lars-Hendrik Röller
Wissenschaftszentrum Berlin für Sozialforschung, and CEPR

Leonard Waverman
London Business School

Romesh Vaitilingam (Editor)

Centre for Economic Policy Research

The Centre for Economic Policy Research (CEPR) is a network of over 400 Research Fellows, based primarily in European universities. The Centre coordinates its Fellows' research activities and communicates their results to the public and private sectors. CEPR is an entrepreneur, developing research initiatives with the producers, consumers and sponsors of research. Established in 1983, CEPR is a European economics research organization with uniquely wide-ranging scope and activities.

CEPR is a registered educational charity. Institutional (core) finance for the Centre is provided by major grants from the Economic and Social Research Council, under which an ESRC Resource Centre operates within CEPR; the Esmée Fairbairn Charitable Trust; the Bank of England; the European Monetary Institute and the Bank for International Settlements; 21 national central banks and 42 companies. None of these organizations gives prior review to the Centre's publications, nor do they necessarily endorse the views expressed therein.

The Centre is pluralist and non-partisan, bringing economic research to bear on the analysis of medium- and long-run policy questions. CEPR research may include views on policy, but the Executive Committee of the Centre does not give prior review to its publications, and the Centre takes no institutional policy positions. The opinions expressed in this report are those of the authors and not those of the Centre for Economic Policy Research.

EUROPE'S NETWORK INDUSTRIES: CONFLICTING PRIORITIES

Telecommunications

Monitoring European Deregulation 1

Centre for Economic Policy Research

90–98 Goswell Road
London
EC1V 7RR
UK

Tel: (44 171) 878 2900
Fax: (44 171) 878 2999
Email: cepr@cepr.org

© Centre for Economic Policy Research, 1998

British Library Cataloguing in Publication Data
A catalogue record for this book is available from the British Library

ISBN 1 898128 37 5

Printed and bound in the UK

SNS

SNS (the Swedish Center for Business and Policy Studies) is a private, non-profit organization with the aim of promoting research on economic and social issues of importance to public decision-makers, and making it readily accessible to a broad audience. SNS was established in 1948 as an association of concerned individuals in the Swedish business community. Today, SNS has more than 5,000 individual members and about 250 corporate subscribers, including Sweden's largest corporations and most important government agencies. SNS engages social scientists at leading universities in applied research on topical policy problems. It is also one of Sweden's major publishers in social sciences.

SNS sees its unique role in Sweden as a bridge between social science research and decision-making in business and public life. It provides an independent forum for discussion of policy issues among prominent individuals in business, the political sphere, the media and the academic community. As an organization, SNS does not take a stand on policy matters.

Traditionally, the activities of SNS have focused mainly on the domestic scene. To an increasing extent we now engage academic expertise from other countries, arrange meetings abroad and collaborate with similar organizations in other countries. The collaboration with CEPR is an important example of this.

July 1998

SNS
Studieförbundet Näringsliv och Samhälle
Center for Business and Policy Studies
Box 5629
SE-114 86 Stockholm
Sweden

Tel: (46 8) 453 99 50
Fax: (46 8) 20 50 41
Email: info@sns.se
Website: http://www.sns.se

Contents

MED Steering Committee Members

Lars Bergman
Stockholm School of Economics

Chris Doyle
London Business School

Damien Neven
Université de Lausanne, and CEPR

David Newbery
University of Cambridge, and CEPR

Lars-Hendrik Röller
Wissenschaftszentrum Berlin für Sozialforschung, and CEPR

Xavier Vives
Institut d'Anàlisi Econòmica, CSIC, Barcelona

Leonard Waverman
London Business School

Reference Group Members: MED 1 (Telecommunications)

Per Olof Åkerberg, *Ericsson*

C Boreggi, *Telecom Italia*

Laurent Citi, *Alcatel*

M W de Jong, *KPN Telecom, Netherlands*

Jürg Eberhart, *Swisscom*

Aimo Eloholma, *Telecom Finland (Sonera)*

Alan Harper, *Vodafone Group*

Hans Munk Jensen, *TeleDanmark*

A C Ketelaars, *Enertel*

Jan Loeber, *Hermes Europe Railtel*

Paul Richards, *British Telecommunications*

Bertil Thorngren, *Telia*

David Twyver, *Teledesic*

Bengt Westerberg, *Telia (Chairman of Reference Group)*

List of Figures

List of Tables

Foreword

The regulation of 'network' industries has emerged as a key issue on the European policy agenda. Yet there has been very little applied, high-quality research capable of guiding European policy-makers on this issue. In the telecommunications sector, the actions of the regulators, at both the EU and national level, will have a vital impact on the growth and prosperity of European firms and the European economy. There is a serious risk that new Europe-wide regulation will tilt the playing field in favour of some competitors, with detrimental consequences for the ultimate consumers of telecommunications services and the long-run development of the industry as a whole.

The Centre for Economic Policy Research (CEPR) and the Swedish Center for Business and Policy Studies (SNS) decided in 1997 to initiate a comprehensive research effort specifically addressed to the issues of regulation and deregulation in European network industries. The aim is to bring together, each year, a team which includes some of Europe's leading researchers in the field of network industries.

We are delighted to introduce the 1998 report, the first product of this collaborative research project examining network industries. The team has produced a survey of the developments in deregulation in network industries in general, as well as a comprehensive review of the telecoms sector in particular. CEPR and SNS appreciate the work of the authors and feel sure that their research will have a significant impact on the industry. This report will be required reading for anyone interested in deregulation issues. We are very grateful to the members of the Reference Group for their unflagging interest at all stages of the research. The Reference Group has been chaired by Mr Bengt Westerberg, former vice-Prime Minister of Sweden and former Chairman of the Board of Telia, and has consisted of representatives from the corporations which, through their financial support, have made the research possible. These corporations are listed overleaf. The views expressed in the report are those of the authors, writing in their personal capacity: the Reference Group has produced a separate statement. Neither CEPR nor SNS take any institutional policy positions.

Richard Portes   Hans Tson Söderström
President   *President and CEO*
CEPR   *SNS*

July 1998

Paying corporations:

Alcatel
British Telecommunications
Enertel
Ericsson
Hermes Europe Railtel
KPN Telecom, Netherlands
Swisscom
TeleDanmark
Telecom Finland
Telecom Italia
Teledesic
Telia
Vodafone Group

Executive Summary

The establishment of a single market and the promotion of competition in Europe's network industries (air, electricity, maritime, natural gas, postal services, telecommunications and rail) have been at the forefront of economic and industrial policy in Europe in recent years. These industries have traditionally been sheltered from competition and operated within national or regional boundaries, but deregulation in the late 1980s and 1990s has greatly changed their structure. Whereas at one time most European consumers had little or no choice over the supplier of a network service, today there is an increasing number of firms operating in most of these industries, none more so than in the airline services and telecommunications industries.

Although deregulation has brought competition to Europe's network industries, regulation is still at the centre stage of activity. Indeed, the conflicts between competition and monopoly, and market forces and regulation, give rise to many challenging policy problems. In this Report these problems are addressed by exploring ten conflicting priorities that European policy-makers face in defining an appropriate competition and regulatory policy framework for the network industries. Throughout the Report it is stressed that appropriate policy should take due account of dynamic considerations for otherwise investment and innovation, and therefore consumer well being and employment, may be adversely affected.

While competition has or is being introduced into Europe's network industries, several factors, if left unchecked, constrain its effectiveness: a history of monopoly control, widespread public ownership and state aids, political and institutional diversity, public service objectives, and the need for network interconnection between rival firms. For these reasons regulatory scrutiny is perhaps needed more in the network industries than in most other European industries.

In the first part of the Report (Chapters 1–7) the general principles governing competition and regulatory policy for the network industries are discussed in detail. In the second part of the Report (Chapters 8–13) the focus is on the telecommunications industry. Appendix 1 gives details of some key European legislation and procedures. Chapter 1 identifies three phases of market structure as being crucial to the network industries. Here it is shown that deregulation means that the network industries in Europe are evolving along a path from monopoly (phase 1), to monopoly and competition (phase 2), and possibly to competition (phase 3). Today in Europe most of the industries lie in phases 1 or 2. Because most of the industries feature monopoly and competition, this gives rise to many problems. Somewhat paradoxically at the beginning of phase 2 when a network industry is opened up to competition more rather than less regulation is required. Over time, however, competition should become more effective during phase 2 and the need for regulation should diminish.

Chapter 2 looks at the vertical structure of network industries and outlines the significance of these industries to the European economy. In Chapter 3 the economic characteristics of network industries are described and the importance of natural monopoly, oligopoly, interconnection, externalities, coordination, standards and convergence are explored.

In Chapter 4 ten conflicting priorities are identified as characterizing the regulatory environment in European network industries in phase 2 where competition and monopoly coexist. These are: short-term versus longer-term objectives; efficiency versus equity objectives; competition versus monopoly; slow versus fast liberalization; public versus private ownership; sector specific regulation versus general competition law; rules versus discretion; permanent versus temporary regulation; centralized versus decentralized regulation; and light-handed versus heavy-handed regulation. Each conflicting priority is examined in detail and implications for policy are discussed.

In Chapter 5 there is a detailed description of deregulation in the network industries in Europe. This commences by looking at the relevant articles in the European Treaty guiding European deregulation policy, which includes a discussion on state aids. This is followed by a detailed exposition on European deregulation in each of the industries. The chapter also contains a discussion on country level deregulation, which includes an assessment of the experience in the United Kingdom.

Chapter 6 provides a thorough account on the economic principles that shape policy in phase 2. This includes a discussion on policies designed to prevent monopoly abuse in both retail and interconnect markets. In addition to policy that is directed towards achieving economic efficiency, the chapter also looks at equity and the role of universal service.

Having assessed the principles of economic policy and the way in which deregulation has occurred, Chapter 7 provides a normative account of the role played by regulators and regulatory institutions. Both the form and level of regulation are discussed in detail. It is suggested that a two-tier regulatory structure, which builds on existing practice in Europe, would be likely to yield a more robust regulatory environment. In particular, it is highlighted that there is a need for more central authority in some areas of competition and regulatory policy. This could be achieved by strengthening existing institutions in Europe rather than through the establishment of new European regulatory authorities.

The second part of the Report focuses specifically on the telecommunications services industry, a sector where shifting patterns of ownership and market structure in combination with extraordinary technological change are creating enormous challenges for regulators at both the EU and national level.

Chapter 8 sets the scene by describing how the industry is shifting in various directions. It is argued that it is no longer straightforward to define what is meant by the telecommunications industry as convergence and other factors are blurring traditional market boundaries. In Chapter 9 European deregulation in the telecommunications industry and the role of the European Commission are discussed. It is pointed out that telecommunications in Europe does not yet comprise a single market as there is much diversity in policy implementation and other areas among the Member States of the EU.

In Chapter 10 the key policy issues surfacing as the industry moves into phase 2 are examined. The obstacles to effective competition are identified and the problem of regulating prices is discussed. In particular, attention is paid to interconnection and unbundling. In Chapter 11 the social impact of telecommunications is assessed with a detailed analysis of policy on universal service.

Having established and discussed the chief areas of concern for policy makers, Chapter 12 addresses the required regulatory regulatory and institutional framework. Here three options for the institutional regulatory framework are considered: (1) A European Communications Commission; (2) Self-regulation through an affiliation of national regulators; and (3) Two-tier regulation aimed at greater harmonization. It is argued that the third option, which implies building on the existing two-tier system of regulation, is the preferred way forward.

In Chapter 13 a variety of policies are presented as suitable for taking the European telecommunications industry forward towards a competitive market structure. The emphasis here is on ensuring that policy is designed and implemented so that objectives are attained while preserving desirable investment incentives. Symmetric regulation between incumbents and entrants is advocated. Universal service is argued to be a problem area and it is suggested that issues like internet for schools properly belong in education policy and not in telecommunications policy. Establishing two-tier regulation and greater consistency in European competition and regulatory policy is also reiterated.

Acknowledgements

The deregulation of Europe's network industries presents many challenging problems for policy-makers. We are grateful to Richard Portes and Hans Tson Söderström for establishing the MED Report. In this Report we have endeavoured to clarify the key problems by identifying the main conflicting priorities in policy and suggesting remedies. This task would not have been possible without help of the CEPR, SNS and the Reference Group.

During drafting we received comments from a wide range of people and are grateful to everyone. In particular, we would like to thank Per Olof Åkerberg of Ericsson, Otto Bjoerklund of Nokia, Claudio Boreggi of Telecom Italia, John Butler of British Telecommunications, Mark de Jong of KPN and the University of Amsterdam, Christian Koboldt of London Economics, Aimo Eloholma of Telecom Finland, Alan Harper of Vodafone, Stefan Sandström of SNS, Bertil Thorngren of the Stockholm School of Economics, Bengt Westerberg former Chairman of Telia, and Stephen Yeo of CEPR. We are also grateful to all those of commented on the Report at its presentation to the International Telecommunications Society Biennial World Conference, Stockholm, June 1998.

We received excellent comments when the Report was presented to the European Commission on 13 July 1998. Special thanks go to Directors Stefan Micossi of DGIII and Robert Verrue of DGXIII and their colleagues, especially Richard Cawley of DGXIII and Alexander Spachis of DGXV.

The authors would like to thank the CEPR for providing excellent administration and support during the writing of the Report. We are especially indebted to Sue Chapman, Joan Concannon, Kate Millward, Constanze Picking and Justine Supple. We should also like to thank Bridget Allen for performing a valiant copy-editing task.

A special thanks is extended to Romesh Vaitilingam who read a draft of the entire manuscript and made numerous comments that helped to improve the Report enormously.

Lars Bergman kindly acknowledges administrative support from SNS. Chris Doyle would like to acknowledge financial support from ACE project 'Emerging Liberalised Telecommunications Market: Interconnection and Tariff Policies in the Central European Countries', grant P96-6100-R and for administrative support from the London Business School Regulation Initiative. Lars-Hendrik Röller is grateful to WZB for providing administrative support during the drafting of the Report.

Finally, the views expressed herein are our own and all errors are, of course, our responsibility.

PART 1: General Principles and European Deregulation

Lars Bergman
Chris Doyle
Damien Neven
Lars-Hendrik Röller

1 Introduction

The internal market shall comprise an area without internal frontiers in which the free movement of goods, persons, services and capital is ensured in accordance with the provisions of this Treaty.[1]

Market forces produce a better allocation of resources and greater effectiveness in the supply of services, the principal beneficiary being the consumer, who gets better quality at a lower price.[2]

In recent years, European economic and industrial policy has been directed towards deregulation through the establishment of the internal market and the promotion of competition.[3] As a consequence, network industries like energy (electricity and natural gas), postal services, telecoms, transport (air, maritime, and rail) and water (domestic supplies and water treatment), which have traditionally been sheltered from competition and operated within national or regional boundaries, have experienced great change. Whereas at one time, most European consumers had little or no choice over the supplier of a network service, today there is an increasing number of firms operating in most of these industries.

Although deregulation has brought competition to the network industries, regulation is still at the centre stage of economic policy. Indeed, the conflicts between competition and monopoly, and between market forces and regulation, give rise to many challenging policy problems. In this Report, these problems are addressed by examining ten conflicting priorities that arise in Europe's network industries. Throughout, it is suggested that careful policy design needs to take account of dynamic and long-term considerations. Otherwise, investment and innovation may be adversely affected, which will in turn have negative implications for consumer well-being and employment.

1.1 Liberalization: constraints on competition

The purpose of introducing competition into Europe's network industries is to promote greater rivalry among firms, leading to improved productivity, wider consumer choice and lower prices. Productivity improvements should also play a crucial role in stimulating the competitiveness of European industry as a whole. While competition has been or is being introduced into these industries, several factors, if left unchecked, constrain its effectiveness and diminish its benefits. The most significant constraining factors are:

- the legacy of monopoly control;
- widespread public ownership and state aids;
- political and institutional diversity;
- public service objectives;
- the existence of natural monopoly (bottlenecks) elements within network infrastructures and the need for network interconnection between rival networks.

Monopoly provision of network services has been the prevailing market structure throughout Europe for most of the second half of the twentieth century. Competition is therefore being introduced to an environment in which there are large and often dominant 'incumbent' firms in many national and regional markets. During the early stages of liberalization, these powerful incumbents may be in a position to exercise monopoly power.

Many of the incumbents operating in the European network industries are wholly or majority owned public enterprises. The considerable involvement of public authorities in these industries, in which private operators are increasingly seeking to enter, raises serious concerns about fairness, particularly with regard to the raising of funds to support restructuring. The role of state aid to publicly owned enterprises is very carefully monitored in Europe, but its effect on new competition in the network industries can be damaging.

The 15 Member States that make up the EU have different political and institutional structures. The existence of national-based competition law and regulations suitable for one country may be less suitable in another. What is more, this diversity increases transaction costs faced by companies and consumers engaged in trade across borders. Where transaction costs are significant, competition may be adversely affected.

Box 1 Generic characteristics of network industries

Network industries share a number of features. In particular, they involve the delivery of products and services to final consumers via a 'network infrastructure'. The infrastructure of a network is comprised of many different elements, linking upstream supply units with customers lying downstream. A typical network industry therefore has three key components: (i) core products; (ii) network infrastructure; and (iii) customer supply and service provision. As shown in Figure 1, these may be aligned to suggest that network industries have a vertical structure: core products and services are supplied into the network infrastructure by firms lying upstream, and final consumers receive services from service providers lying downstream. When a firm operates two or more connected components in a network industry, it is vertically integrated (see also Figure 3 (a) on p. 14).

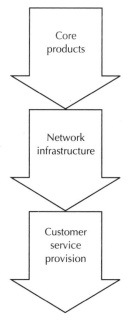

Figure 1 Vertical structure of a generic network industry

Many network industries provide essential services of general economic interest. Few would disagree, for example, that clean domestic water supply is essential and in the general interest. Because of the importance of certain network industries, like the water supply industry, many politicians believe that firms operating in network industries should be subject to special public service objectives. In some cases, political intervention of this kind can be justified in terms of fairness or equity. In practice, intervention has resulted in the imposition of public service obligations. In an environment where competition is being introduced, the setting of public service obligations can, if handled incorrectly, jeopardize competition.

Unlike most other industries, competition in network industries typically requires some degree of cooperation between rival firms to enable the interoperability of competing networks. As entrants will typically need to interconnect infrastructure with that of a dominant incumbent, there is a possibility that an incumbent may abuse its monopoly position either by refusing access to its infrastructure or by offering access on unfavourable or discriminatory terms. As a large fraction of the operating costs faced by entrants are payments made for interconnection, competition is affected significantly by the terms governing interconnection. Indeed, in many instances, competition can only be introduced into a network industry through enforcing network interconnection.

For competition to become effective in the network industries it is essential that policy takes account of these constraints.

1.2 Market structure: three phases

The liberalization of Europe's network industries, which began in the 1980s, has led to a decline in the significance of monopoly. Now, competition and monopoly elements coexist in these industries, and ultimately, deregulation may lead some of them to having fully competitive market structures.

Deregulation of the network industries in Europe means that they are evolving along a path from monopoly (phase 1), to monopoly and competition (phase 2), and possibly on to competition (phase 3). These three phases of market structure are described in Box 2, along with the industries and sectors associated with each phase.[4] It is evident that there is considerable diversity across the industries. Air transport and telecoms, for example, are highly liberalized, but most sectors within these industries have yet to progress into phase 3. Gas and electricity have not yet been liberalized, but both industries should enter phase 2 in the near future. Most industries or industry sectors currently lie in either phase 1 or phase 2 and this is likely to continue for some years to come. What is clear is that effective competition, the hallmark of phase 3, is perhaps only established in the non-reserved postal services sector.

Box 2 The three phases of market structure

Phase 1 – Monopoly
Services are supplied by one firm and regulation is concerned with the prevention of monopoly abuse in retail markets.
Airports, ports, most rail services and rail infrastructure, electricity and gas transmission, reserved postal services and water.

Phase 2 – Monopoly and competition
Competition is gradually introduced into some or all markets and regulation focuses on: monopoly abuse in both retail and interconnect markets by dominant incumbents; emerging competition issues; and public service obligations.
Airport ground-handling facilities, port handling facilities, some rail freight markets, most air services, and residential telecommunications.

Phase 3 – Competition
Here competition is extensive and increasingly effective in some or all markets. Some light-handed regulation is needed, as in other competitive markets, to ensure fair trading practices and the maintenance of public service objectives.
Some air and shipping services, some business telecommunications services, and non-reserved postal services.

There is also considerable diversity in market structure across the countries of Europe.[5] In some countries, like the United Kingdom, competition is more established; in many other countries, such as France and Italy, competition has appeared only recently or has yet to emerge. Ownership structures also vary across Europe. Many firms in Europe's network industries are under public ownership, a considerable number are under mixed public and private ownership, and a growing number are under private ownership.

1.3 Regulatory intensity

Most commentators agree that the introduction of competition into the network industries is desirable. The vertical structure of network industries and the factors constraining competition suggest, however, that much regulatory oversight may be required to ensure that competition can work effectively.

It is phase 2 that involves the greatest intensity of regulation, reflecting the presence of both monopoly and competition. Many of the challenging regulatory problems arising in phase 2 relate to interconnection: the entry of new firms into an industry coincides with demands for interconnection to existing network infrastructures (see Figures 3a and 3c, pp. 14 and 15). Where infrastructure is owned and operated by a vertically integrated incumbent, as is often the case in Europe, interconnection problems are likely to be severe. Many of these problems are compounded when private firms seek interconnection with publicly owned firms, and in Europe public ownership in the network industries remains pervasive.

It is also in phase 2 when public service (fairness or equity) objectives need to be reassessed. Under monopoly provision of services in phase 1, it is relatively straightforward for public authorities to direct firms to provide certain loss-making services. Throughout Europe, prior to liberalization, monopoly firms – incumbents – in the network industries were typically subject to an array of public service obligations. These were usually financed through cross-subsidization. In other words, some customers paid prices above costs to meet the costs of serving customers who were paying prices below cost. The entry of new firms into an industry dramatically changes the incentives for incumbents to engage in cross-subsidization. Thus, regulation is required, particularly in the early stages of competition, to ensure that public service objectives are met.

Phase 2 is also the period in which greater regulation overseeing the way that publicly-owned firms obtain finance will be required.

As liberalization necessarily entails private firms competing against publicly-owned firms, the terms on which capital is provided to publicly-owned firms certainly require greater scrutiny. This is especially sensitive in Europe because many state-owned firms in the network industries have argued for state aid to finance restructuring programmes so that they are better able to compete in newly liberalized markets.

Competition issues and monopoly problems, public service objectives and public ownership in Europe's network industries indicate an important role for regulation during phase 2. Somewhat paradoxically at the beginning of phase 2 when a network industry is opened up to competition, because of the structures described above, *more* rather than less regulation is required. The intensity of regulation during phase 2 would be expected to rise initially, reflecting, for example, problems of abuse in interconnection markets. Over time, however, competition should become more effective during phase 2 and the need for regulation should diminish.

If an industry were to enter phase 3, the market would provide most incentives needed to obtain desirable outcomes. It is likely, however, that some regulation would still be required, as in other competitive industries, to ensure fair trading practices.

The expected path for the intensity of regulatory activity across the three phases of market structure is shown in Figure 2 overleaf. It should be noted that the intensity of regulation is 'humped' in phase 2: at the beginning, regulatory intensity rises before declining when competition is more firmly established. Furthermore, regulatory intensity in phase 3 lies below that in phase 1: unsurprisingly, when an industry structure is competitive there is much less need for regulation. After all, regulation is largely a surrogate for missing competition in phases 1 and 2.[6]

1.4 Ten conflicting priorities

The coexistence of competition and monopoly, competition between private and public firms, interconnection and the setting of public service objectives raise many conflicting priorities for regulatory policy-makers during phase 2. In this Report, ten conflicting priorities are identified as characterizing the regulatory environment in European network industries in this phase (see Box 3 overleaf).

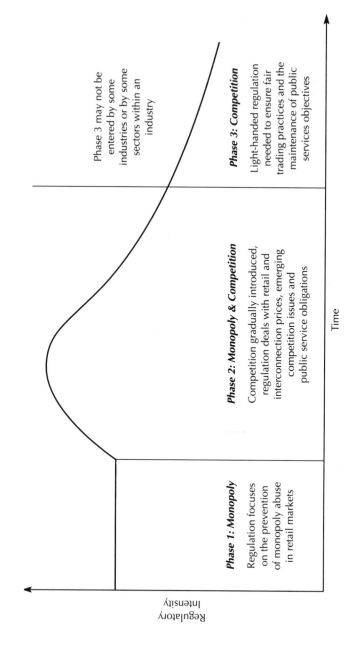

Phase 1: Monopoly

Regulation focuses on the prevention of monopoly abuse in retail markets

Phase 2: Monopoly & Competition

Competition gradually introduced, regulation deals with retail and interconnection prices, emerging competition issues and public service obligations

Phase 3: Competition

Light-handed regulation needed to ensure fair trading practices and the maintenance of public services objectives

Phase 3 may not be entered by some industries or by some sectors within an industry

Regulatory Intensity

Time

Figure 2 The evolution of regulation over the three phases of market structure

Box 3 Ten conflicting priorities

Ten conflicting priorities arise in phase 2 and complicate the problem of designing regulatory policy to govern the network industries:

1. Short-term versus longer-term objectives.
2. Efficiency versus equity objectives.
3. Competition versus monopoly (incorporating infrastructure versus service-led competition).
4. Slow versus fast liberalization.
5. Public versus private ownership.
6. Sector-specific regulation versus application of general competition rules (incorporating horizontal scope of regulation).
7. Rules versus discretion.
8. Permanent versus temporary regulation.
9. Centralized versus decentralized regulation (incorporating geographical scope of regulation).
10. Light-handed versus heavy-handed regulation (incorporating vertical scope of regulation).

Conflicting priorities 1 and 2 relate to society's preferences, 3–5 relate to market structure, and 6–10 relate to regulatory structure.

1.5 The structure of the Report

In this Report, competition and regulation policy affecting Europe's network industries are examined from both a positive and normative perspective. Throughout, there is an emphasis on the dynamic consequences of policy by looking at the relationship between regulation, competition and investment, and at the evolution of market and regulatory structures. The discussion seeks to address the trade-offs encountered where priorities conflict.

The Report comprises two parts: Part 1 which examines general principles; and Part 2 which is a detailed case study of the telecoms services industry. Part 1 is structured as follows: Chapter 2 examines the structure and general significance of Europe's network industries, including an outline of the European Commission's policy on Trans-European Networks. Chapter 3 explores the economic characteristics of network industries, while Chapter 4 goes into greater detail on the ten conflicting priorities. Chapter 5 describes in detail EU policy on liberalization and harmonization in the network industries, as well as providing some history of the industries and of national liberalization policies in these industries. This chapter also features a discussion of the UK experience, where liberalization in the network industries has been the most extensive within Europe.

Chapter 6 focuses on the implementation of liberalization and the design of regulation across the three phases of market structure. Here the objectives of competition and regulation, the instruments available to policy-makers and the issue of universal service obligations are all addressed. Chapter 7 concludes Part 1 with a discussion of the scope, form and level of regulation and the dynamic design of regulatory institutions. In particular, it focuses on the potential for 'regulatory capture' and the appropriate policy response.

Notes

1 Article 7a of the EC treaty.
2 European Commission communication *Services of general interest in Europe,* OJ C 281, 26 September 1996, p. 3.
3 Unless otherwise stated, throughout this Report, Europe refers to the countries comprising the EU (the community) and policy refers to actions taken by the Community as a whole.
4 Chapter 5 below contains full details on the industries. See also Table 2 and Figure 5.
5 For example, see Box 7 below for details on diversity in the European electricity industry.
6 Chapter 7 below re-examines the evolution of regulatory intensity across the three phases from a normative perspective.

2 The Structure and Significance of Network Industries

2.1 Vertical structure

As Figure 1 above shows, network industries have three key elements: upstream production; an infrastructure; and downstream service provision. For this reason, they are often described as vertical industries. Upstream production in the gas industry involves extraction; in the electricity industry, it involves power generation; in the airline industry, it involves aircraft manufacturing; and so on. In many cases, upstream activities are competitive.

The infrastructure of a network industry is an essential input that is combined with the outputs of upstream production to enable services to be delivered to consumers lying downstream. For example, airline services can only be offered when aircraft are used together with airports and air traffic control systems.

Network industries have many possible industry structures, and below are five of the more interesting cases. In cases (i)–(iv), it is assumed that there is only one network infrastructure, possibly due to natural monopoly conditions; in case (v), competition is assumed to be viable in the infrastructure components of the industry. The five cases are:

(i)   Vertical integration and monopoly, where a single firm operates the upstream and downstream components and the network infrastructure.

(ii) Vertical integration with competition in the downstream or upstream components. This is similar to (i) except that the vertically integrated firm faces competition in the downstream and/or upstream components. In some instances, the vertically integrated firm is required to provide separate accounts for its component businesses: so-called accounting separation.

(iii) Vertical separation with upstream and/or downstream competition, but the firm operating the network infrastructure does not operate in either the upstream or downstream components.

(iv) Joint ownership, where the infrastructure is owned jointly by firms competing in the upstream and/or downstream components.

(v) Infrastructure or facilities-based competition: competing vertically integrated firms that may or may not be interconnected.

The five industry cases are illustrated in Figures 3 (a)–(c) where a single arrow denotes the direction in which goods and services flow between *different* firms, and a double arrow indicates a flow between the *same* firm.[1] Figure 3 (c) shows that the two competing vertically–integrated firms are interconnected.

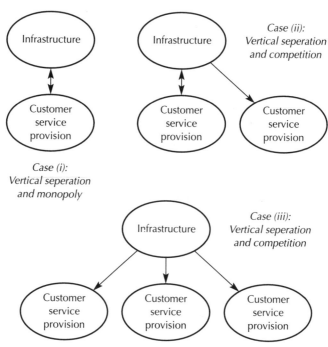

Figure 3(a) Different vertical industry structures

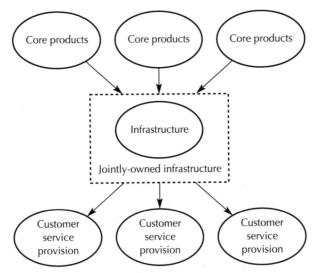

Figure 3(b) Joint-ownership of infrastructure

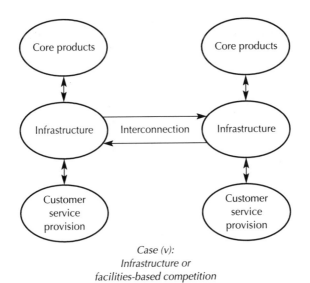

Case (v):
Infrastructure or
facilities-based competition

Figure 3(c) Facilities-based competition

2.2 The significance of network industries

The outputs of the network industries make up around 5% of Europe's GDP and their share of total EU employment is also around 5%.[2] Many of the outputs are essential inputs into production elsewhere in the economy; they are also, in many cases, vital inputs into consumption activities. The relative size and importance of these industries means that they have a significant role to play in influencing European economic growth and competitiveness. The precise relationship between network industries and economic performance is, however, difficult to quantify. Most of the evidence on the link between the network industries and economic performance derives from US experiences. The results vary considerably and the relationship remains a topic of debate.

Early studies of the impact of network industries on economic performance (for example, Aschauer, 1989) find a very significant impact. Others find little or none, certainly in terms of the infrastructure component of the network industries. For example, Hulten and Schwab (1984, see also their 1991 study) estimate a production function for the manufacturing sector on US state-level data in order to measure how much of the variance in value-added growth was attributable to factor accumulation (labour and private capital) versus total productivity growth. The underlying reasoning was that since technological progress was likely to be homogeneous throughout the United States, only differences in public infrastructure provision (transport, communications, etc.) could explain cross-state variations in the rate of total productivity growth. (It is well documented that the so-called 'Snow Belt' has suffered a dramatic decline in public infrastructure investment since around 1968.) These researchers found that public infrastructure capital was irrelevant in explaining differences in productivity growth.

More recent studies have assessed the impact of investment in telecoms and information technology infrastructure on productivity and economic growth. Again using US data, Greenstein and Spiller (1995) investigate the impact of telecoms infrastructure (as measured by the amount of fibre-optic cable employed) on economic growth. They find a positive and significant effect in one industry (output increases of 10% from doubling the amount of fibre-optic cable), but across manufacturing as a whole, the effect was less pronounced.

Lichtenberg (1995) uses firm level data on information technology investments and finds very high growth effects. Röller and Waverman (1998) investigate the impact of telecoms infrastructure (as measured by the penetration rate of exchange lines) on economic growth. Using a sample of OECD countries and accounting for the simultaneous interaction between growth and telecoms infrastructure, they find evidence that there is a positive causal link, with telecoms infrastructure accounting for as much as a sixth of economic growth. Telecoms investment is, however, only beneficial if the total telecoms infrastructure lies above a certain critical mass.

Although there are few rigorous studies quantifying the effect of network industries on performance, it is without contention that these industries are crucial for competitiveness. Europe may be progressing towards a single market, but its potential is undoubtedly handicapped by a patchwork of transport, energy and telecoms infrastructures. These were designed and built according to the needs of individual countries at a time when their economies were far less dependent on each other than they are now. As a result, there are many missing links, some physical (such as motorways that do not join up at national borders) and some technical (such as telephone lines that cannot carry advanced electronic communications).

Because of the deficiencies in some networks across boundaries within Europe, policy-makers at the European level have directed resources at establishing improved interoperability across Member State boundaries. The programme of investment associated with this policy is part of the EU Trans-European Networks (TENs) initiative (see Box 4 overleaf). The programme of support for TENs is due to be completed by the year 2000. Activities include, among other things, the development of trans-border gas, electricity and rail networks. These include electricity interconnections between France and Italy, and between France and Spain, and natural gas networks in Greece and Portugal. In the energy sector alone, 74 projects of common interest have been identified, representing a total investment of ECU 18 billion. Much of the funding is provided by operators in the energy sector, but in some cases aid has been extended.

While it is undisputed that TENs facilitate greater economic integration within Europe, and lower network-transportation costs are good for European competitiveness, the empirical literature suggests that promoting large-scale network investments through such publicly supported initiatives is not necessarily good for aggregate growth and employment.

Box 4 Trans-European Networks (TENs)

At their meeting in Brussels at the end of 1993, the European Council of heads of state and government decided to speed up the development of Trans-European Networks (TENs). They agreed with the conclusions of the European Commission's (1993) White Paper on 'Growth, Competitiveness and Employment : The challenges and way forward into the 21st century'[3] that TENs were essential to efforts to achieve a significant cut in unemployment by 2000.

The Treaty on European Union, which came into force in November 1993, established TENs in transport, energy and telecoms as formal EU objectives. Article 129 (c) (see Appendix 1 of this Report) of the EC Treaty gives the three main tasks:

- to lay down specific guidelines, which must, among other things, identify projects of common interest;
- to take the necessary steps, including technical standardization, to ensure that the networks are 'interoperable';
- to support projects of common interest by financing feasibility studies and providing loan guarantees or interest rate subsidies.

The economic rationale behind such initiatives is threefold:

- to help boost growth and employment;
- to accelerate the integration of European markets and facilitate the convergence of European regions;
- to improve European competitiveness *vis-à-vis* the rest of the world by speeding up the introduction of new technologies and reducing costs, in particular transportation costs.

Notes

1 The upstream component is not considered in Figure 3 (a) but it can be incorporated without difficulty.

2 See 'Network Industries and Public Service', Institut D'Economie Industrielle, Toulouse, Final Report, July 1997 submitted to DG II of the European Commission.

3 European Commission (1993) 'Growth competitiveness and Employment: The challenges and way forward into the 21st century' COM (93) 700, December 1993.

3 The Economic Characteristics of Network Industries

Network industries display a number of special economic characteristics, which influence questions about whether and how they should be regulated. While not *all* network industries display *all* the characteristics discussed in this section, *all* network industries are subject to at least *some* of the characteristics.

3.1 Infrastructure characteristics

The infrastructure of a network is typically a collection of nodes connected by transport links. In the electricity industry, the nodes are power plants and consumers, and the transport links are the wires that transmit electricity from the power plants to consumers. In the air transport industry, the infrastructure comprises airports and air traffic control systems.

Investments in network infrastructure tend to have two key characteristics:

- they are irreversible or 'sunk';
- they are indivisible or 'lumpy'.

The capital investments required to install a network infrastructure are often considerable, upfront, fixed and irreversible. In the gas industry, for example, the infrastructure comprises high-cost extraction rigs, high-pressure national distribution and storage pipelines, and lower-pressure regional and local distribution networks. The installation of such a network is extremely costly and many of the network components, once installed, are sunk investments. In many cases, this is because there are few alternative uses that can be made of the assets. If a nuclear power plant closes, for example, much of the capital equipment is unlikely to be of use elsewhere.

In many instances, network infrastructure investments are also lumpy, that is, they are undertaken on a large scale. Airports and inter-city rail routes are classic examples. Lumpy investments are largely responsible for the economies of scale that make some network industries natural monopolies (see Section 3.2 below).

Because investments are often sunk, it means that over time, assets may become stranded: they are unable to recoup their costs due to changed circumstances. In this regard, network assets may be viewed as idiosyncratic: they are specific to the network for which they were built.

The onset of deregulation in Europe has increased the possibility of stranded costs. These may arise after regulatory change when the costs associated with an asset cannot be recovered. Joskow (1996) defines stranded costs as the difference between the revenues needed to cover the costs of historical investments and contractual obligations made under regulatory regime A, and the revenues that will be received in the future under regulatory regime B. Stranded costs are therefore incurred at the time of liberalization. Assets that may lead to considerable stranded costs tend to be large fixed investments, such as power plants.

The existence of long-term contracts signed before liberalization, such as take-or-pay contracts in the gas industry, may also result in stranded costs. Of course, stranded costs could be positive, for example, liberalization may improve profitability if it involves the lifting of line-of-service restrictions.

3.2 Natural monopoly

Natural monopoly elements are more likely to arise in the infrastructure components of a network industry because of strong economies of scale and scope. Economies of scale are often pervasive because the relatively high degree of lumpy capital investment required to install network infrastructure often contrasts sharply with the relatively low operational costs associated with the transportation of services over the network. For example, once a telecoms network is established and there is plenty of capacity, the cost at the margin of providing a telephone call between two consumers is very small and close to zero. Most network industries are typically characterized as having a high fixed-cost element and low marginal costs. Thus, average costs decline as output increases and production costs are lower for larger scale production.

Furthermore, many network industries involve the provision of many different services sharing a common network. This is clearly the case in telecoms where voice telephony and data traffic share a common network infrastructure. The incremental cost of adding a new service is relatively low for a firm that possesses an infrastructure, whereas the cost facing a new firm is relatively high as it entails the duplication of the network infrastructure. The cost in the latter case is known as the stand-alone cost. Where there are scope economies, incremental costs will lie below stand-alone costs. Such cost characteristics in the network infrastructure result in natural monopoly conditions.

The preceding analysis largely treats the infrastructure of a network as if it were an amorphous mass. Network infrastructures are, however, very often made up of many different components, sometimes involving thousands of different elements. In the railway industry, for example, the infrastructure comprises track, signals, sidings, signalling systems, ticketing systems, tunnels, stations, traction power supply (electricity), bridges, etc. Depending on location and the size of any particular element within a typical railway network, some parts of the infrastructure may exhibit classical natural monopoly conditions whereas other parts may not be a natural monopoly at all. So, it may not be inefficient to duplicate some parts of a network.

In contrast, in telecoms, demand has grown rapidly in recent years and costs have fallen significantly. This has made duplication possible in some parts of the network infrastructure, especially in the high capacity inter-urban routes. Where this is the case, it may be possible to introduce competition into a network industry, something that has already happened in telecoms.

Of course, network industries are affected by technological innovations and these can have dramatic consequences on their structure. What is happening across many of the network industries is a gradual reduction in the significance of natural monopoly in the infrastructure. In telecoms, this has been very stark as changing technological circumstances have allowed far greater competition. In some of the other network industries, developments have been less dramatic.

Water is perhaps the network industry where natural monopoly elements remain considerable and largely static. Few people would advocate that duplicating a water supply network is efficient. Nevertheless, some parts of the water industry are potentially competitive, especially in those areas related to sewerage treatment.

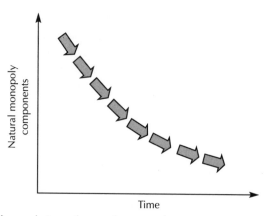

Figure 4 The evolution of natural monopoly components over time

The recent evolution affecting all of the network industries has resulted in the declining significance of natural monopoly, as Figure 4 indicates. The continued presence of natural monopoly conditions in some parts of the network and, in some cases, in many parts of the network, however, continues to complicate the regulatory environment.

3.3 Oligopoly

Even where competition is feasible between firms that possess their own infrastructure, the sunk-cost conditions endemic to network industries tend to favour the operation of only a few infrastructure firms. So even in industry structure (v) shown in Figure 3 (c) above, conditions are likely to be oligopolistic in network industries. According to Sutton (1991), a high degree of market concentration is likely in network industries despite the intensity of competition that might arise in service provision. This is because considerable costs are sunk in network expenditures prior to revenue-generating sales. In many cases, sunk costs reflect expenditure on network plant and R&D. In Sutton's terminology, these represent exogenous and endogenous costs respectively.

An industry with sunk costs clearly exposes firms to the risk that sales may not generate sufficient revenues to cover these outlays. Firms anticipate that if competition is intense in the future, prices will tend to be driven downwards. As more firms enter an industry, competition is likely to become more intense. So, a firm seeking to invest

Box 5 Airline computer reservation systems and oligopoly

On 22 December 1993, the European Commission issued Regulation EC 3652/93 (OJ L 333, 31 December 1993, p. 37) on the application of Article 85 (3) of the EC Treaty to certain categories of agreements between undertakings relating to computerized reservation systems (CRS) for air transport services. These CRS provide detailed information about flight possibilities, fare options and seat availability. They can also be used to make reservations, print tickets and issue boarding passes. In short, CRS are a critical input in the industry and influence consumer choice.

Of course, to facilitate fair competition, it is vital that flight schedules and fare displays are complete and unbiased. According to the Commission, however, the CRS are 'such that few individual European undertakings could on their own make the investment and achieve the economies of scale required to compete with the more advanced existing systems'. Thus, large airlines already operating CRS are likely to have a competitive advantage. To counter this, the Commission permitted cooperation in this field, subject to rules ensuring that no discrimination exists between parent carriers and participating carriers. The Commission stated in the Regulation that 'In order to maintain competition in this oligopolistic market, subscribers must be able to switch from one system to another at short notice and without penalty'. The above Regulation came into force on 1 January 1994 and expired on 30 June 1998.

in infrastructure may be deterred from entering the market because it anticipates that future competition will erode revenues and result in losses. The typical outcome is that the greater the proportion of sunk costs, the weaker the incentives and the fewer the number of firms that choose to participate.

Concentration in network industries may also be strengthened by 'first mover' or incumbency advantages. In Europe's network industries, the legacy of public control and the granting of exclusive rights usually means that there are dominant firms. These firms have been in their industries for a long time and are familiar to customers. Such familiarity may lead to customer inertia, particularly when there might be costs to customers of seeking to change supplier. These costs are known as 'switching costs' and can be particularly strong in tele-coms where number portability is still not generally available. Large firms already in the market may also have deep pockets and may be in a better position to exploit R&D potential.

While powerful incumbency advantages often exist, there may also be incumbency disadvantages, which make entry into an industry easier than would otherwise be the case. For example, large incum-bent firms may be insufficiently flexible to change strategy, particular when moving from the culture of public monopoly to competition. Furthermore, firms in industries where technology has changed dra-matically may have capital that is several vintages old, while entrants can choose from 'state-of-the-art' technology.

3.4 Interconnection and access pricing

As Chapters 1 and 2 indicated, a network industry can be characterized as having three components: an upstream component supplying and/or producing the basic products and services; the network infra-structure; and the downstream service provision businesses. If all three parts of the industry are operated by a single firm (case (i) in Figure 3 (a) above, the vertically integrated monopolist), regulation naturally focuses on the final prices set by the firm. The main purpose of price regulation in this case is to ensure that prices are set equal to marginal costs with an appropriate mark-up allowing for common costs, thus preventing the firm from abusing its monopoly position.

The next cases to consider are when there is downstream competi-tion and a monopoly infrastructure. With the vertically integrated industry structure (case (ii) in Figure 3 (a)), the vertically integrated firm operating the infrastructure also competes against firms that have access to the infrastructure. The infrastructure firm, sometimes known as the 'bottleneck provider', is in a position to act monopolis-tically against its rivals in the downstream sector. It could raise its rivals' costs through setting an excessive access charge for use of the infrastructure, a practice known as foreclosure. By doing this, it would be able to provide a competitive advantage to its subsidiary in the downstream market. This means that the terms of access need to be scrutinized closely so as to prevent monopoly abuse.

Some commentators argue that, where there is accounting separa-tion, the ability of the vertically-integrated firm to practice market foreclosure is weakened. Accounting separation is, however, of little significance unless the infrastructure and the other parts of the business are strictly 'ring-fenced' from one another and costs are verifiable. Accounting separation is not a very strong regulatory requirement since it does not necessarily influence behaviour within an integrated firm. For example, the integrated firm could set an access price for its subsidiary equal to that levied on all other downstream firms, while in practice the subsidiary acts as if the price is lower, knowing that the competitive advantage this provides may lead to greater profits overall. An access charge for an integrated firm is much like a transfer price within a large corporation.

To overcome the problem of undue discrimination and foreclosure by an integrated infrastructure firm, it is usually desirable to implement structural separation or vertical separation. Of course, this pre-supposes that any losses arising from a possible decline in economies of scope are more than offset by the reduced costs of regulation arising from greater transparency.

Vertical separation (case (iii) in Figure 3 (a) above) means that all the firms in the competitive sectors are on a level playing field. There is no reason why the infrastructure provider should favour any one downstream firm. The main problem arising here revolves around the price of access set by the monopolist.

Regulation here needs to concentrate on the setting of access charges by the infrastructure monopolist. To preserve adequate investment incentives, the key regulatory challenge in this setting is identifying the appropriate rate of return the infrastructure firm should earn on its asset base. This requires an assessment of the firm's exposure to risk, which is easier to undertake if the firm's shares are actively traded on a stock market.

An alternative industry structure is joint ownership (case (iv) in Figure 3 (b) above), but in terms of access pricing, this case is, in spirit, equivalent to industry structure (iii). In this case, it is in the interest of the rival firms that jointly own the infrastructure to set a relatively high access price. This is because a higher access price means that prices can be raised in final markets as access costs form a substantial part of the cost base (in telecoms, for example, it can amount to 40% or more). If the firms compete away profits but share in the profits enjoyed through shares in the infrastructure firm, then it can pay them to have high access prices. In effect, the joint-ownership case can lead to monopoly outcomes and so regulation of access charges is also necessary.

Cases (i)–(iv) all feature a single infrastructure provider, and for many of the network industries, notably electricity, gas and rail, there will only be one provider in any given region. In some industries, however, particularly telecoms, it is increasingly likely that the industry structure will be that of case (v) in Figure 3 (c) above: competing vertically-integrated firms or facilities-based competition. For example, competition in voice telephony involves cable TV companies, traditional telecoms companies, and increasingly mobile and wireless in the local loop. Because of the strong private and social benefits associated with interconnecting different telephone networks (see Section 3.5), such competing firms will typically interconnect their networks. Indeed, this has been a feature of international telephony services for many decades. When there are several interconnected network infrastructures with goods and services flowing in both directions, this gives rise to what is called the two-way interconnection problem (see Section 6.5.8 below). In the discussion above, when there is only one network infrastructure, this is known as the one-way interconnection problem.

A good example of two-way interconnection often arises in the maritime transport industry. Suppose that there are two competing ferry operators S_1 and S_2 operating over a route connecting A and B. The operation of the ferry service is the downstream part of the industry and the infrastructure comprises port and harbour facilities. Assume that each firm is vertically integrated, but that firm S_1 owns the infrastructure in A and firm S_2 owns the infrastructure in B. Each firm will set an access price for use of its facilities, assuming that rights of access are granted. Not surprisingly, access prices will be set in excess of costs, reflecting monopoly power. In the final market, however, competition may be very intense and prices may equal costs, where of course costs include the access charge levied by the other firm.

It is perhaps not surprising to see in this simple setting that while final prices may equal costs, each firm may nevertheless make excess profits from its high access prices. In other words, monopoly outcomes may arise despite vigorous competition downstream. Hence, if infrastructure is an essential facility, meaning there is no viable alternative facility, and firms are vertically integrated, competition does not necessarily resolve the access pricing problem.[1] Hence, regulatory oversight is probably needed even in the case of industry structure (v).

High access charges may lead to bypass – the duplication of network resources to enable a firm to access customers without using existing infrastructure. While bypass may weaken the position of the firm selling access to the infrastructure, it does lead to an unnecessary duplication of resources. Such inefficiency may be self-evident in a competitive setting, but when an infrastructure provider is protected by public ownership and exclusive rights, as is often the case in Europe, there may be considerable production inefficiencies. In this case, it is possible that bypass, which enhances competition and therefore drives down final prices, can be socially beneficial. A better method of improving efficiency, however, would be to change the incentives driving the performance of the existing infrastructure firm.

3.5 Network externalities

Several kinds of externalities play a role in competition and regulatory policy towards the network industries.[2] Externalities can occur in a network when the actions of one user affects the well-being of other network users. For example, a person making use of a telephone network may confer benefits or impose costs on others through making telephone calls – a user externality. A club externality arises when the value an individual places on belonging to a network increases with the number of users. For example, belonging to a telephone network may be more valuable for everyone, the more users there are connected to it.

Some network industries, however, may have no network externalities. Indeed, they may even have negative network externalities. For example, in road and air transportation, the club externality may be negative because of congestion.

Network externalities can in principle lead to what are termed 'multiple equilibria'. If there are only a few users on a network, it may be unattractive for others to join because the club effect is too small – there are not enough members of the club to make subscription worthwhile. If there are many users, however, there may be too much congestion, deterring new members.

The club externality depends critically on the size of a network's infrastructure. For a given network size, club effects are likely to be increasingly prominent when the users of a network is small and growing. At some point, however, where membership size leads to more congestion, club effects become smaller and possibly negative.

Another type of externality occurs when a network has spillover effects, sometimes known as investment externalities.[3] This means that the presence of a network in a particular area can lead to benefits spilling over into activities outside the network. Obvious examples are integrated transport systems that allow for efficient access to markets, fast and reliable telecoms infrastructures, and so on. The presence of spillover externalities is often used to justify public participation in large infrastructure projects, such as the EU's TENs programme.

3.6 Coordination, standards and interoperability

Natural monopoly typically lies in the infrastructure of a network industry while competition is often viable in the upstream and downstream segments. When there are potentially many different firms wishing to supply into a network and many potential firms wishing to supply services to customers, this can present coordination problems for the operator of the network. In the energy industries, for example, where security of supply and network integrity are important factors, this can be a complex task.

The costs of coordinating disparate supplies and demand through a network should ideally make use of market mechanisms since this is what the market is especially good at. In the Norway and Sweden electricity market, for example, use is made of a 'pool mechanism' (see Box 6). There may however be considerable transaction costs associated with operating a market mechanism like a pool system. If coordination is relatively costly, competition in the upstream and downstream components of an industry may be compromised. This is because a vertically integrated monopolist would be able to internalize the difficulties thrown up by competition.

Where there are potentially many different users of a network and potentially several different networks, there may well be substantial benefits from establishing common standards within networks to allow for interoperability. This is because strong club externalities can only be exploited through interconnection and this requires interoperability across competing network operators. In digital mobile telecoms, the GSM protocols ensure technical uniformity across the different networks in Europe, thus facilitating interoperability. This has allowed widespread roaming and, as a consequence, encouraged greater use of mobile telephony services.

The success of GSM as an industry standard was, to a large extent, due to cooperation in the telecoms manufacturing industry. Cooperation,

Box 6 The Nord Pool electricity spot market

Since January 1996, there has been a common Norwegian-Swedish spot market for electricity, where wholesale buyers and sellers trade electricity on an hourly basis. While the spot-market trade in effect determines the merit order dispatch of available generating capacity, the grid operating companies, Statnett in Norway and Svenska Krafnät in Sweden, are responsible for the short-term stabilization of frequency and voltage in the power system. The spot market is operated by Nord Pool, which is an independent company owned by Statnett and Svenska Kraftnät. It is open to all sellers and buyers that comply with Nord Pool's rules and regulations, but there is no obligation to buy or sell electricity via Nord Pool. As a result, approximately two-thirds of the deliveries of electricity in Norway and Sweden are based on bilateral contracts.

The Nord Pool electricity spot market is organized in a very simple way. Until noon the day before delivery, the sellers and buyers are allowed to make bids indicating the amount of power they want to buy or sell at different price levels during each one of the day's 24 hours. On the basis of these bids, Nord Pool constructs aggregate demand and supply schedules for each hour and computes the corresponding market-clearing prices. The trades implied by the accepted bids are all settled at the computed market-clearing prices. Formally, the sellers are selling power to Nord Pool, while the buyers are buying from Nord Pool. Thus, from the point of view of a seller, there is no risk that the buyer cannot pay for the delivery, and from the point of view of a buyer, there is no risk that the seller cannot deliver.

Nord Pool also operates a set of futures markets. The contracts traded on the futures markets are entirely financial in nature and aimed at providing buyers and sellers with opportunities to hedge against spot-market price risks. The futures contracts are highly standardized and defined in terms of a given number of megawatts of electricity for delivery during a given future week. The currently available futures contracts make it possible to secure electricity prices up to three years in advance.

however, may not have occurred in the absence of Commission initiatives.[4] While encouraging standards through coordination allows the exploitation of both externalities and scale economies, however, it also diminishes variety. If the 'wrong' standards are chosen, service provision may be less efficient than might otherwise have been the case.

3.7 The legacy problem

Natural monopoly and public service objectives have been used to legitimize public control of most of Europe's network industries. As conditions affecting these industries have changed in recent years, the operation of large public firms with exclusive rights is increasingly undesirable. The consequence of past public policy is, however, a high degree of concentration in many of the final and intermediate markets of the network industries. In many cases, service provision in a given region was the responsibility of one firm, the public utility. So, at the point when liberalization measures aimed at promoting competition are introduced, the market is inevitably dominated by the incumbent operator.

Policy can address this legacy problem in a number of ways. Consideration can be given to the merits of separating the dominant incumbent into smaller companies (horizontal separation), as happened with power generation in the United Kingdom. In this case, the benefits of introducing more effective competition need to be weighed against the costs of sacrificing economies of scope. Alternatively, regulatory conditions may be designed in such a way as to impose on the incumbent the requirement that it reduces its market share over some period of time, as happened in the UK gas industry.

Another legacy issue concerns the role of equity or fairness considerations in network industries. Because of perceived 'spillover' benefits from universal consumption of certain network services, policies have been designed, and are still influenced considerably, with a view to promoting greater accessibility and affordability of network services. The issue of universal service and public service obligations is taken up further in Chapter 6.

Box 7 Diversity in European network industries

Network industries across the EU exhibit many different ownership and vertical structures. This is due to many factors, including market size, population density, geographic considerations and political make-up. The wide diversity in European network industries can be illustrated by the electricity industry. In aggregate, there are fifteen electricity systems in the EU which, in broad terms, share a number of common characteristics in their structures:

- *Market size*:   The large systems are those over 100,000 GWh – in France, Germany, Italy, Spain, Sweden and the United Kingdom. Medium size systems include Austria, Belgium, Denmark, Finland, Greece, the Netherlands and Portugal. The smaller systems include Ireland and Luxembourg.

- *Trade*:   Luxembourg stands out with 95% of its electricity imported from Germany and Belgium. Other Member States had significant levels of imports in 1994 in relation to consumption: Finland (9%), Italy (14%) and the Netherlands (12%). France is by far the largest exporter with 16% of production in 1994. Germany has a significant level of activity with the surrounding countries: Austria, France, Luxembourg, the Netherlands, Poland and Switzerland.

- *Ownership structures*:   Across the EU, these can be very complex, involving different tiers of government (local, municipal, federal and central) as well as private companies and public–private partnerships. Eight of the Member States fall into the loose category of public ownership, with the other seven favouring private ownership or a mixture of public and private ownership. Purely private ownership is very much the exception, found only in Belgium and the United Kingdom.

- *Vertical structure*:   Vertically integrated systems linking generation, distribution and transmission are found in France, Greece, Italy and Ireland. Luxembourg does not have any generation capacity; and Portugal, Spain, Sweden and the United Kingdom have vertically separated industries. The system in the United Kingdom, however, is more complex as there are varying degrees

continued

Box 7 continued

of vertical integration in different parts of the country, and recent developments have seen re-integration (see Section 5.17). Austria and Germany do not have vertical integration in distribution. The Scandinavian countries are restructuring the industry and are developing a Nordic Power Exchange that includes Norway (see Box 6). In Finland, Sweden and the United Kingdom the systems exhibit some form of regulated third-party access (see Section 5.9).

3.8 Convergence

Convergence is occurring in Europe's network industries as a result of three factors:

- technology;
- changes in market structure;
- policy.

Technological convergence is occurring in industries like telecoms as it becomes more closely associated with the information technology and broadcasting industries. As Part 2 of this Report indicates, convergence driven by technological change will have a profound effect on competition and the way in which this industry is regulated. Increasingly, many telecoms services are being made available across computer networks, and many broadcast services can be delivered over telecoms networks.

Technological innovations and market liberalization are leading to convergence in industries like energy. Gas and electricity companies are moving into each other's markets as power generation in the electricity industry increasingly makes use of gas. There is also the likely prospect of some convergence occurring between electricity distribution and telecoms. For example, in the United Kingdom, Norweb, a regional electricity firm, and Nortel, a Canadian telecoms manufacturing firm, have established a joint venture that intends to market data services through low voltage power lines. Other utility industries, notably rail and water, have for some time been able to offer telecoms services.

Policy is also leading to convergence in some areas, especially in the transport industries. The EU is seeking to encourage the delivery of more freight over inter-modal transport systems to relieve congestion on roads and reduce adverse environmental emissions. Investments in TENs are therefore partly directed towards stimulating integrated port, railway and road facilities. Recent market developments in the transport industry have also seen a rise in inter-modal company operations.

Notes

1 A more sophisticated approach to the two-way interconnection problem is undertaken in Laffont, Rey and Tirole (1998) and Laffont and Tirole (1998).

2 See Economides (1996) for a discussion on network externalities, and on standards, coordination and interoperability. See also Besen and Farrell (1994).

3 See Krugman (1990) on the spatial effects on investment.

4 The Commission is currently encouraging coordination for the next generation of digital mobile telephony, UMTS (see Part 2 of this Report).

4 Deregulation: Ten Conflicting Priorities

The coexistence of competition and monopoly, competition between private- and public-sector firms, interconnection, and the setting of public-service objectives raise many challenging conflicting priorities for regulatory policy-makers during phase 2 (see Box 2 above). Ten conflicting priorities can be identified as characterizing the regulatory environment in European network industries in this phase.

4.1 Short-term versus longer-term objectives

The infrastructure of network industries is often capital intensive and, in many cases, involves large-scale investment projects, such as the building of major power plants or airports. Completing investments of this kind may take many years and hence a long-term outlook is essential to weigh up the pros and cons of such undertakings.

Many of the costs associated with large-scale infrastructure investments are irreversible. Firms engaged in investment programmes where costs are sunk usually expect to recoup costs through setting prices for new services above observed *ex post* (after the event) costs. If a firm can set its prices above observed *ex post* costs to recover the costs of past investments, this provides *ex ante* (before the event) incentives which may encourage desirable investments.[1] For example, investments may result in higher quality, lower cost services.

If regulation is overly concerned with the welfare of current consumers (say for short-term political reasons or because it concentrates too much on static rather than dynamic efficiency considerations), it may result in prices being set equal to observed *ex post* costs. Indeed, once an investment is sunk it is optimal *ex post* to set prices equal to marginal or incremental costs. Such *ex post* optimality, however, conflicts with *ex ante* incentives. If firms anticipate that too much emphasis is placed on *ex post* optimality and regulatory structures are not conducive to credible commitments that safeguard against opportunism, investments in network infrastructure will be adversely affected and ultimately consumers (current and future) may be worse off. The preferred forms of regulation are those that strike the right balance between *ex ante* incentives and *ex post* optimality. If regulation puts too much emphasis on setting prices equal to costs rather than establishing market conditions that would deliver such prices, investment incentives may be dented due to disagreements about what constitute costs.

4.2 Efficiency versus equity objectives

The price and quality of outputs supplied by network industries significantly affect the competitiveness of European industry and the standard of living of European consumers. Policy-makers and politicians, therefore, take a very keen interest in these industries and have done so for many years. Indeed, policy-makers have enshrined in the EC Treaty that the services supplied by network industries are 'services of general economic interest'.[2] According to the Commission, 'Europeans have come to expect high quality services at affordable prices. Many of them even view general interest services as social rights that make an important contribution to economic and social cohesion'.[3]

The expectations regarding services of general economic interest mean that the formulation of regulation and competition policies affecting network industries takes account of equity objectives as well as efficiency objectives, giving rise to another conflicting priority. The Commission recognizes this conflict:

> 'The real challenge is to ensure smooth interplay between the requirements of the single market in terms of free movement, economic performance and dynamism, free competition, and the general interest objectives. This interplay must benefit individual citizens and society as a whole. This is a difficult balancing act, since the goalposts are constantly moving: the single market is continuing to expand and public services, far from being fixed, are having to adapt to new requirements.'[4]

Economic efficiency entails setting prices equal to some measure of costs. In the network industries, costs comprise a significant fixed component and rigidly adhering to efficiency objectives may mean that for certain services, prices should be set at relatively high levels. For example, pricing the provision of air and railway services to remote rural areas efficiently may result in very high air and rail prices for some users, thereby leading to social exclusion. Because social cohesion is an objective within Europe, it may mean that to achieve equity or fairness objectives of this kind the prices of certain network services should not be set solely with efficiency criteria in mind.

As is often the case with economic policy, when fairness or equity considerations affect decision-making, differences of opinion surface and conflicts with policies directed towards achieving efficiency can arise. Two aspects of equity or fairness that impact most on competition and regulation policies in the network industries are:

- the concept of public service;
- universal service.

Public service usually takes the form of specific public service obligations imposed by public authorities on undertakings rendering network services. Public service obligations usually require firms to provide certain services that they would otherwise choose not to supply. Universal service is an 'evolutionary concept, developed by the Community institutions, [which] refers to a set of general interest requirements which should be satisfied by operators of telecoms and postal services, for example, throughout the Community. The object of the resulting obligations is to make sure that everyone has access to certain essential services of high quality at prices they can afford.'[5]

The difficulty with the concept of universal service is that it leaves open for interpretation what constitutes 'an essential service', 'high quality' and 'affordable prices'. Such nebulous terms unfortunately provide too much discretion for political interference that can undermine regulatory commitment and adversely affect *ex ante* incentives. In many cases, it would be better for policy-makers to target social objectives using tax and benefit instruments.

4.3 Competition versus monopoly (incorporating infrastructure versus service-led competition)

The services supplied by network industries can be brought to consumers via competitive or monopolistic market structures. Even if competition is acknowledged to be the superior market structure, there can be differences of opinion about the nature of competition.. Competition in a network industry may be symmetric, in the sense that all firms invest in network infrastructure, or it may be asymmetric in that competition prevails downstream among service providers that rely extensively on the infrastructure provided by an upstream monopolist.

Opinions may differ as to which is the best market structure to meet efficiency and equity objectives. Because most network industries have some elements of natural monopoly, competition is not necessarily the optimal market structure. A natural monopoly element exists within a network when the costs of supplying services to customers are minimized when one firm supplies (or a group of firms jointly supply) this element.[6] The costs of delivering domestic water supplies, for example, are certainly minimized by having only one pipe connecting each household to a distribution system.

Natural monopoly elements tend to pervade network industries because of economies of scale and scope. Scale economies mean that the average costs of supplying services tend to decline as output expands. Under competition, when potentially many firms share total industry output, economies of scale are necessarily sacrificed. Economies of scope imply that the costs of supplying services may benefit from 'joint production'. As firms in network industries may supply many different services and products over a common network, there may be advantages from having large multi-output firms.

Natural monopoly implies that the duplication of assets, which tends to arise under competition, is wasteful. Traditionally, natural monopoly arguments have been used to justify the operation of vertically-integrated monopoly firms in Europe's network industries. The case for monopoly is founded on efficiency: a monopolist can take advantage of scale and scope economies to attain productive efficiency – least cost production. The absence of competition, however, can give rise to monopoly abuse and allocative inefficiency: where output is sold at prices above costs.

Conditions in the network industries have changed considerably in recent times. The combination of increased demand for many network services and declining operating costs have diminished the significance of natural monopoly elements in network industries. These changes have made it increasingly feasible for competition to take place, particularly in areas lying outside of the main network infrastructures, for example, in downstream service provision.

In some industries, notably telecoms, it is increasingly feasible, and many would argue that it is desirable, for infrastructure (or facilities-based) competition to take place. Infrastructure competition implies that the existence of natural monopoly in an industry is insignificant. Conflicts tend to arise in policy circles about the merits of infrastructure competition as different parties often hold different views about the prevalence of natural monopoly elements in network industries.

Where it is thought that natural monopoly elements are significant, it is often argued that competition is best accommodated via service providers being granted access to a monopoly network infrastructure. Although this type of competition may deliver benefits in the short run as prices move closer to cost, it may undermine *ex ante* investment incentives on the part of infrastructure firms, particularly if access is granted on relatively favourable terms.

Table 1 Competitive and monopoly components in the network industries

Industry	Natural or near natural monopoly components	Competitive or potentially competitive components
Air Transport	Some ground-handling services, airports, air traffic control, computer reservation systems.	Many passenger and freight air services, some ground-handling services, airport slots, airport retail outlets.
Electricity	Transmission and distribution.	Generation, many supply services, such as billing and maintenance.
Gas	Transportation.	Extraction, many supply services, such as billing and maintenance; and storage.
Maritime transport	Ports, some harbour facilities.	Ship services, some harbour facilities.
Postal services	Local delivery network.	High value services, sorting.
Rail transport	Track, signalling, stations, timetabling.	Passenger and freight services.
Telecoms	Some elements of the local loop, scarce resources (for example, spectrum).	Voice and data services, high capacity, high-speed infrastructure.

The diminished significance of natural monopoly elements in network industries means that competition is now recognized to be a more powerful means of achieving both efficiency and equity objectives than monopoly. Differences in opinion about the form competition should take do arise, however. If policy-makers encourage competition via service providers, terms of access must be set so as not to undermine *ex ante* investment incentives. This is especially important in dynamic network industries like telecoms.

Box 8 Competition versus monopoly in network industries

Many studies support the hypothesis that competitive markets lead to greater efficiency than monopolistic markets. Although a regulated monopolist can be coerced to choose output levels equivalent to those that would arise under competition, the absence of rivalry typically means that innovation is less likely to be as dynamic and costs are likely to be higher. Winston (1993) examined several US network industries that have been subject to deregulation in recent times and concluded that encouraging competition generally leads to greater dynamism and welfare gains. The OECD showed in a 1997 report that considerable price reductions have been achieved in many network industries where competition has increased (OECD, 1997a).

Political attitudes in Europe have generally shifted towards supporting market forces. For example, on 11 September 1996, the European Commission, in its communication *Services of general interest in Europe*, stated that 'market forces produce a better allocation of resources and greater effectiveness in the supply of services, the principal beneficiary being the consumer, who gets better quality at a lower price.'

4.4 Slow versus fast liberalization

In general, the move in Europe has been towards greater competition in the network industries. The pace at which competition is being introduced, however, varies across the industries and across countries. In each industry, liberalization has resulted in competition being introduced gradually. This gradual and sometimes slow approach to liberalization is a result of three main factors:

- tensions arising between efficiency and equity objectives;
- lobbying by incumbents and Member State governments;
- resistance by workforces within incumbent firms.

In moving to competition, it is recognized that prices for services provided by a network industry should move increasingly in line with costs. Where prices have historically been unbalanced for social reasons, meaning that some customers face prices below costs and others face prices greatly above costs, competition should lead to the 'rebalancing' of prices. As this entails some prices increasing, it may result in some customers being worse off. If politicians perceive that the number of losers is likely to be significant, this may result in them favouring slower liberalization.

In some instances, incumbent monopolists have argued against rapid liberalization. It is usually reasoned that time and aid is needed to restructure operations in readiness for changed market conditions. This is particularly argued by publicly-owned firms that have been used by Member State governments as instruments of social policy. On the other hand, some incumbent managers in public firms welcome liberalization as it provides an opportunity for greater commercial freedom.

Liberalization is sometimes viewed sceptically by employees in firms that have traditionally operated under exclusive rights. It is argued that liberalization will lead to job losses and therefore employees should resist change. If politicians are sensitive to these claims, this too may result in slow liberalization.

The introduction of competition into Europe's network industries has proceeded at a relatively moderate pace. Political legitimacy required for market reforms has perhaps stood in the way of a more desirable fast track approach to liberalization. Delaying liberalization to allow restructuring, through derogations for example, seems particularly counterproductive as competition is usually a more effective means of bringing about necessary and desirable restructuring. Furthermore, the granting of state aids to public undertakings to enable restructuring runs against the spirit of liberalization and should be resisted.

4.5 Public versus private ownership

The importance attached to network industries by politicians (through the imposition of public service objectives) and the

Box 9 Public versus private ownership in network industries

Many of the services provided by network industries in Europe have traditionally been supplied by publicly-owned monopoly firms. Even today, there remains considerable public ownership in these industries, although there has been a gradual shift towards privatization since the late 1980s. In some industries, like telecoms, privatization has been undertaken extensively, whereas in other industries, such as rail, public ownership continues to predominate.

From a static perspective, economic theory is generally agnostic as to whether private ownership is superior in efficiency terms compared to public ownership. A key determinant of a firm's performance, for any given industry structure, is the relationship between the firm's owner (the principal) and the firm's management (the agent). Because of the nature of informational asymmetries, this principal-agent problem is not necessarily easier to solve under private ownership (see Laffont and Tirole, 1993, Chapter 17).

From a dynamic perspective, however, the threat of takeover and the role of capital markets under private ownership can provide very powerful efficiency incentives for management. It is very difficult to find surrogates for these features under public ownership, and therefore private ownership is generally superior in efficiency terms to public ownership.

Public ownership has traditionally been argued to be a better safeguard than private ownership for the attainment of equity objectives. This is particularly the case when equity objectives entail loss-making activities. The regulation of private firms, however, can usually result in equity objectives being satisfied.

From a cost (productive) efficiency view, empirical studies have tended to favour private ownership in some of the network industries. For example Good, Röller and Sickles (1993) showed that US private airlines were around 15–20% more efficient than European publicly-owned airlines. In analysing a variety of network industries, Galal *et al.* (1994) found that privatization is associated with greater efficiency and welfare gains.

Policy-makers in Europe are neutral with regard to ownership structures, as enshrined in the EC Treaty under Article 222. Because of this, Community liberalization does not favour a specific form of ownership, although the Commission is inclined to favour private ownership over public ownership in the network industries.

existence of natural monopoly elements have in practice led to regulatory structures in Europe where public authorities directly control monopoly firms through ownership. Public ownership of firms in the network industries is extensive in Europe.[7]

The legacy of monopoly in network industries and the scale of public ownership in Europe's network industries can present problems when competition is introduced. The existence of publicly-owned dominant incumbent firms in many national and regional markets may induce conflicting priorities within the public sector. To some extent, priorities can be better focused if the boundary between the state as owner and the state as regulator are drawn more clearly.

Many publicly-owned network firms experienced financial difficulties during the 1970s and 1980s. This has been particularly evident in the European airline industry where several operators have relied on state aids to enable the restructuring of their businesses. At the outset of competition, therefore, some publicly-owned firms may be in a possibly disadvantageous position. Where state aids are extended to publicly-owned network firms to enable them to compete more effectively within newly liberalized markets, great care has to be taken to ensure that this does not constitute unfair competition.

Where publicly owned or mixed private- and publicly-owned firms compete against privately-owned firms in network industries, as is increasingly the case in Europe, regulatory structures must be transparent and independent from political structures. It seems, however, an unsustainable and undesirable position to retain publicly-owned firms in competitive network industries. The increased likelihood of private firms seeking legal recourse against the funding of public undertakings will be to the detriment of publicly-owned firms, to the industries concerned and to European consumers more generally.

4.6 Sector-specific regulation versus application of general competition rules (incorporating horizontal scope of regulation)

As many European network industries feature large dominant incumbent firms, close attention will need to be paid to the setting of prices in both retail and wholesale markets. Furthermore, for many firms entering into newly liberalized markets they will be seeking interconnection with an incumbent's facilities and this too will require scrutiny. As network industries are large and very complex, these detailed regulatory tasks are probably best undertaken by sector-specific agencies. This is because regulators will be better able to focus on the knowledge needed to address problems within a specific industry. In any case where a network industry is like any other competitive industry, then regulation can be undertaken through an application of general competition provisions.

The more regulation is specialized, however, the greater the prospect of capture, where regulatory decision-making can become adversely affected by vested interests. If civil servants accumulate important industry-specific knowledge, their understanding of the industry and hence the quality of their decisions can be expected to improve. The industry specificity of the civil servants' human capital also implies, however, that their main alternative employment opportunities are in the industry that they regulate, or closely related to it (such as management consultancy). Civil servants may therefore have an incentive to accommodate the firms that they regulate in order to ensure adequate future opportunities – the practice of 'revolving doors'.[8] General regulatory agencies can overcome the problem of the revolving door, but at a cost of possibly less effective regulation. The revolving doors phenomenon can, however, be offset through clauses written into labour contracts that may constrain future employment opportunities, but this requires greater remuneration for regulatory officials.

Where sector-specific regulation is desirable, as will be the case in phase 2 for most network industries, this raises the problem of defining the boundaries of a sector. Should the regulation of railways be undertaken separately from regulation of air transport? Should the regulation of the electricity and gas industries be undertaken by the same agency? Should the converging telecoms and broadcasting industries be regulated by a communications agency? The horizontal scope of regulation depends on the 'closeness' of the markets. It would seem sensible to consider broader regulatory agencies when there are strong complementarities (rail and air) and/or the services in question are close substitutes (electricity and gas).

Sector-specific regulation is likely to be optimal when there are large dominant incumbent firms operating in complex network industries. Defining the horizontal scope of sector-specific regulation may be difficult, however, especially where convergence is occurring. Therefore, industry-specific regulatory structures should be reviewed periodically.

4.7 Rules versus discretion

There is a trade-off between on the one hand, the degree of precision in the implementation of regulation, and on the other hand, the scope for regulatory or bureaucratic capture. In principle, implementation of regulation through precise rules (say, via licensing) can be monitored without difficulty but is likely to result in inflexiblity. In contrast, the implementation of regulation through general rules (say, via general competition rules) leaves a great deal of discretionary decision-making to civil servants and allows greater flexibility, but it may compromise regulatory commitment.

Where regulation allows for discretion, it can be adapted to the peculiarities of a given situation. It is, however, difficult and costly to evaluate discretionary decisions *ex ante* and accordingly, the scope for capture is enlarged. The balance between rules and discretion will thus depend in part on the benefits of flexibility and the cost of capture. Capture problems need not increase when regulatory rules are made more flexible, however, as long as there is sufficient transparency in regulatory procedures and adequate accountability.

Where rules are made very precise and governance structures constrain discretion, regulators will be able to commit more credibly to policy. Regulatory commitment is of vital importance to network industries because of the scale and duration of investments.[9] Commitment can help to lower regulatory risks, thereby favourably affecting the cost of capital and overcoming difficulties related to stranded costs. The price of commitment is inflexibility. This is not a problem if network industries operate in stable environments. In reality, however, these industries are operating in a climate of change. Indeed, liberalization itself is a major structural change.

In considering rules versus discretion in regulatory policy, it is important that due account is taken of the trade-off between flexibility, which raises the prospect for regulatory opportunism and capture, and regulatory commitment.

4.8 Permanent versus temporary regulation

In Europe's network industries, liberalization is occurring gradually. As a consequence, over time competition is increasingly significant in most of the industries. Furthermore, as markets evolve, competition also becomes more effective: rivalry between firms in an industry begins to lead to lower prices, better quality services and improved productivity. When competition is more established within an industry, regulation ought to become less relevant. After all, regulation is largely a surrogate for absent competition. Thus, sector-specific regulation should be phased out as competition takes hold in an industry.

To ensure that regulation diminishes in significance as competition becomes more effective, regulatory structures ought to include 'sunset clauses'. In practice, sunset clauses may result in less powerful (less heavy-handed) regulatory structures so as to prevent regulatory entrenchment.

4.9 Centralized versus decentralized regulation (incorporating geographical scope of regulation)

The appropriate geographical scope of regulation depends on the extent to which decisions by national or regional authorities fail to internalize important external effects across jurisdictions. If interjurisdictional externalities are significant, regulation should be more centralized.

Local civil servants may, however, be better informed about the specifics of regulatory problems because of more efficient observation. Furthermore, when decisions are taken at the local level, regulatory authorities face stronger incentives to compete against one another. This may improve the quality of regulation and reduce the scope for capture if local regulators care about the well-being of all European consumers and shareholders. In practice though, national or regional regulatory authorities are subject, to a greater or lesser extent, to political control, and are likely therefore to place more weight on the welfare of those residing within their respective political jurisdiction. This could give rise to unhealthy competition between regulators, particularly if it means sacrificing some control over the activities of firms in order to attract investments. As investments in network industries can be substantial, this is a cause for concern.

Decentralized regulation could also lead to too much diversity and inconsistency. This is evident in the telecoms industry as discussed in Part 2. Diversity can result in 'forum shopping', whereby companies seek out a regulatory authority that is more likely to support its case.

In practice, centralized and decentralized regulatory structures are both substitutes and complements.[10] Thus, regulation will involve both centralized and decentralized authorities – two-tier regulation – and it is the balance between these two that matters for policy. Too much power at the centre may lead to slow decision-making (because of imperfect information), whereas if power is too decentralized it can result in fragmentation, inconsistency and inefficient resource allocation.

If regulatory bodies are sufficiently independent of political control, there is a presumption in favour of decentralized regulation, particularly with regard to regulating the conduct of firms. This presumption can be overturned in the presence of important external effects or inter-jurisdictional externalities. These effects, which include competition for investments, mean that centralized direction overseeing market structure is likely to be desirable in Europe. Two-tier regulation, where the centre sets the framework and local authorities deal with detail, will prevail in practice. It is important, however, that only the minimum necessary tasks should be allocated to central authorities.

4.10 Light-handed versus heavy-handed regulation (incorporating vertical scope of regulation)

In addition to the horizontal and geographical scope of regulation, concern should also be given to the depth or vertical scope of regulation. Qualitatively, regulation can be either light-handed or heavy-handed. Light-handed regulation means that rules and regulatory institutions are relatively few.[11] In most instances, light-handed regulation means the application of general competition rules. In Europe, this would in practice mean the application of Articles 85 and 86, the State Aid Regulation, and the Merger Regulation.

In contrast, heavy-handed regulation means that specific rules and institutions are established to regulate an industry. It may also mean that the rules are very detailed (including lengthy licences, which of course imply inflexibility) and that the actions taken by dominant incumbent firms are given very close scrutiny. Whether heavy-handed regulation is required depends on the conditions prevailing in a given industry. It also depends on how effective general competition rules are in practice.

In Europe, the application of general competition rules is the duty of the Commission.[12] Decisions made by the Commission can be challenged in the European Court of Justice (ECJ). Legal procedures in European competition cases are, however, notoriously slow. A reliance on general competition provisions to police emerging competition in the network industries may not resolve uncertainties for some period of time when cases are contested in the European Court. To reduce uncertainties of this kind, more heavy-handed regulation may be desirable.

To date, the application of general competition rules in Europe to specific problems in the network industries has been hampered by slow legal procedures. This means that specific regulation and typically more heavy-handed regulation is likely to be better suited to driving the industries over the hump in phase 2 and forward to phase 3. Serious consideration should, however, be given to measures that can improve the speed of legal decision-making in the competition field so as to enable more desirable light-handed regulation of these industries.

Notes

1 This is precisely the motivation for patents in other industries that exhibit large-scale sunk investments.

2 Article 7 (d) of the EC Treaty, see Appendix 1.

3 'Services of general interest in Europe', 96/C/281/03, OJ 281, 26 September 1996.

4 Preface to Notice from the Commission 'On the application of the competition rules to the postal sector and on the assessment of certain state measures relating to postal services', Brussels, OJ C 39, 6 February 1998.

5 *Op cit.*, note 3 above.

6 Whether a natural monopoly occurs in practice depends on both the demand and supply sides of the market. In other words, it is a property of both the cost functions of firms and market size (see Baumol, Panzar and Willig, 1982).

7 In some industries (notably telecoms), and in some Member States (especially the United Kingdom), the state has shifted away from the public ownership model.

8 See Adams (1981), and Laffont and Tirole (1993), Chapter 11.

9 See Sappington (1994).

10 This issue is examined in greater detail in Chapter 7.

11 Light-handed regulation of network industries is not practised in many countries, though New Zealand is an exception (see Box 19 below).

12 See Appendix 1 for details on Community laws, procedures and institutions.

5 Deregulating Network Industries in the EU

The Community's aim is to support the competitiveness of the European economy in an increasingly competitive world and to give consumers more choice, better quality and lower prices, while at the same time helping, through its policies, to strengthen economic and social cohesion between the Member States and to reduce certain inequalities.[1]

Policy in the EU affecting the network industries is achieved by implementing the founding treaties of the EU. These have been revised three times: in 1987 (the Single Act), in 1992 (the Treaty on European Union, TEU or Maastricht Treaty) and in 1997 (the Treaty of Amsterdam). Community law affecting network industries has its legal basis in the EC Treaty.[2] The ultimate goal of the EU is 'an ever closer union among the peoples of Europe, in which decisions are taken as closely as possible to the citizen'. This implies that policymakers in Europe are seeking the establishment of a single market in which decision-making is decentralized. The TEU states that policies should be designed to achieve this goal by promoting balanced and sustainable economic and social progress.

The first major initiatives in the EU to affect the network industries gathered momentum after the 1987 Single Act. In order to devise a single market in sectors like communications, transport and energy, this required a legislative programme to bring about liberalization and harmonization. The programme of reforms was strengthened with the signing of the TEU at Maastricht in 1992. In particular, Article 7 (a) of the EC Treaty states that:

> The internal market shall comprise an area without internal frontiers in which the free movement of goods, persons, services and capital is ensured in accordance with the provisions of this Treaty.

With such a clear objective, the Commission accelerated its programme of liberalization and harmonization in the network industries.[3] Liberalization means establishing the conditions, or market rules, necessary for the operation of an internal or single market; and harmonization is aimed at bringing consistency across what had hitherto been industries predominantly shaped by national markets. The Maastricht Treaty also established the objective of creating TENs to enable 'citizens of the Union, economic operators and regional and local communities to derive full benefit from the setting up of an area without internal frontiers'.[4]

Policy affecting network industries is enacted through Community law.[5] The legislative process begins with a Commission proposal – Community law cannot be made without one – and in devising its proposals, the Commission has three constant objectives:

- to identify European interest;
- to consult widely as is necessary;
- to respect the principle of subsidiarity.

Subsidiarity is enshrined in the TEU and is applied by the Commission in such a way as to ensure that the EU takes action only when it is deemed to be more effective than if left to individual Member States. Once the Commission has formally sent a proposal for legislation to the Council of Ministers and the European Parliament, the EU's law-making process involves close cooperation between these institutions. In addition, the opinion of the Economic and Social Committee and the Committee of the Regions may be sought. The role of the latter two institutions in the legislative process was strengthened after the signing of the Treaty of Amsterdam in 1997.

5.1 Articles of the EC Treaty relevant to the network industries

The EC Treaty contains the principles and objectives governing the shape of policy in the European Community. Many articles in the EC Treaty are applicable to network industries, but some are more directly relevant than others: over time, some articles have become more relevant following liberalization, in particular the articles outlining the rules on competition, especially Articles 85 and 86.

Box 10 Articles of the EC Treaty relevant to the network industries

- **Rules on competition:** Articles 85 (restrictive practices), 86 (dominance) and 90 (exclusive rights).
- **Aids granted by states:** Articles 92–4.
- **Approximation of laws:** Article 100 (a) (internal market).
- **Trans-European Networks:** Articles 129 (b) (interconnection and interoperability), 129 (c) (guidelines and standards) and 129 (d) (consultation procedures).
- **Industry:** Article 130 (competitiveness and adjustment).

Undertakings may, however, be exempt from Articles 85 and 86 if they hold exclusive rights. As discussed above, many governments in Europe granted exclusive monopoly rights to many network industry firms. The policy of exclusive rights was, and in some instances remains, sensible where a network industry exhibits natural monopoly attributes both upstream and downstream, and where services are considered vital and universal service is desirable. In recognition of these features, the EC Treaty under Article 90(2) allows for the possibility that undertakings operating 'services of general economic interest or having the character of a revenue producing monopoly' are exempt from the rules on competition in the EC Treaty.

For many years, firms operating as monopolists in markets where the services were deemed to be of *general economic interest* were protected from Articles 85 and 86. Not surprisingly, most of the network industries studied in this Report have been associated with exclusive rights as Member States have claimed, in many cases justifiably, that services were of general economic interest. In practice, though, it is a matter of dispute as to what is meant by services of general economic interest. This theme is discussed further in Chapter 6 below.

As European objectives have shifted increasingly towards promoting a single competitive market, the Commission has applied Article 90(3) to remove exemption rights in these industries. This has resulted in the passage of directives aimed both at liberalization and harmonization. Progress towards a single competitive market is most marked in the air transport and telecoms industries, where competition has been strongly encouraged. In the energy industry, measures are currently being drafted (in the case of gas) and implemented (in the case of electricity) to develop greater competition through open access and common carriage. Pro-competitive measures have also been applied to postal services, railways and maritime transport.

While Article 90 directives determine the essential principles for the liberalization of network industries, Article 100 (a) enables the Commission to propose directives designed to harmonize liberalized markets. In effect, measures taken under Article 100 (a) complement liberalizing measures pursued under Article 90. Article 100 (a) directives are focused on establishing common rules applicable to market participation (licensing) and in particular deal with the problem of interconnection and interoperability, as well as with the thorny issue of universal service.

Cohesion, in both an economic and social sense, is viewed as an important aim of EU policy. In 1992, a desire for greater cohesion resulted in politicians agreeing to the insertion into the EC Treaty of three articles dealing with TENs. Article 129 (b) states that:

> To help achieve the objectives referred to in Articles 7 (a) and 130 (a) and to enable citizens of the Union, economic operators and regional and local communities to derive full benefit from the setting up of an area without internal frontiers, the Community shall contribute to the establishment and development of trans-European networks in the areas of transport, telecoms and energy infrastructures. Within the framework of a system of open and competitive markets, action by the Community shall aim at promoting the interconnection and interoperability of national networks as well as access to such networks. It shall take account in particular of the need to link island, landlocked and peripheral regions with the central regions of the Community.

With regard to the speed of structural change in network industries, Article 130 measures can be adopted. This Article states that 'in accordance with a system of open and competitive markets action shall be aimed at: speeding up the adjustment of industry to structural changes'. While liberalization is, however, acknowledged to be necessary to establish a single market, and harmonization is necessary to ensure a level playing field, it is also recognized that a period of transition is needed to ensure the successful working of a competitive single market. This is especially relevant to the network industries, where there is a considerable legacy of monopoly and state involvement.

5.2 State aids

Many firms in the European network industries have been loss-makers (in the case of railways, substantially so), and through public funding, they have received state aid. When most of the network firms held exclusive rights and operated largely within national territories, or were protected from competition, the provision of state aid was a matter for Member States alone. The single market programme and the commitment to opening up network industries to greater competition mean, however, that the granting of state aid is a more sensitive issue. This is particularly important when competition takes place between public and private enterprises. If a Member State grants aid to a public firm operating in a liberalized network industry, it may provide the firm with an unfair competitive advantage, and this could be considered incompatible with the common market.[6]

Articles 92–4 of the EC Treaty deal specifically with aids granted by Member States. Article 92 outlines terms under which state aid 'may be considered to be compatible with the common market'. In particular, state aid affecting network industries may be compatible with the common market if it is seen 'to promote the execution of an important project of common European interest'.[7]

The opening up of European network industries to greater competition is undeniably a project of common European interest. State aid has therefore been granted by Member States to some firms in the network industries where it is deemed to be compatible with the common market, especially where it facilitates restructuring and complements pro-competitive measures. There are instances, however, where the Commission has ruled that state aid extended to some firms operating in the network industries is incompatible with the common market. This has occurred most prominently in the air transport industry where state aids have been extended by some Member States to airlines (see Box 14 below).

As Articles 92–4 are rather general, the Commission has sought to clarify and disseminate its rules applicable to state aid.[8] The Commission has also confirmed that the public financing of infrastructure, particularly regarding transport and energy or water distribution, is not aid provided the utilization of the infrastructure is open to all the firms in the relevant area without discrimination. Despite such clarification, state aids have been problematic in some areas affecting the network industries.

5.3 Community policy affecting specific network industries

It is evident that the Commission has taken an increasingly active role in the liberalization of the European network industries. The approaches used to accommodate liberalization have varied, however. In the air transport and maritime industries, the Commission relied on regulations, whereas in the other industries, directives have been issued mainly through applications of Articles 90 (3) and 100 (a) of the EC Treaty. Since the Maastricht Treaty in particular, the Commission seeks wherever possible to coordinate and promote liberalization and to leave implementation to individual Member States. This is in accordance with the principle of subsidiarity. Conflicts do arise, however, because of decentralization, and it is likely that a number of competition policy problems will surface over the next few years in Europe because of different forms of implementation.

A description of liberalization and harmonization measures in each of the major network industries now follows.

5.4 Air transport

Since 1983, the air transport industry in Europe has been gradually liberalized. Liberalization began with a limited initiative on interregional air services in 1983, followed by two consecutive packages of liberalization measures in December 1987 and July 1990, as well as rules for the free provision of air cargo services between Member States in early 1991. A third and final package of measures for Europe's internal air transport market took effect from 1 January 1993.[9] Since 1997, the domestic markets of Member States have also been opened up to competition. The 'third package' largely replaced bilateral agreements between Member States and paved the way for a much more competitive and liberalized industry. Arguably, the air transport industry is the most liberalized of all the network industries in Europe.

The rules governing air transport and air services in particular have led to a much more competitive industry in Europe, although the ownership requirement (see point 1 in Box 11 overleaf) is unnecessarily restrictive and should be abolished. It is now possible for an air carrier to be set up anywhere in the EU in accordance with one single set of rules and to operate between two airports within the EU without generally being subject to any restrictions on capacity, frequency or pricing. As mutual recognition of air carrier licences operates within the EU, it means an operator needs only to apply for one licence in order to provide services anywhere within Europe.

Box 11 The third package of liberalization in air transport

---

1. **Common rules on the licensing of air carriers.** Any undertaking that complies with the rules, including the obligations of being majority owned and effectively controlled by Member States or nationals of Member States, is entitled to receive an operating licence.

2. **An air carrier holding a licence generally enjoys free access to all intra-Community routes.** A Member State is allowed, under the control of the Commission, to intervene through safeguard clauses in the market for public policy reasons such as, serving routes to remote regions, airport policy and the environment. For example, in the case of Orly Airport in Paris the French authorities initially obstructed access on the grounds of airport policy in the Paris airport system. The Commission intervened and found the French measures to be discriminatory and disproportionate in relation to the policy objectives pursued. Access was subsequently made available.

3. **An air carrier is free to set its fares and rates for services in the Community.** Member States may intervene under safeguard clauses allowing them to withdraw excessively high prices or to stop downward spirals in prices.

In contrast, mutual recognition of licences remains elusive in telecoms. Although the telecoms industry was fully liberalized on 1 January 1998 (as described in detail in Part 2), unlike the air transport industry, regulation is much more diverse. This is because the liberalization of telecoms was undertaken using directives and these have been implemented by individual Member States. Liberalization of the air transport industry, however, has been driven largely by the Commission through the application of regulations, which are directly applied without the need for national measures to implement them. Nevertheless, the air transport sector is usually subject to specific regulation (covering economic regulation, safety and the environment) within a Member State.

Although air services are almost fully liberalized (except for owner-ship conditions), conditions still prevail in the industry that impede the effectiveness of competition. These stem largely from bottlenecks like airports. The Commission has been concerned that the benefits flowing from a liberalized internal market are not compromised by monopolistic and/or discriminatory practices regarding infrastructure and essential services. In particular, airports and services provided in airports, such as the allocation of airport slots, ground-handling activities and the operation of computer reservation systems (see Box 5 above), have been the focus of attention.

In dealing with some of these bottleneck issues, the Commission has chosen, under the principle of subsidiarity, to issue directives rather than regulations. In October 1996, the Council adopted Directive 96/67/EC on ground-handling activities at airports in the EU.[10] The directive aimed to liberalize this part of the industry through the introduction of competition, but for certain services (baggage handling, ramp handling, fuel and oil handling) Member States may limit operators to two, of whom at least one must be independent of the airport and the dominant carrier. Accounting separation has been mandated so those suppliers of ground-handling services to third parties are subject to transparency to deter undue discrimination through cross-subsidization. The directive is coming into force gradually, depending on the type of activity involved and the size of the individual airports. Derogations may be granted if there are serious problems concerning capacity and available space at some airports. (See Box 12 for some problems involving ground-handling.)

The main challenge facing the Commission currently is the establishment of rules appropriate to the development of a competitive air transport industry, which is close to entering the phase 3 of market structure. Three areas are critically important here: alliances and mergers, slot allocations and infrastructure charging.

Alliances are prominent in the airline sector because of complex and out-dated ownership regulations, which often prevent non-nationals from holding an operating licence. Instead of mergers seen in other global industries like accounting, airlines resort to close collaboration through alliances. Alliances between airlines may fall foul of Article 85(1), but if operational costs and efficiencies can be generated to the extent that consumers would be expected to benefit, an alliance may be exempt from Article 85(1) under Article 85(3). In

Box 12 Ground-handling problems at Athens and Frankfurt airports

Ground-handling facilities at Athens airport were supplied on a monopoly basis by Olympic Airways (Greek national carrier) and alleged poor quality of service resulted in complaints to the Commission. The Commission began investigating under Articles 90 and 86 and concluded in 1997 that the poor quality of service and a lack of transparency in charges were the result of an abuse of a dominant position. The Greek authorities responded by improving facilities at Athens airport and by abolishing the monopoly in the supply of ground-handling facilities from 1 January 1998. Olympic Airways has also devised and published a new cost-based charging structure.

On 14 January 1998, the European Commission took two decisions that in practice ended a ground-handling monopoly at Frankfurt Airport. The first decision related to complaints brought under Article 86 of the Treaty by Air France, KLM and British Airways that Frankfurt airport was abusing its dominant position by not granting airlines the right to provide self-handling. The Commission upheld the complaints and Frankfurt airport must now demonstrate to the Commission that it intends to open the market. The second decision was based on the Ground-Handling Directive 96/67/EC. Frankfurt airport had applied for a derogation from the timetable for staggered liberalization of ground-handling services until the end of 2000 on the grounds of space and capacity constraints due to construction works. The Commission rejected the request for a total derogation, though agreed that because of heavy reconstruction work a partial exemption for one terminal (Terminal One) was justified.

practice, it may be difficult to assess the costs and benefits of an alliance, because there is usually at least one counterfactual.

Nevertheless, an alliance between SAS and Lufthansa operating a joint venture on routes between Scandinavia and Germany was approved in January 1996 for a period of ten years.[11] Several transatlantic air agreements, notably those between British Airways with American Airlines; Lufthansa with United Airlines; SAS with United Airlines; and Swissair/Sabena/Austrian Airlines with Delta have all come under the scrutiny of the Commission with regard to Article 85. In these cases, the involvement of firms in countries outside the EU makes the issue more complex.

Box 13 Market imperfections in the air transport industry:
alliances and slots

In 1996, British Airways and American Airlines announced that they wanted to form a close operational alliance. As each airline has a significant presence in the transatlantic market (around a 60% share of the business traffic), the proposed alliance may fall foul of Article 85(1). Four jurisdictions commenced investigations into the merits of the proposed alliance: the UK Office of Fair Trading, the US Department of Transportation and the Competition Directorate DG IV of the Commission in parallel with the Department of Trade and Industry in the United Kingdom.

In July 1998, the Commission published its preliminary ruling on the proposed alliance giving qualified approval. The Commission has stated that it would exempt the alliance from Article 85(1) under Article 85(3) if a number of conditions were satisfied. It has proposed that British Airways and American Airlines surrender 267 slots at London's Heathrow and Gatwick airports, and reduce frequencies on routes between London and American's three main US hubs (Chicago, Dallas/Fort Worth and Miami) during the first six months of the alliance. Furthermore, they face restrictions on frequent flyer programmes and ticketing practices, and will not be compensated for giving up slots.

The next stage in the process will involve further negotiations between the various parties. Which slots should be surrendered have yet to be decided. As slots are allocated through an administrative process rather than via the price mechanism, bureaucratic haggling over slot divestiture is likely to lead at best to an imperfect outcome.

Although the Commission and third party authorities (more often than not the US Department of Transportation) examine different proposed alliances on a case-by-case basis, the Commission should also re-examine the merits of imposing shareholder restrictions on airlines. Furthermore, as a matter of urgency, consideration should be given to devising ways in which slots can be allocated through the price mechanism rather than by concession bargaining over proposed alliances.

Although the Commission claims that the air services industry is fully liberalized, this is not the case *de facto* and *de jure*.

As many European airports face increased congestion, and a significant expansion in the number and capacity of airports is unlikely, the issue of slot allocation is a growing concern. In 1993, the Commission established some common rules for allocating slots at European airports, but these have not been sufficient to deal with the problem. Indeed, if anything, things are getting worse.

One point of controversy are so-called 'grandfather rights' which reinforce the *status quo* and favour incumbent operators. Prior to liberalization, slots at airports were usually granted through some administrative procedure and not surprisingly each Member State tended to favour allocating the majority of slots or the best slots to airlines based in its territory. In many cases, it would be the usually publicly owned 'flag carrier' that would be the chief beneficiary. The legacy problems created by the administrative allocation of slots are probably very great. Grandfather rights that protect the interests of the incumbent certainly act to impede competition by restricting the effectiveness of entrants. The Commission is aware of this and is currently making proposals to help develop a means of facilitating the transfer of slots (although this seems currently to be intertwined with other issues, see Box 13). The allocation of slots can be achieved in various ways and several commentators have suggested the use of auction mechanisms. If an auction procedure were to be used, it would probably be very complex, but assuming transaction costs are not too great, auctions should deliver greater benefits than the present system.

Another area of concern for competition policy is the pricing of infrastructure. Infrastructure costs account for around 25% of airlines costs and in the EU, these are 40% above those in the United States.[12] Later this year, the Commission will publish a White Paper on Infrastructure Charging setting out principles for fair and efficient pricing.

In April 1997, the Commission proposed a directive on airport charges. Having liberalized air space, attention has now turned to the liberalization of ground-handling facilities and services provided by airports such as landing, lighting, parking, refuelling, storage and freight services. Charges for these services can vary widely from airport to airport and represent on average 5% of the operational costs of airlines. Although the variation in charges between different airports need not cause alarm and may be justified on efficiency grounds, concerns have been raised, especially with regard to discrimination at individual airports (see Box 11). For example, there is often a considerable difference in charges and treatment between domestic and international flights. The Commission is not seeking to harmonize airport charges; rather, it is establishing a framework of basic rules governing the levy of charges that accords with three principles: non-discrimination; cost-relatedness; and transparency. Of course, costs are expected to reflect the cost of congestion.

The transition to a fully liberalized internal market for air services has been marked by a number of cases of state aids which were deemed to be incompatible with a common market. It is without doubt that state aid in the air transport sector is a highly contentious policy issue. As many airlines in Europe prior to liberalization were publicly owned, inefficient and indebted, rules were established permitting the granting of state aid to ease the path for these companies into a more competitive environment. The Commission only justifies aid in this context when it is 'an integral part of a programme for achieving the financial viability and competitiveness of the recipient airline'.[13]

In cases where state aid is granted, the Commission monitors the implementation of restructuring plans and compliance with the conditions it lays down in its decision authorizing aid. The Commission has recently authorized final aid payments to Air France and the Portuguese airline TAP, but in the case of Olympic Airlines of Greece, it re-opened proceedings because it found some conditions were not being complied with. In 1994, the Commission issued guidelines on the application of Articles 92 and 93 of the EC Treaty and Article 61 of the EEA Agreement to state aids in the aviation sector. They can be summarized as follows:[14]

- Direct operating aid is *prima facie* prohibited. It can only be acceptable as a reimbursement for meeting public service obligations or as aid of a social character under Article 92 (2)a.
- Any other aid can only be authorized if it forms part of a comprehensive self-contained restructuring programme designed to restore a carrier's financial health within a reasonable time period.
- Authorization of restructuring aid will include conditions preventing market distortions.
- Restructuring aid to an airline that has previously received aid will only be allowed under exceptional circumstances, unforeseeable and external to the company (the so-called 'one-time-last-time' principle).

It was under the above guidelines that the Commission sanctioned FFr 20 billion of state aid to Air France in 1994 (see Box 14).[15]

Box 14 The controversy surrounding state aid extended to Air France

In 1994, the European Commission approved a FFr 20 billion restructuring state aid package to the state-owned airline, Air France. As European air services were already liberalized at this time, many of Air France's competitors believed that the aid was unfair. British Airways and six other commercial airlines opposed the Commission's approval and brought a suit to the European Court of Justice (Court of First Instance) against the Commission. The plaintiffs claimed that the state aid gave Air France an unfair advantage against other firms in the industry that had to rely on open markets for capital. Four years later, on 25 June 1998, the ECJ has delivered a judgement condemning the aid.

The judgement cancels the 1994 approval, and the Commission must decide what course of action to take. One option would be to return to the Court with new legally acceptable arguments retrospectively justifying its original decision; an alternative option would be to appeal against the ruling. Both would be retrograde courses of action. There seems little benefit to European consumers from approving large aid packages to companies operating in markets where commercial incentives ought to be sufficient to bring about efficient company operations. If individual Member State governments choose to subsidize commercial operations heavily, in the long run this can only be to the detriment of European competitiveness.

The excessively long time taken by the ECJ to arrive at its judgement means, however, that it will be very difficult for the Commission to demand that Air France hand back the aid. Indeed, Air France has made clear that it will use all available means to avoid returning the aid. A further twist in the tail is caused by the imminent partial privatization of Air France due in September 1998. The ruling by the ECJ has served to increase uncertainty over Air France's net worth, and this is likely to result in intense political lobbying in Brussels to oppose the judgement made by the ECJ.

The approval of state aid to Air France and the controversy it has generated serves to show that large-scale government intervention in competitive and increasingly commercial network industries is likely to become more difficult to justify. Certainly the judgement made by the ECJ is welcome, if a little late in the day.

The liberalization of air services in Europe is advanced but not yet complete. Competition is increasingly becoming effective in many parts of Europe: by 1996, 6% of routes were served by three operators or more, compared to 2% in 1993.[16] Many new airlines have entered the industry and there has been a favourable downward effect on some prices. Nevertheless, many prices remain stubbornly high, particularly on certain routes and for certain (fully flexible) classes of tickets. The remaining impediments to competition are bottlenecks lying in the airport infrastructures and in the systems used to control air traffic in the air space over Europe. A variety of measures are being considered at the European level to deal with these important outstanding issues. Clearly, much remains to be done.

5.5 Maritime transport

Liberalization in the EU maritime industry is based on an open market, non-protectionist philosophy.[17] In 1996, the Commission communicated to the Council a new policy on the maritime industry, in which it emphasized the importance of this industry for European competitiveness.[18] In December 1997, the Commission published a Green Paper on seaports and maritime infrastructure in which it states that ports are vital to trade and transport in the EU and its global competitiveness.[19] It acknowledged that the position of ports in the wider transport policy debate had for too long been on the sidelines. The Green Paper envisages various ways of improving port infrastructure, increasing the efficiency of ports and their integration into the EU's transport network.

The main policy concerns in this industry arise in the context of· access to port facilities, and the financing and charging for ports and maritime infrastructure. Access to port facilities is increasingly being deregulated. For passenger services, many ports, by virtue of their location, are natural monopolies and therefore essential facilities: no rival port is sufficiently close that it lies in the same market. Problems have arisen where port authorities have refused access to harbour facilities, a clear case of the restriction of competition.

Whether such refusals to supply are detrimental is not necessarily a straightforward matter to resolve. If competition were free to take place, free-rider problems may lead to an inadequate infrastructure. This is because competing operators may gain in the short run by not investing or contributing towards the costs of harbour facilities. As a long-term consequence, the provision of infrastructure may suffer. On the other hand, protecting a route from competition can result in cost inefficiencies, poor customer service and monopoly abuse. Although some of these problems may be alleviated through carefully designed regulation, it may not always be cost-effective to undertake such regulation whereas opening up a route to competition may yield net benefits.

As with the other industries, state aids and public service obligations are also prominent in this industry. Public service obligations are, however, permitted usually only for scheduled services to ports serving peripheral EU regions or thinly served routes which are considered vital for the economic development of that region, in cases where the operation of market forces would not ensure a sufficient service level.

Box 15 Refusal to supply in Scandinavian car ferries

An example of blocking access to essential infrastructure occurred in a case involving car ferries between Denmark and Sweden. Port authorities at Helsingør denied access to harbour facilities to operators wishing to compete against Scandlines A/S, a firm jointly controlled by the Danish State enterprise DBS and a Swedish firm SweFerry. Scandlines enjoyed exclusive rights to operate car ferry services between Helsingør and Helsingborg in Sweden. The Commission investigated the refusal to supply following a complaint lodged by the Danish ferry operator Mercandia. In its judgement, the Commission regarded the refusal to grant access to an essential infrastructure constituted a state measure protecting and strengthening the position of a public operator and a breach of Articles 90 and 86 of the EC Treaty. Following discussions with the Commission, the Danish Government agreed to provide access to the harbour facilities at Helsingør to a new ferry operator on the basis of a tendering procedure.

5.6 Railways

European railways share an attribute found in railways across the world: in general, they are loss-makers. Railway debt in the EU in 1994 amounted to 1.8% of the EU's GDP. Although competition from other forms of transport, notably cars and lorries, has diminished considerably the position of railways, the Commission has sought to revitalize them. In its 1996 White Paper on railways, the Commission stated that:

> A new kind of railway is needed. It should be first and foremost a business, with management independent and free to exploit opportunities, but answerable for failure. For this it should have sound finances, unencumbered by the burden of the past. It should be exposed to market forces in an appropriate form, which should also lead to a greater involvement of the private sector. A clear division of responsibilities is required between the State and the railways, particularly for public services.[20]

The White Paper also states that railway finances should be organized according to the following principles:

- Member States should relieve railways of the burdens of the past;
- the railways should be run on a commercial basis;
- Member States should pay full compensation for public services and exceptional social costs.

Except for public service provision and specific infrastructure investment, the railways should self-finance their operations. The purpose of this policy is to put greater discipline on the players involved. It is acknowledged by many that efficiency in European railways is relatively poor and costs could be reduced substantially. Where state aid is received to offset the burdens of the past; this is subject to Article 92 of the EC Treaty.

From the perspective of European competition, it would be beneficial to foster an interoperable and interconnected railway for freight and international passenger services. Measures are being proposed to promote the separation of infrastructure management from transport or service-provider operations, as has already happened in Sweden and the United Kingdom. Particular urgency is being attached to the improvement of international freight transport with the Commission promoting the establishment of trans-European rail freeways, which will feature open access and have simplified arrangements. One sector of the industry that would significantly benefit from liberalization is the freight market. At present, freight rail is generally the sum of national services: rarely does a single operator have responsibility for the whole international service from terminal to terminal. This fragmented mode of transport contrasts sharply with the major competitor, road transport, which is seamless.

The first step towards open access in railways took place with Directive 91/440/EC, which covered four areas of policy:

- greater autonomy for railway managements;
- vertical separation of infrastructure from service provision, at least at an accounting level;
- debt and state aid;
- access rights to rail infrastructure.

The implementation of this directive was hindered to some extent by uncertainty over licensing and other issues (capacity allocation and charging) and required complementary Directives 95/18/EC and 95/19/EC.[21] These later directives, however, were only transposed in June 1997. The Commission is also encouraging the introduction of market forces into domestic passenger transport in a way that respects public service objectives. As yet, it is not clear what policy would best deliver the objectives. Open access is seen as possibly desirable over long-distance services, but on regional and urban routes it may not be an attractive solution.

Problems of allocating fixed and common costs, typically at least 75% of the costs associated with operating rail infrastructure, and the coordination of timetables, allocating train paths and ticketing greatly complicate the problem. An alternative approach would be to retain exclusive concessions and introduce a tendering process, as has happened in the United Kindom (see below). With regard to public service, the Commission prefers to apply the principle of subsidiarity, allowing each Member State authority to decide on the organization, level and definition of a public service as long as Community principles are respected.

Charges levied for access to the infrastructure requires clear principles, and if a single market is to emerge in some areas of the rail industry, some degree of harmonization will be needed across the EU. Different systems have already emerged, however: for example, in Germany and the United Kingdom, access charges are intended to recover all costs, whereas in the Netherlands and Spain operators only pay avoidable costs. The Commission is keen to promote fair and efficient pricing in transport and has published a Green Paper on this theme.[22] In this, it states that, as far as possible, charges should reflect private and social costs.

The Commission recognizes in the White Paper that separating the operations of the infrastructure from service provision is essential if railways are to benefit from market forces. It is stated that 'an undertaking cannot at the same time be both a competitor and the judge determining access to any relevant market.'[23] The Commission is considering a modification of Directive 91/440/EC to allow for accounting separation of integrated railway companies. The Commission is also considering the establishment of a European Railway Agency. It is claimed that such an institution would be better able to coordinate European dimension issues, such as infrastructure capacity allocation, technical harmonization, safety rules and the creation of a single market for railway equipment.

In March 1998, following a timetable established in the White Paper, the Commission published a report on the state of the rail sector in the EU.[24] The report identifies the key economic issues that need to be addressed in the rail industry. It states that the EU needs to define better the framework conditions for the internal railway market. To this end, in May 1998, the Commission proposed an 'infrastructure package', establishing guidelines for infrastructure charging and trainpath allocation, and in the second half of 1998 the Commission will also provide detailed rules on state aid. In terms of market liberalization the Commission is proposing that, as a first step, it should be possible to open up the market in each Member State by · at least 5% immediately, building to 25% after 10 years.

5.7 A common transport policy

The liberalization of the air, maritime and rail industries in the EU and the policy on TENs has prompted the Commission to adopt a better coordinated policy on transport. At the heart of this policy is the objective of an integrated inter-modal transport infrastructure in Europe. This was outlined in a Commission White Paper 'The Future Development of the Common Transport Policy'.[25]

5.8 Energy markets

Before looking at the electricity and gas industries in detail, it is useful to outline the status, in general terms, of the energy markets in the EU. Although some competition exists in upstream activities, particularly in natural gas extraction, the energy markets in Europe are much less competitive than those in the United States. It has been estimated that in the chemicals sector, European companies pay up to 45% more than their US competitors.[26] Apart from differences in tax treatment, the lack of competition is a key factor in explaining the cost differential. It has been calculated that full liberalization of the European internal electricity market will provide substantial benefits, which would amount to ECU 10–12 billion per annum, or twice as much as gains anticipated from the opening already agreed.

It is also claimed that third party access in gas to be introduced throughout the EU may lead to benefits amounting to ECU 900 million per annum.[27] A key challenge for energy policy is therefore to ensure further integration of the EU energy market, based on the principle of open and competitive markets. One of the objectives of the single market in energy, as set out in the Commission's 1988 working document, is to introduce competition between the suppliers of energy products.[28] The need to take account of security of supply, the environment and defend consumer interests makes this a more complex challenge than in some other sectors.

> The Commission believes that the absence of a single liberalized market in energy is a serious competitive disadvantage for European businesses as compared with those of its main trading partners, who generally enjoy lower costs.[29]

5.9 Electricity

Any system of electricity supply is divided into three segments: generation; transmission; and distribution and supply. Generation lies upstream and is the process by which fuels (mainly gas, coal, nuclear and, to a lesser extent, renewable sources of energy) are converted into electric energy. Transmission constitutes the large network infrastructure and it is the process by which the generated electricity is moved in bulk (high voltage) from the generation plant to large customers, usually wholesale purchasers. Lying downstream is distribution, which is the process of delivering medium–low voltage power from wholesale purchasers to final consumers. Also lying downstream is supply, which deals with billing, maintenance, meter readings and other customer-related services. In many cases, the distribution firm undertakes supply, although this need not be the case.

Deregulation in electricity sectors around the world has so far led to two basic models of competition, which can take a number of forms: the competitive pool and the grid access model. In general, these models involve some vertical separation between the monopoly components (transmission and distribution) and the potentially competitive parts (generation and supply). In practice, vertical separation can be achieved through accounting or corporate separation. Accounting separation permits an undertaking to operate in both the monopoly and competitive sectors of the industry, but requires considerable regulatory oversight to ensure that cross-subsidy and undue discrimination are not occurring. Corporate or structural separation is a more effective way of ensuring that the competitive playing field is level.

In December 1996, the European Council adopted Directive 96/92/EC on common rules for the internal market in electricity, which came into force on 19 February 1997.[30] This provides for a gradual opening of the electricity market. The first opening, to be effective by 19 February 1999, provides for the market in each Member State to be opened for a proportion that is represented by the share of EU consumption accounted for by customers using more than 40 GWh/year per site in 1997, around 25.37%.[31] This threshold will be reduced to 20 GWh/year on 19 February 2000 increasing the minimum market opening to around 28%. A third reduction to 9 GWh/ year will take place by 19 February 2003, equivalent to a market opening of around 33% or turnover of roughly ECU 45 billion. A further opening will be proposed later by the Commission. The figures with respect to opening the electricity markets up to competition are, of course, minimum requirements. According to DG XVII, at least 60% of the EU electricity will be open to competition by 2000.[32]

The liberalization of the electricity market provides Member States with two broad options regarding access to the network to the transmission and distribution network:

- third party access (TPA);
- single buyer system (SBS).

Whichever approach is adopted by a Member State, it shall operate in accordance with objective, transparent and non-discriminatory criteria. To facilitate these criteria, the directive incorporates measures related to accounting separation so that vertically integrated undertakings cannot practice undue discrimination, cross-subsidization or distort competition.

TPA is where producers and consumers contract supplies directly with each other. This comes in two variants: negotiated third party access (nTPA) and regulated third party access (rTPA). In the case of nTPA, access to the network is negotiated with its operator. Thus, an independent generator may contract with a steel plant and negotiate terms of access to the transmission network for delivery of power. The rTPA variant is identical to nTPA except the terms of access are not negotiable; instead, access to the system is governed by published tariffs for 'eligible customers'. Under nTPA, however, system operators must publish indicative prices in the form of average prices, whereas under rTPA, prices must be published in advance.

SBS is defined in the directive as a legal person who is responsible for the unified management of the transmission system and/or for centralized electricity purchasing and selling. In electricity systems for which a Member State chooses the SBS, independent producers and self-suppliers can use TPA to supply their own premises and those of their subsidiaries situated within the system and to supply any eligible customer outside the system. The single buyer is, however, obliged (except in the case where the single buyer principle is combined with TPA or in the case of lack of capacity in the system) to purchase electricity contracted by an eligible customer from a producer at a price which is equal to the sales price offered by the single buyer minus the price for the use of the network. The single buyer is not informed of the price in the contract between the producer and the eligible customer. This is intended to generate an outcome equivalent to rTPA.

Because the electricity industry in some Member States is vertically integrated, the directive requires accounting separation and a requirement on transmission and distribution operators not to discriminate in favour of their own subsidiaries. Operational separation is also required where a transmission operator is involved in other activities. It is not, however, a legal requirement to structurally separate any vertically integrated firm.

The directive also contains a provision for supply through direct lines by any producer or electricity supplier (where these are authorized) of their own premises, subsidiaries and eligible customers under certain conditions. Member States will decide the categories of electricity buyers ('eligible customers') who will be able to choose a supplier under the directive. The directive provides that customers using more than 100 GWh/year must be included. It also provides that distributors will be eligible to purchase electricity from alternative suppliers in order to supply it to their own customers who are themselves eligible. The directive provides for reciprocity: that customers may be prevented from obtaining electricity in another

Box 16 Liberalization brings globalization in the electricity market

The liberalization of European energy markets is leading to some profound changes in the industry's structure. European companies are venturing outside their traditional market territories and US companies are making significant investments in Europe.

So far the gradual liberalization of the European electricity industry is largely affecting the power generation market. Many of the new IPPs (independent power producers) entering the European market are US companies. This is because the United States is also liberalizing its energy markets and, as a consequence, permitting US companies to compete in markets outside their traditional service territories. For example, Entergy is engaged in a joint venture with British Petroleum to build a 1,000 MW power station, and Shell Oil plans to make significant investments in Europe, particularly in the United Kingdom. Many European companies are also investing in markets lying outside their traditional territories. The UK's National Power has expanded its global investments to around $1 billion in eight countries: Australia, China, the Czech Republic, India, Pakistan, Portugal, Spain and the United States. The Energy Group of London acquired Citizen's Lehman Power, the fifth largest US power producer, and Sithe Energies (60% owned by the French utility group Generale des Eaux) is to pay $675 million for 12 power plants belonging to Boston Edison, the Massachusetts electricity utility. Sithe Energies already operates 22 US power plants. Germany's RWE Energie AG has expressed an interest in the acquisition of up to 25% of Finland's IVO when it is privatized. At the end of 1996, Sweden's Vattenfall entered the German electricity market, through a joint venture with Kommunalfinanz to establish a new energy company, Vasa Energy, which will generate and distribute heat and power in the Hamburg region. In 1997, Southern Electric acquired 20% of Bewag, Berlin's electricity company, and Enron formed a joint venture with Italy's Enel.

Although distribution remains a natural monopoly, liberalization through privatization is shaking up ownership structures, most notably in the United Kingdom The majority of the distribution companies in the United Kingdom, the regional electricity companies, have been acquired by US interests with seven of the eleven companies having been sold to US companies: Central and South West, GPU/Cinergy, Southern Company, CalEnergy, Dominion Resources, Entergy and AEP. RWE is seeking to invest in the Finnish distribution system.

Member State if they would not be eligible there. The Commission may, however, overrule such a refusal at the request of a Member State. This provision will be valid for nine years, but is to be reviewed after half this period.

The directive also contains provisions designed to protect public service obligations. Member States are allowed to define public service obligations imposed upon electricity undertakings. These obligations may relate to security, including security of supply, quality, prices, system reliability, and environmental factors. The article dealing with public service obligations only allows Member States to derogate from the rules of the directive when the social obligations would otherwise be compromised. Any public service obligations must be notified to the Commission, clearly defined, transparent, non-discriminatory, verifiable and published. The use of public service obligations allows Members States to balance efficiency and equity objectives. An example would be an obligation on a distribution firm to supply all customers in its area at a uniform price per kWh.

The Electricity Directive significantly extends competition into the EU electricity market. The steps in the directive, however, are designed to implement partial liberalization. It is probable that the Commission will seek to liberalize the market further. The directive includes a revision clause that requests the Commission to review the application of the directive with a view to possible further liberalization in 2006. The experience from complete opening of markets as has largely happened in the Nordic countries and the United Kingdom will probably be important in this respect.

5.10 Gas

A proposed directive concerning common rules for the internal market in gas will be implemented in the near future.[33] The approach towards common rules in the gas sector follow very closely the rules that have been established in the electricity market. In scope the rules extend over transmission, distribution, supply and storage of natural gas. As in the case of electricity, the market will be opened up to competition gradually. Eligible customers will include gas-fired power generators and final customers consuming more than 25 million cubic metres per year. Member States will, however, ensure that the definition of eligible customers results in an opening of the market equal to at least 20% of the total annual gas consumption of the national gas market. It is intended that after five years, the competitive part of the market should have expanded to 28%, and after ten years be 33% or more. To achieve these targets, the threshold consumption defining an eligible customer will decline accordingly.

Access to the transmission system can either be through nTPA or rTPA, which must operate in accordance with objective, transparent and non-discriminatory criteria. Under nTPA, eligible customers and gas suppliers will be able to enter into commercial agreements and access to the system must be negotiated with the relevant natural gas undertakings. To promote transparency and discourage discrimination, however, terms for use of transmission systems must be published. Under rTPA, contracts can be struck between gas suppliers and eligible customers and access to the system is a right based on published tariffs.

As many gas undertakings in Europe remain vertically integrated, the directive is proposing unbundling. This means vertically-integrated undertakings will be required to publish separately audited accounts for natural gas transmission, distribution and storage activities, and, where appropriate, consolidated accounts for non-gas activities.

In the gas extraction industry, investments require considerable upfront sunk-expenditures. To reduce the risk exposure of these investments, contracts between gas suppliers and gas transmission undertakings are often of a take-or-pay form. Many of these contracts were drafted prior to deregulation. In an environment of greater competition and increasing gas supplies, spot prices for gas typically lie significantly below the prices stipulated in take-or-pay contracts. Incumbent operators, usually those exposed to take-or-pay contracts, are therefore vulnerable to new entry. Indeed, this was the case in the United Kingdom where British Gas was paying considerably more for gas than many of its new competitors. Take-or-pay contracts can be renegotiated, although with some difficulty as happened in the case of British Gas, but while they remain in force they constitute a stranded cost at the time of deregulation.

If the burden of take-or-pay contracts were to present serious economic and financial difficulties, a gas undertaking may submit to its Member State or designated competent authority, a request for a temporary derogation from the requirement to grant access to the system. The Member State or designated competent authority decides on whether to grant a derogation and must notify the Commission of its decision. The Commission may request an amendment or withdrawal of the decision. In determining whether a derogation should be granted, various criteria will be taken into account. Significantly, these include the need to ensure the achievement of a competitive gas market and the need to fulfil public service obligations and ensure security of supply. Derogations may also apply to emergent gas markets, particularly in Greece and Portugal.

The proposed Gas Directive could radically change the European gas industry. The current structure of the gas industry in Europe is highly concentrated, dominated by twelve large gas utilities and a similar number of gas producers. Some countries, however, are completely dependent on a single supplier (for example, currently Finland is entirely dependent on Russian gas). New entrants into the gas industry, which tend largely to be power generation companies, are very much providing extra impetus behind the liberalization process.

Box 17 Price Waterhouse survey of executives in the gas industry

In July 1997, Price Warehouse surveyed 150 top executives at 34 major gas companies in Europe. Respondents were divided into two groups: established gas suppliers (incumbents) and recent or potential entrants. The most significant obstacles to the successful implementation of the proposed Gas Directive were found to be take-or-pay contracts and the negotiation of access with the transporter. The overwhelming view among those questioned was that the process of gas liberalization would lead to more competition. The incumbents were much more convinced of strong competition developing (77%) than the recent or potential entrants (47%). 62% of the respondents stated that a true pan-EU gas market would be a reality within 10 years. (See also Box 20 below.)

Source: *Price Waterhouse Survey of Utility Executives on the Liberalisation of the EU Gas Market* (1997), London: Marketline International Ltd.

5.11 A common energy policy

In some countries that have progressed significantly towards establishing competitive energy markets, notably the Nordic countries and the United Kingdom, it has increasingly been recognized that an integrated approach to energy policy may reap benefits. This particularly makes sense given that much of the new generating capacity being installed in the electricity market is reliant upon gas supply. Thus, the electricity and gas supply industries are very closely related and converging. Furthermore, in countries like the United Kingdom, horizontal integration is taking place across the gas and electricity supply businesses. In November 1997, the Commission put forward a proposal to the European Parliament for a common energy policy.[34] The objectives of the common energy policy are as follows:

- to guarantee the security of energy supplies;
- to ensure competitiveness;
- to develop the energy market, while at the same time ensuring the protection of the environment.

5.12 Postal services

Discussions with regard to the liberalization of postal services began in 1991 with the Commission publishing a Green Paper.[35] In July 1995, the Commission proposed a directive on common rules (harmonization measures) for the development of postal services and a draft Notice on the application of competition rules in this sector. The Postal Directive aims to introduce common rules for developing the postal sector and improving the quality of service, as well as gradually opening up the markets in a controlled way. Universal provision of postal services has played a key role in shaping the directive, therefore impinging directly on the likely evolution of industry structure.

The Postal Directive aims to safeguard the postal service as a universal service in the long term. A minimum harmonized standard of universal service, including a high quality nation-wide service with regular guaranteed deliveries at prices 'everyone' can afford, is imposed on Member States. This universal service covers collection, transport, sorting and delivery of letters as well as catalogues and parcels within certain price and weight limits. It also covers registered and insured ('valeur déclarée') items and applies to both domestic and cross-border deliveries. The 'reserved sector' for letters covers items weighing less than 350 grammes and/or costing less than five times the basic tariff.

The imposition of universal-service obligations in the Community necessarily raises funding issues. Member States may grant exclusive rights to undertakings if this is necessary to guarantee the maintenance of universal service. To safeguard measures aimed at promoting greater competition, the Postal Directive places an upper limit on the reserved sector. If, as a consequence, an undertaking providing universal service is unable to fund its obligation, a Member State can establish a universal service fund. Article 9 of the directive allows for cross-subsidy through levies on commercial operators. Firms operating in the competitive sector may be required to make financial contributions to a universal-service fund (compensation fund) administered by a body independent of the beneficiary or beneficiaries.

The Postal Directive clarifies considerably the legal context in which firms operate in this sector. Significantly, the directive has established a minimum common standard of universal services and placed an upper bound on the reserved area. There are, however, state measures that are not dealt with in the directive, which can be in conflict with the EC Treaty's competition rules addressed to Member States. In particular, the thorny issue of exclusive rights and exemption from competition rules, permissible under Article 90(2) as discussed above, may give rise to problems. The exemption from the EC Treaty rules is, however, subject to the 'principle of proportionality'. This principle is designed to ensure the best match between the duty to provide general interest services and the way in which the services are actually provided, so that the means used are *proportional* to the ends pursued. The principle is intended to ensure that the means used to satisfy universal service requirements do not *unduly* interfere with the running of the single European market and do not affect trade to an extent that would be contrary to the Community interest.[36]

The EC Treaty articles dealing with the behaviour of undertakings (e.g. Articles 85 and 86) and state aids (Articles 92–4) are implemented on a case-by-case basis. Until cases are resolved in court, there is the potential for much legal uncertainty in the postal services sector.[37] Uncertainty is likely because of an inability to make precise what is meant by *proportional* and *undue*. Competition takes place between private firms operating in the non-reserved areas; typically, publicly-owned firms operate in both the reserved and non-reserved areas; and the industry structure is a mix of cases (ii) and (v) discussed in Chapter 3 above. Any heightened uncertainty will raise the cost of capital and probably dampen the effectiveness of competition.

For these reasons, the Commission has published a Notice in which it seeks to explain to the players in the market the practical consequences of the applicability of the competition rules to the postal sector, and the possible derogations from the principles.[38] This is a welcome move by the Commission as it seeks to diminish uncertainty by setting out the position it would adopt in assessing individual cases or before the ECJ in cases referred to the Court by national courts.[39]

5.13 Telecommunications

Since January 1998, the telecoms markets in the EU have become one of the most competitive network industries. Following the UK approach, the incumbents have not been unbundled, but third party access has been ensured. Furthermore, competition has been strengthened by alternative terrestrial (trunk) networks and mobile services, which provide (from the customer's point of view) competing end-to-end services. In most Member States, privatization is on its way or envisaged.

As in other network industries in most countries, the changes were initiated or underpinned by EU legislation. Part 2 of this Report provides a detailed overview of the telecoms industry.

5.14 Water

The water industry is largely based within national territories and trade between Member States is negligible and is likely to remain so in the foreseeable future.

5.15 Liberalization, regulatory intensity and competition

Figure 5 overleaf highlights where the various industries and industry sectors lie in relation to the intensity of regulation over the three phases of market structure (see also Chapter 6, Section 3 below). The figure is intended to show where an industry or sector lies on average. It should be noted that all industries lie in phases 1 or 2, except for non-reserved postal services. Table 2 on p. 77 indicates the extent of liberalization in the various industries at EU level, as well as the degree of competition they have achieved to date.

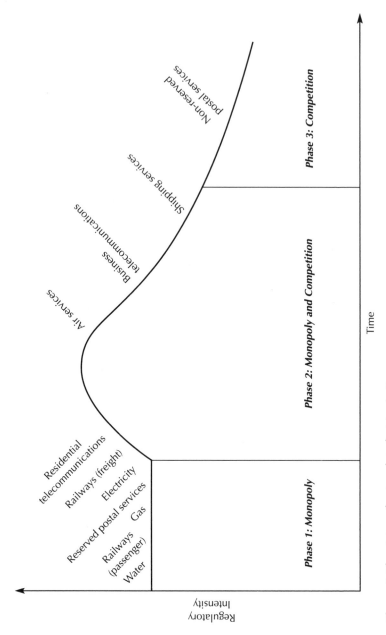

Figure 5 The status of network industries in Europe

Table 2 Summary of liberalization in Europe's network industries

Industry	Liberalization and competition measures	Current status of competition in Europe
Air transport	Three packages of Regulations between 1983 and 1993. Directive 96/67/EC on ground-handling.	Air services liberalized. Remaining impediments to competition (infrastructure bottlenecks) being liberalized. Much of the industry in phase 2. International alliances are a major issue.
Maritime transport	Regulations in 1986.	Services liberalized. Bottlenecks carefully monitored. Shipping services in phase 2; some in phase 3.
Railways	Three directives (91/440/EC; 95/18/EC; 95/19/EC) opening parts of the industry.	Policy still being developed. The industry is largely in phase 1, but some parts (for example, freight services) are in the early stages of phase 2.
Electricity	Some measures in the early 1990s. Directive 96/62/EC opening up the market.	Gradual liberalization benefiting large users initially due in January 1999. Industry approaching phase 2.
Gas	Proposed directive along the same lines as in the electricity industry.	Gradual approach to liberalization, industry in phase 1. May enter phase 2 in 2000.
Postal services	Directive 97/67/EC and Notice on the application of competition rules.	Segmented market: very competitive high value (non-reserved) sector mainly in phase 3; reserved sector in phase 1.
Telecoms	Various liberalization and harmonization measures between 1987 and 1998 (see Part 2 of this Report).	Services fully liberalized and market structure in phase 2, some elements moving towards phase 3.

5.16 The degree of deregulation of network industries by individual Member States

Deregulation initiated at an EU level has in some cases been preceded by measures taken within individual Member States. The Nordic countries and especially the United Kingdom have generally been ahead of developments taking place across the EU as a whole. Nevertheless, liberalization is now occurring throughout the EU and elsewhere in Europe, especially in the former Communist countries of East and Central Europe. In many cases, liberalization within individual countries has observed the experience of the United Kingdom. For better or worse, liberalization in the United Kingdom has been an important driver, if not explicitly then implicitly, of deregulation in the EU.

This section provides an overview of the degree of liberalization in major network industries in selected European countries. For this purpose, liberalization is defined broadly in order to capture the variety of issues involved. The degree of liberalization in a network industry thus reflects the extent to which measures have been taken in order to promote competition.

The reduction or abolition of institutional or regulatory barriers to entry is the most evident and one of the major measures of liberalization. Other actions by governments or regulators, however, may be just as important in promoting competition, such as the creation of a level playing field and structural measures. The understanding of liberalization used here includes the opening of the market for competitors, the creation of a level playing field and measures regarding the industry structure designed to promote competition in the industry.

Using this concept, Table 3 on p. 80 classifies the degree of liberalization (very low, low, medium, high, very high) in five network industries in Germany, France, Italy, Spain, Sweden and the United Kingdom. One arrow indicates that further liberalization is expected within the next five years, two arrows underline that the measures will be significant. The survey intends to provide qualitative information based on expert opinion. The degree of liberalization is judged according to the most liberal structure of the industry that can be envisaged in that particular industry. The underlying issues vary from industry to industry as has been described above. When interpreting Table 3, the following two points must be kept in mind:

• Market liberalization may be achieved in different ways: obviously, an assessment of the degree of liberalization will always involve subjective judgements with regard to the relative 'value' of different types of liberalization and the importance of different aspects of liberalization as well as the relevant vision of the 'most liberal organization'.

• A high degree of liberalization does not guarantee that competition works in that particular industry and country: further aspects that have not been captured in Table 3 would have to be considered in order to judge the impact of liberalization on effective actual and/or potential competition.

Given that less than a decade ago, most network industries were generally characterized by a very low degree of liberalization, Table 3 shows the efforts undertaken to liberalize the market since then. The degree of liberalization varies across industries as well as across countries, however. In all countries and almost all sectors that are not yet characterized by a high degree of liberalization, further reforms are envisaged.

As indicated above, liberalization is often accompanied and underpinned by privatization of the incumbent. Besides removing potential conflicts of interests that may result in asymmetric regulation, privatization is often motivated by efforts to enhance the efficiency of the organization. Table 4 overleaf provides an overview of the current ownership patterns in each of the industries and countries.

In the airlines, postal services, rail and telecoms sectors, the ownership pattern refers to the incumbent. In electricity, most countries were historically characterized by decentralized systems with a number of public operators. The labels 'state-owned' and 'privatized' imply 100% or almost 100% state or private ownership, partly privatized refers to any ownership pattern in-between. The term 'mixed' implies that there are several operators and ownership pattern varies.

It is clear that experience with liberalization in Europe is very mixed. While some governments have been keen to divest assets, others have continued to interfere directly into the operations of firms in the network industries. Even where assets have been privatized, however, governments through regulatory agencies often continue to play a key role in the development of these industries.

Table 3 Degree of liberalization in five network industries in selected European countries, Spring 1998

	Germany	France	Italy	Spain	Sweden	United Kingdom
Air transport	High	Medium	High	Medium ↑	High	High
Electricity	Medium ↑	Low ↑	Low ↑	Medium ↑↑	High ↑	Very High
Postal services	Medium ↑↑	Low ↑	Very Low ↑	High ↑	Very High	Medium ↑
Rail	Low ↑	Low ↑	Very Low ↑	Very Low ↑	High	Very High
Telecoms	Very High	High ↑	Medium ↑↑	High ↑	High ↑	Very High

Table 4 Ownership patterns in five network industries in selected European countries, Spring 1998

	Germany	France	Italy	Spain	Sweden	United Kingdom
Air transport	Privatized	State-owned ↑	State-owned	State-owned ↑	Partly privatized	Privatized
Electricity	Mixed	State-owned	Mixed	Mixed	Mixed	Privatized
Postal services	State-owned ↑	State-owned	State-owned ↑	State-owned	State-owned	State-owned ↑
Railways	State-owned ↑	State-owned	State-owned	State-owned	State-owned	Privatized
Telecoms	Partly privatized	Partly privatized	Partly privatized	Privatized	State-owned	Privatized

In Europe, there is patchwork liberalization of the network industries. There remains a lot to do before effective competition is established in all the industries across the EU as a whole.

5.17 Deregulation in the United Kingdom

Tables 3 and 4 above indicate that the United Kingdom has undertaken considerable deregulation. Although the United Kingdom may lag behind the rest of Europe in some areas of economic convergence and policy, in its policy towards the network industries, it has in most instances been ahead of Commission initiatives. For this reason, the Commission and other Member States have kept a close eye on developments in the United Kingdom. The principal features of the UK programme of liberalization in the network industries are shown in Table 5 overleaf.[40]

Effective competition was only allowed to take hold in the UK's telecoms sector in the 1990s, ten years after the first move to liberalize the industry. Even today, there are those who claim that the policy of encouraging infrastructure competition, rather than third party access and competition in service provision, has not delivered significant gains. Nevertheless, after a slow start, competition now appears to be developing in most parts of the industry, with competition for business and high value residential users becoming more effective.

The experience of UK gas liberalization has been fraught with difficulty. In 1982, the UK government passed legislation to enable negotiated third party access to the infrastructure operated by a publicly-owned and vertically-integrated operator, British Gas. Competition failed to materialize and in 1986, the UK government privatized British Gas without vertically separating the firm.

Three major regulatory enquiries have looked at various aspects of competition in the gas industry. In the 1993 review, the Monopolies and Mergers Commission (MMC) recommended that before any extension of competition into the household sector, the transport infrastructure of British Gas should be separated from its supply business.[41] In the event, the UK government chose to extend competition in the industry without restructuring British Gas. Not surprisingly, further difficulties arose and another enquiry was undertaken by the MMC in 1997.[42] This focused on infrastructure charges and in particular on the allowable rate of return. Ironically, British Gas decided to

Table 5 Liberalization in the United Kingdom

	Liberalization	Industry structure	Regulation	Principal events
Telecoms	Privatization began in 1984, completed 1991. Liberalization began 1981; market fully liberalized by 1996.	Incumbent BT is vertically integrated and operates nationally. Entrants vary in size, services and locality.	Retail prices of BT regulated, a position likely to end in 2001. Many BT interconnect prices regulated.	1991 review extends competition. 1995 MMC review on number portability. Introduction of Fair Trading Condition in 1996. 1998 MMC enquiry on mobile.
Gas	Privatized in 1986. Liberalization began in 1982 with access rights to infrastructure established. Phased liberalization of retail supply began in 1996, to be completed by mid-1998.	Incumbent British Gas privatized as a vertically integrated entity. In 1997, the incumbent vertically separated supply and transport operations. Entry considerable and extensive competition to occur in retail markets in 1998.	Final prices of British Gas regulated. Transport prices on the gas transmission and storage network also regulated. 1995 Gas Act separates pipelines from supply business.	Four MMC referrals: in 1988, on supply in competitive sector; in 1993, two referrals examining British Gas in the gas market; in 1997, on infrastructure charges. 1991 Office of Fair Trading report on competition. 1997 British Gas divests itself of infrastructure business.
Water	Privatized in 1989, except in Scotland and Northern Ireland.	Regional franchises. No national grid.	Prices and quality yardstick regulated.	Complaints about excessive profits. Mergers.

	Liberalization	Industry structure	Regulation	Principal events
Electricity	Privatized in 1990 (except for nuclear component). Liberalization in 1990 occurs in generation. Phased in for retail supply and expected to be fully liberalized in September 1998. Majority of nuclear power privatized in 1996 to form British Energy.	Vertically-integrated public firm vertically separated at privatization into: generation; transmission and dispatch; and public electricity supply companies responsible for regional distribution.	Separate price regulation of transmission, distribution and supply. Dispatch and market operated via a pool mechanism.	Generation viewed as insufficiently competitive and in 1994, under threat of industry review, incumbents (National Power and PowerGen) divest some power plant. Limited price regulation introduced in pool. Takeovers and mergers, various MMC referrals due to proposed mergers.
Railways	Complex privatization in 1993, except for rail infrastructure which was subsequently privatized. Freight markets fully liberalized under open access. Passenger services operated on a franchized basis with exclusive rights, open access competition permitted in the near future.	Vertical separation of the industry occurred at privatization. Infrastructure operated by a national private monopoly, Railtrack. Entry has occurred on a small scale in freight transport markets. Competition likely to develop in passenger services largely between existing franchise companies.	Regulation of infrastructure charges and passenger prices. Quality of passenger services monitored closely, with performance incentives.	Problems of service quality on passenger service operations. Freight market very concentrated, one operator (EW&S) with around 80% of market. Railtrack fails to meet investment commitments. Infrastructure charges under review.

break itself into two separate companies in 1997 as a way of overcoming the regulatory costs associated with ring-fencing its transportation business from its trading (supply) business.

The experience of gas liberalization in the United Kingdom was not a great success from a regulatory perspective. Perhaps the main lesson from this case is the need to undertake structural separation before introducing widespread competition. As this has now occurred in the United Kingdom, competition may indeed flourish.

The approach taken when liberalizing the electricity industry did take heed of the problems encountered in gas. At privatization, the industry was vertically separated into its main constituent parts: generation, transmission and distribution and supply. Transmission and distribution, being the natural monopoly elements, were privatized as monopoly enterprises. Competition was introduced immediately into the generation sector through horizontal separation, although at privatization only two non-nuclear companies were created: National Power and PowerGen.[43]

Dispatch is organized through a pool mechanism that solicits bids from generators and establishes a *system marginal price* (SMP). The SMP is the key incentive for entry into the generation sector. The biggest problem that arose shortly after deregulation was a lack of effective competition in the pool establishing the SMP. The existence of two very large generating companies meant that the SMP could be influenced to the detriment of final consumers. Green and Newbery (1992) have argued that ideally the generation sector should have resulted in five symmetric generating companies.[44] Competition in supply has been phased in gradually, as in the case of gas, with large customers being the first to be able to shop around. During 1998–9, it is expected that competition in electricity supply will be extended to all customers, and thus the supply market will be fully liberalized.

The UK's water supply and sewerage treatment industries were privatized in 1989. As a national grid in water-supply did not exist, the industry had always been organized into distinct regional units holding exclusive rights. Ten water and sewerage companies were privatized in 1989 joining another 29 smaller water-only companies that were already privately owned. Tariffs are subject to a price cap implemented through yardstick regulation. The last major network industry to be deregulated in the United Kingdom was rail in 1993. As in the case of electricity, the railway industry was vertically separated. A complex industry structure was established, but recent developments have wit-

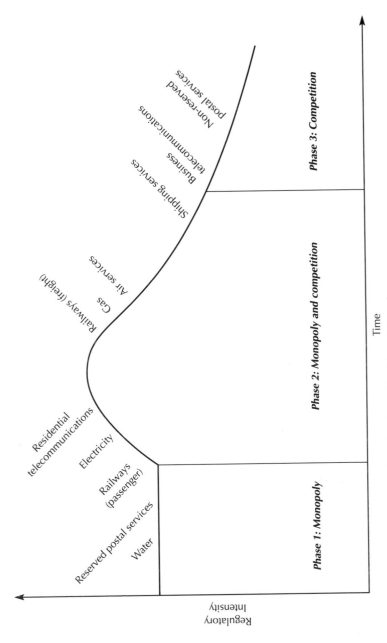

Figure 6 The status of network industries in the United Kingdom

nessed increased concentration in the industry through alliances, mergers and takeovers.

The experience of liberalization in the United Kingdom has met with mixed success.[45] The enthusiasm for privatization in the 1980s and early 1990s seemed to dominate efforts to implement appropriate structural measures needed to stimulate effective competition. The number of enquiries into competition problems in the energy industry is a testament to this. Despite the obvious flaws in policy, liberalization has delivered better quality services at lower prices to many customers.[46] Whether this would have occurred as impressively in less competitive settings, is doubtful.

Figure 6 on the previous page indicates that the network industries in the United Kingdom are much more deregulated than in Europe as a whole. Despite this, most of the industries currently lie in phase 2, although many are advancing towards phase 3.

Notes

1 *Op cit.*, see note 3, Chapter 4.

2 The EC Treaty (or the Treaty) is used to denote the founding treaties of the EU. Appendix 1 provides the full text of the key Articles of the Treaty that are commonly associated with policies related to network industries.

3 The European Commission has three distinct functions: initiator of proposals for legislation, guardian of the EC Treaty, and manager and executor of Union policies and international relationships. See Appendix 1 for further details.

4 Article 129 (b) EC Treaty.

5 See Appendix 1 for a brief description of Community law and procedures.

6 Article 92 (1) defines what is meant by incompatible, see Appendix 1.

7 Article 92 (3b). Article 92 (3e) provides the Commission with discretion to propose other categories of aid which may be compatible with the common market.

8 The Commission has published 'Competition Law in the European Communities – Rules Applicable to State Aid' on the Internet and published a user's guide 'Explanation of the Rules Applicable to State Aid'. Various guidelines have been published by the Commission on state aid in specific industries, for example, 'Community guidelines on State aid to maritime transport', (97/C 205/05) OJ C 205, 5 July 1997. Recently, the Commission has proposed a Council Regulation laying down detailed rules for the application of Article 93 of the EC Treaty, COM(1998) 73 Final, Brussels, 18 February 1998.

9 The third package comprised three Regulations 2407/92 (OJ L 240, 24 August 1992, p.1), 2408/92 (OJ L 240, 24 August 1992, p.8) and 2409/92 (OJ L 240, 24 August 1992, p.15), see Box 11 for details.

10 OJ L 272, 25 October 1996.

11 See *European Community competition policy*, XXVIth Report, 1996.

12 EC Press release IP/96/950.

13 Speech by Commissioner Neil Kinnock of Transport Directorate DG VII at Forum Europe, Brussels, 27 January 1998.

14 OJ C 350, 10 December 1994, p.5.

15 OJ L 254, 25 February 1994, p. 30.

16 *Op cit.*, see note 11 above.

17 The Community's approach to the maritime industry was outlined in a 1986 package, OJ L 378, 31 December 1986, pp. 1, 4, 14 and 21, consisting of four Regulations: Regulation (EEC) No. 4055/86 applying the principle of freedom to provide maritime transport between Member States and between Member States and third countries, as last amended by Regulation (EEC) No. 3573/90 (OJ L 353, 17 December 1990, p. 16); Regulation (EEC) No. 4056/86 laying down detailed rules for the application of Articles 85 and 86 of the Treaty to maritime transport, as last amended by the Act of Accession of Austria, Finland and Sweden; Regulation (EEC) No 4057/86 on unfair pricing practices in maritime transport; and Regulation (EEC) No. 4058/86 concerning coordinated action to safeguard free access to cargoes in ocean trades.

18 'Towards a new Maritime Strategy', COM(96) 81 Final, 13 March 1996.

19 Brussels, 10 December 1997 [Press release IP/97/1099].

20 White Paper 'A Strategy for Revitalising the Community's Railways', COM(96)421, paragraph 3.

21 Council Directive 95/18/EC on the licensing of railway undertakings, OJ L 143, 27 June 1995 and Council Directive 95/19/EC on the allocation of railway infrastructure capacity and the charging of infrastructure fees, OJ L 143, 27 June 1995.

22 'Towards Fair and Efficient Pricing in Transport', Green Paper.

23 Paragraph 53 in the White Paper, *op cit.* note 20 above.

24 See EC Press release IP/98/306.

25 COM (92) 494 Final.

26 *Fourth Report of the Competitiveness Advisory Group*, December 1996.

27 Figures taken from European Commission Communication COM(97) 'An overall view of energy policy and actions', Brussels, draft 21 April 1997.

28 COM (88) 238 Final, 2 May 1988.

29 Paragraph 27 in XXVIIth Report on Competition Policy, Brussels 1998.

30 'Concerning common rules for the internal market in electricity', OJ L 27, 30 January 1997, p. 20.

31 Derogations have been applied to Belgium and Ireland, which have extensions of one year, and Greece, which has a two-year extension to transpose the Directive.

32 'Will the EU Gas and Electricity Directives offer a sound basis for wider consumer choice?', speech by Klaus Thostrup, EC DG XVII, November 1997.

33 'Amended proposal for a European Parliament and Council Directive concerning common rules for the internal market in natural gas', COM(93) 643 Final, OJ C 123, 4 May 1994. Council reached a common position on the Directive proposal on 12 February 1998 and it has now gone back to Parliament for its second reading, OJ C 91, 26 March 1998.

34 'Proposal for a Council Decision adopting a Framework Programme for actions in the energy sector (1998–2002)', COM (97) 550 Final, OJ C 46, 11 February 1998.

35 COM (91) 476 Final.

36 See judgement of 23 October 1997 in Cases C-157/94 to C-160/94 'Member State Obligations – Electricity' *Commission* v *Netherlands* (157/94), *Italy* (158/94), *France* (159/94), and *Spain* (160/94).

37 See Chapter 6, Section 7.6.

38 'Notice from the Commission on the application of the competition rules to the postal sector on the assessment of certain State measures relating to postal services', OJ C 39, 6 January 1998.

39 The Commission has also published Notices dealing with uncertainty arising in other network industries. For example, it published a Notice on the status of voice on the internet under Directive 90/388/EC, see OJ C 140, 7 May 1997, p.8 and Part 2 of this Report.

40 See Armstrong, Cowan and Vickers (1994) and Helm and Jenkinson (eds) (1998) for a detailed exposition on the UK approach to deregulation.

41 Four reports were published by the MMC in 1993 on the status of gas competition and the role of British Gas.

42 *British Gas Plc* (1997), London: Monopolies and Mergers Commission.

43 Nuclear generation remained in public ownership and is largely passive, in a strategic sense, as it supplies baseload power to the market.

44 Symmetric in terms of fuel mix and size.

45 The Labour government in the United Kingdom is currently reviewing the regulation of the utility network industries, see Department of Trade and Industry (1998).

46 See OECD (1997a) for details on price reductions.

6 Phase 2 and the Need for More Regulation

Regulation can take two basic forms: an *ex ante* 'before the event' role, such as the setting of rules for corporate behaviour and mergers; and an *ex post* 'after the event' role, such as monitoring behaviour and resolving disputes. As seen in the previous chapter, the Commission has largely played an *ex ante* role in the programme of liberalization of Europe's network industries. Its primary activities have been:

- the setting of common rules to govern the single market;
- the formulation of guidelines, for example, on the application of competition rules and state aids.

Applying the principle of subsidiarity means that the detailed implementation of Community legislation is undertaken by Member States. Of course, as the previous chapter made clear, some national liberalization initiatives have preceded the initiatives of the Commission. Consequently, liberalization has not been applied uniformly across the EU: some countries, such as Sweden and the United Kingdom, have applied policies ahead of Commission directives, while others, such as Greece and Italy, have liberalized in response to Commission directives. The driving force behind liberalization is therefore moving in two directions: bottom-up in some Member States; and top-down when the Commission takes the lead role.

In this chapter, the focus is on the objectives of regulation and on the instruments used by Member States to achieve these objectives. The discussion focuses on phase 2, as most of the industries currently feature both competition and monopoly elements. Of course, monopoly problems are likely to diminish in significance over time as illustrated in Figure 2 above. As a result of interconnection, however, other difficulties will surface, particularly in relation to entry. Furthermore, dominance is an issue and social objectives complicate matters. Much of the discussion on monopoly in phase 2 is applicable to the treatment of monopoly in phase 1.

In phase 3, competition is more extensive and where it is effective, the need for detailed regulatory instruments wanes. Here the issue is largely concerned with choosing the right instruments for policing competition. As this topic is extensively covered elsewhere, only a brief treatment is given here.

6.1 The efficiency and equity objectives of regulation

Regulation is about constraints designed to influence the behaviour of powerful economic actors so as to achieve the best outcomes for society, taking account of both efficiency and equity considerations. Achieving allocative and productive efficiency is a relatively straightforward ambition, but equity is concerned with the distribution of resources across households and, due to distributive politics, can give rise to serious disagreements.

During phases 1 and 2, regulation of Europe's network industries is essential because of the absence of effective competition. With effective competition, rivalry would lead firms to undercut one another and drive prices towards costs, thereby achieving allocative efficiency. Because of dominance in network industries, however, rivalry is unlikely to be significant within national or regional markets at the outset of liberalization. Incumbents are likely to possess significant market power, and prices may not therefore be driven down to costs.

In phases 1 and 2, regulation could achieve allocative efficiency through instruments that control prices (and perhaps other variables like investment, line of service restrictions, etc.) set by dominant firms. This would require an omnipotent and omniscient regulator, however. In practice, regulators are imperfectly informed because of asymmetries in information, and are unlikely to possess the instruments necessary to control firm-level decisions perfectly. Much of regulation is therefore concerned with the acquisition of information, like identifying costs. Furthermore, imperfect control means that the application of instruments inevitably involves trade-offs giving rise to conflicting priorities.

In competitive markets, rivalry drives out high-cost firms, thus ensuring productive efficiency. Competition is an effective mechanism because the incentives faced by firms align with those of society. In the absence of effective competition, a feature of phase 1 and much of phase 2, productive efficiency may not be realized. A firm protected from competition may be less inclined to operate in the most efficient manner due to managerial slack – what is called X-inefficiency. Whether this is the case in practice depends very much on the economic relationship between a firm's management and its owners. In Europe's network industries, ownership has largely resided with the state. Because of this, political influence has affected the operations of firms, often, but not always, to the detriment of productive efficiency.

As the managers of incumbent network firms gain greater operational independence under liberalization, and some are exposed to stock market discipline following privatization, the incentive relationship between the firm's owners and its management is changing. This ought to help in terms of productive efficiency. Until effective competition is realized in phase 3, however, there will be a need for regulation and this will in part focus on productive efficiency. Thus, a regulator will need to devise instruments that provide desirable incentives to managers so that productive efficiency is achieved. The biggest problem regulators face in this area is asymmetric information: managers in dominant firms will know more about the relationship between effort and the way in which costs respond than external regulators.

Productive efficiency can be evaluated in a 'static' sense by examining whether output is produced using the most efficient combination of inputs at any moment in time. Over time, however, the capital stock can change because of depreciation and investment and the focus can switch to 'dynamic' efficiency. Dynamic efficiency occurs when resources are allocated optimally over time. Much of dynamic efficiency is therefore related to investment incentives. In the network industries, investment can be substantial, especially in the infrastructure component. Where a network industry is undergoing liberalization, investment incentives are critically affected by policies directed towards promoting greater competition. In seeking to promote competition, if regulators attach too much significance to short-term or static efficiency objectives, long-term or dynamic efficiency may be compromised – the first of the ten conflicting priorities.

Regulation may give rise to problems of under-investment, particularly in phase 2 where incumbents operating infrastructures are of the view that competitors are not contributing sufficiently in access charges towards investment risks. Furthermore, incumbents may be reluctant to provide innovative new services that rely upon developments within the infrastructure if they believe that regulatory *opportunism* is an acute problem (an issued addressed in Chapter 7).[1]

For example, if a regulator mandates that all firms in an industry have access rights to all new services provided by the incumbent, this may lead the incumbent to divert too many investment resources elsewhere (for example, to overseas investments, other industries, etc.). Notwithstanding the desirability of efficiency, pricing regulation in network industries is in practice influenced heavily by notions of fairness. Public service obligations are designed in many cases with fairness in mind, for example, demanding geographically uniform prices for services with non-uniform costs, and universal service, which may result in the provision of some services that are not *economically viable*.

It is not obviously *fair* to charge different consumers the same for a product, the supply of which to one consumer uses more scarce economic resources than supply to the other. For political or other reasons, however, such policies are likely to be important in the EU for the foreseeable future, and certainly during phases 1 and 2. The Commission affirmed its support of universal service in an opinion presented to the Intergovernmental Conference:

> Europe is built on a set of values shared by all its societies and combines the characteristics of democracy – human rights and institutions based on the rule of law – with those of an open economy underpinned by market forces, internal solidarity and cohesion. These values include access for all members of society to universal services or to services of general benefit, thus contributing to solidarity and equal treatment.[2]

The instruments used to achieve equity objectives, like mandating geographically uniform prices, may conflict with efficiency objectives. Similarly, outcomes that are efficient may not be desirable from a distributional perspective. In practice, there will be a trade-off between efficiency and equity (the second conflicting priority), and this problem will likely be more acute in phases 1 and 2. Once competition is effective in phase 3, the market will in most instances act in society's best interest.

6.2 Gradual liberalization

Liberalization is about transforming monopolistic industry structures into competitive markets. Chapter 5 showed that in Europe, liberalization is gradual and competition is being phased in to all the industries. This approach is undertaken partly to give incumbent operators time to restructure and partly because the scale of investments needed in some of the industries makes entry a relatively slow process. Allowing time for restructuring purposes may seem counterproductive since competition provides powerful incentives for restructuring. Protecting an incumbent for some period of time to allow for restructuring, however, avoids the problem of stranded costs (although this problem is often exaggerated for strategic reasons). It also enables Member States to deal with political legitimacy problems that may present obstacles, such as trade union opposition. Where restructuring involves the structural break-up of an incumbent, this will invariably be a lengthy process.

The typical path towards competition in Europe begins with monopoly in phase 1 followed by gradual liberalization of markets in phase 2. During the early stages of phase 2, an industry structure will tend to feature a dominant incumbent facing competition in some but typically not all markets. Here regulation needs to focus primarily on the incumbent's choice of prices. In practice, this ought to mean 'business as usual' since the incumbent's prices are likely to have been subject to scrutiny prior to liberalization. There are, however, several significant differences in the regulatory environment between the pre- and post-liberalization phases.

Since liberalization entails the move to a more market-oriented world and with the entry of new firms taking place, the way in which the incumbent's common costs are allocated to its services becomes much more critical. If an incumbent allocates its common costs disproportionately onto the services provided in the protected or monopoly markets, it may be in a position to set lower prices in the competitive markets. By creatively cross-subsidizing certain services, the incumbent gains an unfair competitive advantage.

As noted in Chapter 3, common costs can be considerable in network industries and their allocation is a key regulatory concern. So at the beginning of liberalization, regulation will focus on the incumbent's cost-allocation procedures as well as its price-setting behaviour. The Commission recognizes the potential problems that can arise from the way in which common costs are allocated in network industries, and it has instituted rules that should lead to greater transparency. When a Member State liberalizes a particular industry, it must usually implement some form of 'unbundling' of the incumbent's operations. A minimum requirement is that separate accounts are published for activities in the competitive and monopolistic sectors.

Another key difference between the pre- and post-liberalization regulatory environment centres on the relationship between the incumbent firm and the regulatory authorities. Commission directives implemented in this area require a separation between the day-to-day management structures of the incumbent and the regulatory authorities. Prior to liberalization, regulation is concerned with preventing monopoly abuse and meeting social objectives; and under public ownership, regulatory objectives are largely aligned with the interests of managers.

In the more market-oriented environment following liberalization, however, the managers of an incumbent firm will shift their priorities to the prospect of competitive entry. This means that managerial interests within the firm will no longer align with broader social concerns. Consequently, after liberalization, it is essential to remove many regulatory functions from the firm so as to prevent 'capture' and to lend credibility to the regulatory regime.[3]

The emergence of competition in phase 2 of network industry liberalization also demands that attention be devoted to meeting public service objectives. Before liberalization, these are typically met through obligations placed exclusively on the incumbent, but with competition, it may become necessary to impose obligations on new entrants. In most cases, however, public service obligations continue to be placed disproportionately on incumbents, even after liberalization. If entrants are not required to meet them, however, how should they be funded? In particular, if entrants benefit indirectly because of the incumbent's public service obligations, it may seem reasonable that they contribute to their costs. At the same time, if entrants are expected to contribute to their costs, careful scrutiny will be needed of the costs alleged to be associated with them.

Once a programme of liberalization is firmly established, a network industry sees the opening up to competition of more markets. During phase 2, competition is widened and greater entry is likely to arise. It is also probable that the regulatory structures established at the beginning of phase 2 will need to be reviewed and possibly restructured in the light of experience and new information.

The final phase of liberalization, phase 3, is where competition becomes extensive and increasingly effective, and correspondingly regulation diminishes. For many of the industries or industry sectors, this phase may not be entered for a considerable period of time, if ever. Nevertheless, even in phase 3 there will remain a need to apply rules on competition to prevent restrictive practices taking hold. In network industries, this necessarily means keeping a close eye on vertical restraints.

6.3 Regulatory intensity over the three phases of market structure

The gradual phasing of liberalization means that the scope and intensity of regulation are likely to vary and its emphasis shift as an industry moves through phase 2 and on towards phase 3. In the early stage of phase 2, much attention will focus on preventing monopoly abuses by incumbents, whereas in the latter stage, the emphasis will be more about policing competition.

It must be noted, however, that the prevalence of natural monopoly characteristics, particularly in the infrastructure, means that there may always remain some elements of regulation to deal with monopoly abuse. This is because competition may not develop or become effective in interconnection markets. Indeed, it may be the case that liberalization is predicated on the promotion of competition in either or both of the upstream and downstream components of an industry. If competition is promoted through encouraging competition between downstream service providers, this will require the scrutiny of an incumbent's access charges. Such scrutiny will be all the more essential in those industries where an incumbent is integrated into the competitive downstream markets.

Having characterized network industries as going through three phases, it is possible to identify the principal regulatory tasks that will be associated with each phase. It must be emphasized that the activities in each phase are likely to overlap.

The rest of this section probes deeper into the main competition and regulation policies that are needed in some or all of the three phases of regulation.

6.4 Preventing monopoly abuse in retail markets

Monopoly during phase 1 and dominance during much of phase 2 means that regulators will choose instruments that focus on the prices set by incumbents in final markets, assuming that an incumbent is vertically integrated and operates in the downstream part of the industry. It has been argued above that where prices reflect costs, or more precisely equal incremental costs, a condition needed for efficiency is achieved. Hence it is desirable to equate prices with costs. A firm with monopoly power in final markets can obtain greater profit by setting prices above costs, and therefore regulation is needed to prevent this from happening.

Thus, regulating the *level* of prices set by a dominant incumbent is a feature of regulation that is prominent during phase 1, and continues to a lesser extent in phase 2. As most network industries feature firms selling many different outputs, however, the prevalence of common costs, which may be substantial, presents a problem: how does one evaluate the costs associated with an individual output? The problem of how to allocate common costs is endemic in network industries and raises the issue of the appropriate *structure* of prices. Regulation of final prices therefore needs to address both the level and structure of prices.

Consider the case of a dominant network firm selling n different services, x_1 through to x_N. Let F denote the firm's common costs associated with the network infrastructure, and let c_i be the marginal or incremental cost of production for each service i produced. If the price level of each output is set equal to marginal cost, as allocative efficiency requires, the firm would make a loss. Such a loss could be offset by the granting of a subsidy, but in practice this may be politically infeasible and in any case is likely to have detrimental incentive effects working against productive efficiency. In the absence of subsidy, it will be necessary for the firm to include a mark-up above marginal cost in its prices so that fixed costs are recovered.

There are many possible ways in which a mark-up can be applied to costs and, therefore, there are many possible price structures. From an efficiency perspective, however, it is well known that the setting of *Ramsey prices* is the preferred method for recovering fixed costs. Ramsey prices are structured in a way that enables efficiency to be maximized while allowing the common costs to be covered. Efficiency is maximized in a constrained sense, meaning that allocative efficiency losses due to prices deviating from marginal cost are kept to a minimum. This is achieved by setting the structure of prices such that services having a low elasticity of demand (demand is less sensitive to price changes) will have a higher cost mark-up than services with a high elasticity of demand.

Where there is monopoly or dominance in final markets and subsidy is not possible, regulation should seek to attain a structure of prices consistent with those that would be chosen by a so-called *Ramsey welfare maximizer*. To achieve Ramsey pricing through regulation, however, requires a tremendous amount of information. A regulator would need to know in detail about costs and price elasticities of demand. When regulation is integrated within the firm or closely associated with it, as was and often is the case before liberalization, this information may be more readily available. In the early stages of liberalization, however, regulatory functions are made independent and management within dominant incumbents change priorities. Because of this it may be very difficult to achieve Ramsey prices directly. Regulators must instead appeal to indirect methods which steer or provide incentives for dominant firms to choose a structure of prices consistent with Ramsey prices.

The use of indirect methods to regulate the prices set by dominant firms in network industries has been a feature of US regulation for many years. In the United States, until recently, the most common method of controlling the prices set by dominant network firms was through a control on the rate of return earned on the assets employed by a firm. Rate of return (ROR) regulation is an instrument available to regulators in Europe.

There has been much research conducted on the efficacy of ROR regulation. The earliest contributions, notably a seminal piece by Averch and Johnson (1962), show in a theoretical setting that ROR regulation may promote a desirable structure of prices but it tends to promote productive inefficiency through inducing an excessive or inefficient level of investment in capital. More popularly, the phrase *gold-plating* is used and in the economics literature it is termed the Averch-Johnson (A-J) effect. The A-J effect arises because a ROR regulated firm finds it is profitable to inflate the capital base, because at a given output level higher absolute profits can be obtained. The consequence of this is that the capital-labour mix is different to that consistent with productive efficiency. ROR regulation provides insufficient incentives for the firm to be productively efficient. In the parlance of economic theory, ROR regulation is described as a *low powered incentive scheme*.

Although theoretical models may predict productive inefficiency, the problem of gold-plating is more elusive to find in empirical studies. This is due in part to a phenomenon known as *regulatory lag*, which increases the incentives for a firm to be cost efficient. In practice ROR regulation is applied by calculating the value of the firm's assets employed in regulated markets and then estimating a *rate base* that would be applied to this value which would enable the firm to earn a fair rate of return.[4] The regulated firm submits its proposed prices to the regulator, and the regulator uses demand data consistent with the asset valuation to make sure that the firm does not exceed a return in excess of the rate base. Hence, data used in implementing ROR regulation, is historical and because it tends to be based on audited company accounts is at least a year old. Between rate-base reviews, therefore, the firm has an incentive to become more efficient, and this incentive increases the greater the lag between reviews. In practice rate-base reviews were frequent and this dented productive efficiency incentives. Furthermore, a ROR regulated firm knew that it would always be possible to earn the return allowable because costs could be passed through to consumers.

It is important to note that while regulatory lag contributes towards improvements in productive efficiency, with regard to allocative efficiency, it works in the opposite direction. In practice there is a trade-off between a short regulatory lag that promotes allocative efficiency but is bad for productive efficiency, and a long regulatory lag that is good for productive efficiency but bad for allocative efficiency. Although regulatory lag may provide better incentives when ROR is applied in practice, there may be alternative forms of price regulation with higher-powered incentives. One such mechanism is price-cap regulation.

6.4.1 Price-cap regulation

Price-cap regulation came into prominence in the United Kingdom where it has been applied to the prices set by privatized incumbent firms operating in network industries. The first price cap was applied in the telecoms industry on British Telecom (BT). The application of price-cap regulation in the United Kingdom followed an assessment made by Professor Stephen Littlechild, commissioned by the UK government, on the best approach to regulate the profitability of monopoly firms. Littlechild advocated the adoption of price caps, which he claimed dominated ROR regulation in terms of restraining monopoly power, promoting competition, reducing X-inefficiency and providing incentives for cost reductions. It was also argued that it would lead firms to choose more efficient price schedules by allowing firms greater discretion over the setting of prices.

Price-cap regulation works by setting explicit ceilings on prices charged for services supplied in monopoly markets or in markets where competition is ineffective. Due to inflation, in practice it works by constraining the rate of change in real prices. Once a price cap has been set, a firm faces strong incentives to minimize costs and therefore productive efficiency should be attained. The power of this incentive is greater the longer the period over which a price cap operates without review. In this regard, price-cap regulation explicitly takes advantage of regulatory lag, whereas under ROR regulation it arises because of practical limitations.

Price caps can be applied directly to the tariffs of different services for a multi-output firm. In the case of BT, a price cap constrains the weighted average of price increases for regulated services to be no greater than RPI-X, where RPI is the inflation rate and X is an adjustment factor reflecting *inter alia* expected technological developments. (See Chapter 10, Section 4 for a discussion on price caps in telecommunications.) The weights used when calculating the average price increase across services are usually based on revenue shares for each service generated in the previous year. This price cap is known as the 'revenue weighted form of RPI-X'. Since these are known in the current year, it gives the regulated firm some discretion to influence weights in the future through prices set in the current period. More significantly, a revenue-weighted form of price cap induces an efficient price structure, that is, Ramsey prices (see Box 18 overleaf). If a firm supplies a largely homogeneous product, as may be the case in the gas and electricity industries, a so-called 'revenue yield RPI-X price cap' can be applied. A revenue yield is defined as the revenue generated from the regulated sector divided by some measure of the volume of business in that sector. Thus, the price cap constrains the change in the average price of the good. The weights in a revenue-yield constraint are some measure of current quantity and can therefore be influenced by the firm's current pricing policy. Revenue-yield price caps have been applied in the United Kingdom on the revenues generated by the dominant airport company (BAA), the gas transportation company (Transco) and the electricity transmission firm (National Grid Company).

In practice, ROR regulation and price-cap regulation are not too dissimilar. This is because when setting a price cap, the value chosen for X takes into account a firm's rate of return. Whereas ROR regulation is backward looking, however, price-cap regulation is forward-looking. Furthermore, price-cap regulation provides a firm with greater discretion over the setting of individual prices because the regulator only needs to care about the average price. Price-cap regulation is also arguably more transparent than ROR regulation, as it clearly signals to consumers through the setting of X the direction, on average, in which prices will move. Price-cap regulation also allows the regulator greater flexibility through the setting of the weights. While both ROR regulation and RPI-X price-cap regulation are applied to the subset of services supplied by a firm that is dominant in the markets where these goods are sold, it is very difficult under ROR regulation to target specific consumer groups without controlling individual prices. In price-cap regulation, specific consumers can be targeted by setting weights in a price cap on the basis of the revenues generated from these consumers. In the United Kingdom, the weights in BT's current price cap are based on the revenues of the first 80% of residential households by bill size. Thus, while the price cap is applied to services

Box 18 **Revenue weighted form of RPI-X**

The RPI-X price cap as applied to BT is a Laspeyre index constraint on tariffs. Thus BT's tariffs are constrained as follows:

$$\sum_{i=1}^{n} \frac{(p_{i,1} - p_{i,0})}{p_{i,0}} \left\{ \frac{p_{i,0}\, q_{i,0}}{\mathbf{p_0 q_0}} \right\} \leq \frac{RPI_1}{RPI_0} - X - 1$$

where the i subscript denotes the service, the 0, 1 subscripts refer to time and variables in bold denote vectors. The left-hand side of the expression shows that the change in price for each service i is multiplied into the revenue share associated with the service ($\mathbf{p_0 q_0}$ is total revenue and the weights sum to one). These are summed to measure the average price increase, which is constrained to be no greater than the term on the right-hand side. The right-hand side is a measure of inflation minus the offset factor X. Inflation is the value of the current price index over the previous price index less one. Thus in the absence of inflation (that is $RPI_1 = RPI_0$), the weighted sum of price changes cannot exceed $-X$. Thus, whenever X is positive real prices decline on average. The expression simplifies to yield:

$$\frac{\mathbf{p_1 q_0}}{\mathbf{p_0 q_0}} \leq \frac{RPI_1}{RPI_0} - X$$

continued

Box 18 continued

The left-hand side of the equation above is a Laspeyre index of the regulated firm's prices. In this regard, the price cap has a backward-looking component (that is, the weights are based on the revenues generated in the previous year).

The revenue-weighted price cap can achieve Ramsey outcomes as it has a property similar to a 'regulatory mechanism' first described by Vogelsang and Finsinger (1979). Suppose a firm can choose its prices each period, subject to the constraint that overall it can only choose prices in the current period that would not have generated positive profits using last period's costs and outputs. This mechanism constrains prices in period 1 to generate non-positive profits if applied to period 0 quantities and costs, that is:

$$\mathbf{p}_1\mathbf{q}_0 - C(\mathbf{q}_0) \leqslant 0$$

This expression can be rewritten as follows:

$$\frac{\mathbf{p}_1\mathbf{q}_0}{\mathbf{p}_0\mathbf{q}_0} \leqslant \frac{C(\mathbf{q}_0)}{\mathbf{p}_0\mathbf{q}_0} = 1 - \frac{\Pi_0}{\mathbf{p}_0\mathbf{q}_0}$$

where Π_0 are profits and $C(\mathbf{q}_0)$ is the firm's total cost in period 0. Note the left-hand side is a Laspeyre index and on the right-hand side the term $(\Pi_0/\mathbf{p}_0\mathbf{q}_0)$ is fixed in period 1 and therefore performs the same role as X opposite. Vogelsang and Finsinger showed that this mechanism would lead to Ramsey prices. This implies that the revenue-weighted price cap should induce an efficient price structure.

The revenue yield form of RPI-X establishes weights in current terms and does not share the Ramsey pricing property. The firm's optimization problem when faced with a revenue-yield constraint is to maximize profits by choosing prices as follows:

$$\max\Pi(\mathbf{q}) = \sum_{i=1}^{n} p_i(\mathbf{q})q_i - C(\mathbf{q})$$

$$s.t. \quad \frac{\sum_{i=1}^{n} p_i(\mathbf{q})q_i}{\sum_{i=1}^{n} q_i} \leqslant \bar{\mathbf{p}}$$

where $p_i(\mathbf{q})$ is the inverse demand function for each good or service $i = 1, \ldots, n$ and the term on the right-hand side of the inequality is the price cap.

used by all households, the weights in the cap reflect a segment of the market where competition is not yet effective.

In practice, price-cap regulation, as applied in the United Kingdom, has sometimes been criticized for enabling managers and shareholders to obtain a disproportionate share of the benefits obtained from efficiency gains. This raises a difficult distribution issue between shareholders and consumers. The incentives behind price caps are such that managers are encouraged to search for efficient production methods, this should of course benefit shareholders. Once a price cap is in place, however, circumstances may change in a direction that favours management and shareholders. For example, an unexpected technological development may lead to a dramatic fall in production costs. In this case, the reduction in production costs is not due to the effort put in by management. Thus, is it fair that the gains from such an innovation should flow largely to shareholders?

One solution to such problems would be to allow for adjustments to be made to price caps by altering the value of X. This unfortunately is not very desirable because it raises the prospect of regulatory risk and opportunism. An alternative remedy might be to have some profit-sharing arrangement for unexpected outcomes, something that has been termed *sliding-scale regulation*. Typically, sliding-scale regulation lengthens the period of regulatory review to preserve incentives for cost reductions while at the same time introducing an explicit sharing of the benefits flowing from these cost reductions. Mayer and Vickers (1996) have expressed scepticism about sliding-scale regulation:

> Profit sharing has perhaps been an unduly hasty response to a problem that could alternatively be treated by modifying rather than abandoning price-cap regulation. For this to be achieved, more attention needs to be devoted to measures of performance and the identification of exogenous influences on performance.[5]

6.4.2 Asymmetric information

In the previous section, the effect of asymmetric information was ignored. In practice, a regulated firm's managers will know more about demand and cost conditions than the regulator. Under a price cap, asymmetric information is likely to come into prominence at the time when X is evaluated. Suppose that the chosen X is positive, so that real prices are expected to decline. In telecoms, this is the case because technological progress is dramatically reducing real costs. It is clearly in the interests of a regulated firm to try and obtain the smallest value possible for X, a so-called loose cap. By doing this, real price reductions can be kept to a minimum and the firm can obtain more monopoly rent. Where the firm is better informed, it may choose to hide information from a regulator so that it can obtain a better value for X. In doing this, the firm may obtain rents due to asymmetry in information.

In practice, asymmetric information means that there will be strategic interaction in the regulatory relationship. What tends to occur when X is being evaluated is a game involving the regulator, the regulated incumbent and other firms in the industry. The posturing in this game may involve the regulated incumbent making claims about its cost base in the regulated sector, and in particular arguments in favour of a relatively high return to reflect the risks associated with investments. It may be the case that entrants competing against the incumbent will also argue in favour of a low X. Such an outcome is likely where entry is immediate over all services but phased in over customers according to their value. Typically, liberalization means that competition opens up the markets for lucrative high spending customers (that is, business and high-value residential customers) before the lower-value customers. In this setting, entrants would welcome a loose cap because the incumbent may not reduce prices much in view of entry, especially where it faces geographic uniformity.

The regulatory game will involve signalling with the regulated firm possibly following a cycle of cost reductions just after a review, and then minor cost reductions just before a review. Because of this, the firm will obtain some *informational rents* on its private information. For example, a firm might prefer to be thought of as a high-cost firm when in truth it is a low-cost firm, so that the regulator may treat it leniently.

6.5 Phase 2: Interconnection and the regulation of access to infrastructure

In phase 2, entry into a network industry takes place and this gives rise to interconnection problems. The natural monopoly elements found in the infrastructure, in most cases operated by an incumbent in phase 2, necessarily calls for instruments to control monopoly excess. In an ideal world, regulation should ensure that there is perfect allocative and productive efficiency. This occurs when all prices – including access prices – are set equal to the minimum possible marginal (or incremental) costs of providing the various services. For, if an access charge is set above the associated marginal cost, then firms that consume this access will choose to buy too little of the service compared to the productively efficient outcome.

A serious problem with this policy is, however, that firms operating infrastructure in network industries have often considerable economies of scale and scope, therefore pricing services at marginal or incremental cost will usually result in losses. In such cases, firms practising marginal-cost pricing must receive subsidies in order to remain profitable. Such subsidies, though, cannot be funded without causing distortions elsewhere in the economy – for example, virtually all taxes that raise government revenue cause prices somewhere in the economy to diverge from marginal costs. In the presence of such distortions, it would no longer be certain that marginal-cost pricing of access constitutes an efficient policy.[6] Thus, as in the case of regulating final prices discussed above, access charges will usually entail a mark-up above marginal cost to allow for the recovery of common and fixed costs.

The economics literature concerning access pricing has developed significantly in recent years. In what follows, there is a discussion looking at some of the contributions that have been made to the literature, highlighting their strengths and weaknesses.[7] Two industry structures are examined: vertical separation; and the more complex case of vertical integration where the incumbent infrastructure owner operates downstream.

On reflection, it should not be surprising to observe firms disagreeing over the terms of access. There are clear foreclosure incentives on the part of incumbents: they can influence the speed of implementing interconnection, are in a good position to affect the quality of the access services provided and, because of asymmetric information and common costs, have an opportunity to influence accounting costs used to compute the price of access. These actions have the effect of raising rivals' costs. Furthermore, the provision of interconnection gives the incumbent valuable information about its rivals' marketing plans.

On the other hand, entrants have an incentive to exaggerate the scale of incumbency advantages, in the hope of obtaining generous entry assistance, and an incentive to understate the incumbent's true costs of providing access. In short, the interests of an incumbent and those of the entrants are very often, but not necessarily always, diametrically opposed.[8] In these circumstances, both parties may adopt strategies that are detrimental for welfare and hence inefficient. Indeed, such positions of conflict can result in resources being diverted into rent-seeking activities, such as lobbying. The difficulty facing regulatory authorities when seeking to promote efficient competition is to balance *fairly* the competing claims of the incumbent and entrants, and to ensure that *reasonable* access prices are established. The added emphasis is meant to suggest that this is far from being an easy task. In the rest of this section, the discussion focuses on the efficiency aspects related to the setting of interconnection and access prices.

6.5.1 Vertical separation

Regulating access in a vertically-separated industry is fairly straightforward: the regulator needs to ensure that monopoly power is not abused by the infrastructure operator. For example, consider the case where the ground-handling facilities at an airport are provided by a monopolist. Regulation ought to ensure that the monopolist sets its prices equal to cost, allowing for mark-ups to recover fixed and common costs. In principle, the regulatory problem does not differ from the case of regulating monopoly in retail markets. Thus, regulation should aim for a structure of prices consistent with Ramsey prices. It may also be desirable in practice to put into place incentives that encourage productive efficiency. As discussed above, both these objectives may be achieved through the operation of a price cap. It is also important that a level playing field is maintained in the setting of access charges by ensuring that undue discrimination is not practised. A level playing field requires transparency and, in practice, this may be achieved by insisting on the publication of infrastructure charges.

If regulation can succeed in achieving (constrained) efficient prices for access, it does not follow that overall efficiency will be achieved. In other words, efficient access prices are necessary but not sufficient for overall efficiency. If competition is not effective downstream, say it is oligopolistic, firms in this part of the market will be able to earn some excess profit through a mark-up on costs. Ideally, regulation should use the instruments discussed in the previous section to influence prices in markets where firms have monopoly power.

If this is infeasible, however, an alternative approach might be to influence final prices indirectly through altering the level of access charges. For example, lowering the price charged for ground-handling facilities at an airport enables airlines to set lower fares, and hence may drive final prices closer to costs. Although access charges can be used to influence final prices in this way, regulation should use other instruments to deal with monopoly in downstream markets. This is because using access charges in this way is likely to result in losses being incurred by the infrastructure provider. As these would probably be offset by a subsidy, the transaction costs and distortions arising may more than offset the welfare gains from lower final prices.

6.5.2 Vertical integration

In a vertically-integrated industry, where the firm operating the monopoly or near monopoly infrastructure also competes in the downstream markets, the regulation of access charges is made more complicated by the presence of costs that may be common to both the infrastructure and the downstream market operations. Common costs are, however, largely a practical difficulty that may be overcome through accounting separation and greater scrutiny of cost allocation methods. What is important is that the principles governing the regulation of access prices should be predicated on achieving efficient outcomes, just as in the case of vertical separation above. A number of theories on efficient access pricing have been developed, but as indicated below, it is possible to construct a synthesis relating the key theories.

6.5.3 The efficient component pricing rule

The efficient component pricing rule (ECPR)[9] is a method for setting access charges designed to ensure efficient entry. If it is assumed that price regulation takes place in two stages with retail prices chosen first and then access charges determined to maximize welfare given the retail prices. The concern here is with the second problem, so suppose that retail prices are fixed at some given level. Since retail prices are fixed, consumer welfare and allocative efficiency are not affected by access pricing policy. Therefore, the regulator can focus policy on minimizing total production costs. In other words, access charges should be chosen that ensure that entry occurs if, and only if, the entrant is at least as efficient as the incumbent firm.

Consider a hypothetical example using the air transport industry. An incumbent firm called Big Airline (BA) operates a service connecting two cities X and Y. BA is vertically integrated and operates the ground-handling facilities at both airports. Because the airports are small, the ground-handling facilities are a natural monopoly. Another firm called Entrant Jet (EJ) wishes to operate a service over the route connecting X and Y. EJ requires access to the ground-handling facilities in order to serve custom on the route.

Suppose that BA's average incremental cost of operating ground-handling facilities is $10. More generally, let b denote the incumbent's average incremental cost of access. Assume that the average incremental cost of providing the final output, the airline service between X and Y, is $60 of which $10 is the marginal cost of access. Assume that the price charged by BA for the final service is $75. The reason why the price is set above incremental cost could be because the common costs of running a wide network need to be covered, or because the firm must fund loss-making public service obligations. Suppose that EJ's average incremental cost for operating services between X and Y is given by the charge levied for access to the infrastructure facilities plus $Z. Denote the access charge as a. EJ is more efficient than BA if $Z < 50$.

What access charge a ensures that entry takes place if and only if EJ is more efficient? Given an access charge a, EJ's incremental cost is $a + Z$ and entry is profitable if the price exceeds costs, that is, $75 \geq (a + Z)$. Entry will take place therefore if and only if $Z \leq 75 - a$. Since the regulator wishes to encourage efficient entry, the optimal access charge is $a = 25$. Thus EJ's incremental cost of providing the final service will be $Z + 25$. The optimal access charge exceeds the incremental cost associated with providing ground-handling facilities due to the final price exceeding cost. If the final price were in accordance with allocative efficiency and therefore equal to the incumbent's incremental cost $60, the optimal access charge would necessarily equal cost $10.

More generally, if the price of the service is p and the incumbent's incremental cost of providing the competitive part of the service (air transport) is c, then the optimal access charge is given by $a = p - c$. This is known as the *margin rule* as it implies that the margin between the final price and the access charge is set equal to the incumbent's incremental (marginal) cost in the competitive activity. It ensures that (i) entry takes place if, and only if, $Z < c$, and (ii) if entry does take place the incumbent continues to receive the contribution $[p - (b + c)]$ towards its common costs and/or loss making activities. The term $[p - (b + c)]$ is the opportunity cost due to entry, that is, it is the profit foregone by the incumbent due to entry. The ECPR can be written in terms of the opportunity cost:

$$a = b + [p - (b + c)]$$

The access charge equals the direct cost of providing access plus opportunity cost. In words:

optimal access charge = direct cost of providing access + opportunity cost of providing access

Box 19 The ECPR and controversy in the New Zealand telecoms industry

The ECPR received much attention in the mid-1990s because of a legal battle that took place involving the incumbent and an entrant in the New Zealand telecoms industry. In New Zealand, the regulation of interconnection in the network industries is light-handed through the application of general competition legislation (the Commerce Act).

In the early 1990s, the incumbent, Telecom New Zealand, sought to implement the ECPR when setting its access charges. The entrant, Clear Communications, objected to the access charges proposed and pursued a legal battle claiming that Telecom New Zealand's application of the ECPR (through the setting of an 'access levy') would constitute an abuse of dominance. The final court interpreted the ECPR as a proposition stating that: 'in a fully contestable market, someone selling to a competitor the facilities necessary to provide a service that the seller could otherwise provide himself would demand a price equal to the revenue he would have received if he had in fact provided the service himself "the opportunity cost"' (Privy Council, 1994, p. 8).

The legal battle over the alleged abuse of dominance culminated in New Zealand's highest court (which, for historical reasons, is the Privy Council in the United Kingdom) judging the question of whether the presence of actual or potential monopoly rents weakens the validity of the ECPR. As shown here, even if the retail price charged by an incumbent incorporates monopoly rent, the ECPR nevertheless ensures that entry is efficient. In its judgement on the New Zealand dispute, the Privy Council agreed with this view: 'the risk of monopoly rents has no bearing upon the question whether the application of the Baumol-Willig Rule prevents competition in the contested area' (Privy Council, 1994, p.27).

Note the ECPR detailed on p.107 is a cost-based rule and it can be implemented without the need to gather information about demand elasticities. This feature, however, is a reflection of the simplified structure of the problem addressed. In a more complex setting with a closer resemblance to reality, shown in the next section, demand elasticities appear in the formula.

Although the ECPR is designed to guarantee efficient entry, it does not resolve the problem of allocative inefficiency when the final product price lies above cost. This is because it relies on one instrument, the access price, to target one objective, efficient entry or productive efficiency. To tackle allocative efficiency, the regulator would also need to influence the final price in the market.

6.5.4 Ramsey access prices

In the previous section, access prices were discussed in which the vertically-integrated incumbent was offering a fixed retail-tariff, a tariff that may not have accurately reflected the underlying costs. Because consumer prices were not affected by access pricing policy, the only issue was that of productive efficiency. Clearly, the regulator should choose two instruments to target two objectives: productive and allocative efficiency. This can be achieved by choosing retail and access prices simultaneously in order to maximize welfare. Since the incumbent firm must at least break even, it may be desirable to have higher access charges in order to enable the setting of lower retail prices. In other words, it may be worth sacrificing a little productive efficiency to obtain a greater degree of allocative efficiency. This trade-off is the familiar trade-off encountered in Ramsey welfare problems, like the one examined above in the context of regulating final prices.

The previous section contained another rather extreme assumption: namely, that entry was of the 'all or nothing' form. While this may make sense in some circumstances, in other contexts, it would be expected that entry would take only a fraction of the market, with a lower access charge (or a higher retail price) leading to greater market penetration by the entrant. An entrant like EJ would choose its output such that its marginal cost was set equal to the margin $m = p - a$. The greater the margin m, the greater the degree of entry made by EJ. Productive efficiency is achieved by ensuring that the entrant's and incumbent's marginal cost of air transport are equal. Since the entrant's marginal cost by its actions will equal m, productive efficiency is assured when m is set equal to the incumbent's marginal cost of air transport. In other words, a should be set equal to the retail price p minus the incumbent's marginal cost of air transport, the Baumol-Willig rule. This ignores, however, the fact that increasing a beyond this level could enable the retail price to be reduced, thereby benefiting consumers. On the other hand, the access charge could be lowered to stimulate greater entry and therefore promote product diversity assuming the services are differentiated between the two firms.

Optimal regulation should ensure that some combination of price p and access charge a is chosen so that the incumbent firm just breaks even. Since the incumbent firm's profit is increasing in both p and a, raising a naturally enables a lower p to be feasible. A regulator concerned with consumer welfare would take this trade-off into account. This may lead to an access charge that is *higher* than that set under the Baumol-Willig rule. The precise choice of the access charge will depend on (i) the benefits of reducing the retail price, which will depend on the elasticity of demand; and (ii) the effects of raising the access charge on productive inefficiency, which will depend on the elasticity of the entrant's supply.

The discussion above is an example of the more general problem of maximizing welfare subject to a break-even constraint for the incumbent firm. The solution to this problem results in *Ramsey access prices*.[10] The form of the Ramsey access prices is as follows:

$$a = b + SRT$$

where SRT is a Ramsey term involving super-elasticities.[11] The structure of Ramsey access charges appears to be rather different from the access charges using the ECPR. There is, however, a relationship between the two approaches as shown by Armstrong *et al.* (1996).

The ECPR above was derived implicitly using some key assumptions. In particular:

- **homogeneous final products**: the incumbent and entrant offer identical services;
- **fixed coefficient technology**: constant returns technology between the infrastructure good and the final output;
- **no bypass**: the infrastructure is exclusively provided by the incumbent.

Relaxing these assumptions, which seems plausible, and in the absence of a fixed cost recovery problem, leads to an optimal access price:

$$a = b + \sigma [p - (b + c)]$$

where σ is the *displacement ratio* defined as the change in the incumbent's retail sales as the access charge varies divided by the change in the incumbent's sales of access services to its rival as the access charge varies. The only difference between the expression above and that shown in the case of the ECPR is the presence of the displacement term. When $\sigma = 1$, the two expressions are identical. This occurs when the above three assumptions hold, otherwise $\sigma < 1$. Thus, the optimal ECPR access price is likely to be less than that implied by the simple margin rule formulation above.

Suppose instead that the entrant airline EJ wishes to offer service between X and W, where W is far from Y. Thus EJ is offering a different service to that provided by the incumbent. Assume that a service between X and W is not provided by BA. Although the entrant would still need to purchase ground-handling facilities at the airport located in X, its service is unlikely to displace any passengers from the service offered by the incumbent. In this case it is likely that σ will be very small and it can be seen therefore that the optimal access charge should be set close to the incremental cost associated with ground-handling at X.

If the incumbent needs to recover fixed costs, then the optimal access charges will look like:

$$a = b + \sigma \left[p - (b + c) \right] + RT$$

where RT is a Ramsey term involving the own-price elasticity of demand. Armstrong *et al.* (1996) show this expression is equivalent to the optimal Ramsey access charges derived by Laffont and Tirole (1994).[12]

To implement optimal Ramsey access prices in practice would place a considerable informational demand on regulatory authorities, as they would need to obtain data on bypass, factor substitution possibilities, and supply and demand elasticities. This would imply a degree of intrusion into the market that would seem to run counter to the spirit of liberalization, where the emphasis is on delegating matters to those in possession of the relevant information. Laffont and Tirole (1996) propose the global price cap as a way of achieving Ramsey outcomes without the need for such regulatory intrusion.

6.5.5 Global price-caps

A global price-cap works like the retail price-caps discussed above, but it gives the regulated firm much greater discretion over the structure of prices. A global price-cap includes, however, access services in the basket of services regulated. Thus, in the air transport example, a global price-cap would act to constrain both the final price and the access price. Unlike the Ramsey problem above, a global price-cap delegates to the firm a simple rule that does not, at least on first inspection, require as much detailed information as in the Ramsey case.

The global price-cap works as follows. For given weights w_1 and w_2, the regulated firm chooses prices p and a to maximize profits subject to a constraint:

$$w_1 \times p + w_2 \times a \leq \bar{p}$$

where $\bar{p}$ is fixed and set by the regulator. In other words, the weighted average of the access price and the final price cannot exceed some value determined by the regulator. This form of regulation induces a structure of prices identical to those in the Ramsey problem if the correct weights are chosen: these should be *exogenous* and *proportional* to the quantities realised under Ramsey efficient pricing.

Despite its theoretical appeal, however, the concept of a global price-cap suffers in much the same way as Ramsey prices. The informational burden may be lighter in some respects, but the selection of correct weights poses a considerable informational burden. Furthermore, allowing the incumbent wide discretion over prices raises the prospect of predatory behaviour. A global price-cap could allow an incumbent to set low final prices and relatively high access charges, while meeting the price-cap constraint. To date, a regulatory authority has not yet implemented a global price-cap.

6.5.6 Accounting approaches to access pricing

A regulator attempting to implement optimal access prices would probably find it a very difficult task. Because of this, regulators have tended in practice to rely upon accounting methods to establish access prices. The accounting approach to the setting of the access and retail prices uses a method that allocates total costs, including the common costs, across the different services, including access services. There are various ways of doing this, but once this has been done the procedure, roughly speaking, is to set prices equal to the allocated costs. In practice, this results in access charges being set equal to the incremental cost of providing access plus some 'appropriate' share of the common costs of the incumbent firm. The favourite method is to set prices equal to some measure of forward-looking long-run average incremental costs.

Although some proportion of costs are easily associated with the provision of specific services, in network industries there are likely to be considerable residual common costs. For example, in the UK railway industry, around 90% of costs associated with the operation of the infrastructure are fixed or common. There are various methods that can be used to allocate common costs, and these may include measures using output shares, revenue shares or incremental cost shares.[13] Inevitably, all of these involve a degree of arbitrariness. Economists have traditionally criticized these accounting approaches to pricing on the grounds that the mark-up over incremental cost is not based on any principle of efficient resource allocation. The Ramsey procedure, by contrast, involves setting mark-ups to cause the least allocative inefficiency by trading off productive efficiency against allocative efficiency in an optimal manner.

What then accounts for the popularity of these accounting approaches? There are two possible explanations. The first is that accounting methods for setting access prices correspond to the regulator's (or the public's) conception of what is equitable. It is viewed as fair that all consumers of the incumbent's services – including the consumers of access services – should contribute towards covering the firm's common costs. Accounting methods are appealing in this respect because of their relative simplicity and familiarity. The second, as already mentioned, is the practical difficulty of establishing optimal or even approximately optimal mark-ups over incremental costs.

6.5.7 Unbundling

Until now, the analysis has characterized a network industry as having three distinct components with natural monopoly conditions typically found in the infrastructure. In practice, of course, many infrastructures are immensely complex, none more so perhaps than in telecoms. In this industry (a typical modern network infrastructure is described in detail in Part 2), a network might be comprised of many hundreds of segments. Conceivably, some parts of the infrastructure are potentially competitive while other parts are naturally monopolistic.

In a liberalized setting with these conditions, it is likely that competing firms will invest in some network elements. Few entrants, however, will find it worthwhile to duplicate every aspect of a network and under open access, they will tend to rely on the incumbent for some infrastructure components or interconnection services. The degree to which an entrant can pick and choose from the incumbent's infrastructure is determined by the rules governing *unbundling*. The rules on unbundling affect the scope, location and disaggregation of interconnection services:

- **scope** refers to the amount of infrastructure that is made available for interconnection purposes;
- **location** are the points in a network where interconnection can take place;
- **disaggregation** refers to the degree of partitioning of a network infrastructure for interconnection purposes.

Where the scope of interconnection is wide and the degree of disaggregation high, interconnection services are said to be highly unbundled. In this setting, an entrant may pick and choose from a detailed menu of interconnection services. In practice, this may result in entrants choosing different entry and exit points for interconnection, and even choosing multiple entry and exit points.

The more unbundled interconnection is made, the greater are the transaction and coordination costs. Furthermore, when interconnection services are highly unbundled, and if the (regulated) prices for interconnection services take insufficient account of the risks associated with network innovations, *ex ante* investment incentives may be adversely affected. This is likely to have its biggest impact in those industries that are changing very dramatically, like telecoms.

In this context, a further complicating factor may arise in relation to intelligence in networks and new services. Software is making new services possible in some networks, especially telecoms where intelligent networks are leading to more sophisticated services. When, however, one firm, say the incumbent, is in a position to exploit fully the development of these services because of economies of scale and scope, mandating access and interconnection to other firms so that they can also market these new services may undermine the incumbent's incentives to innovate.

If an incumbent feels that the rewards from innovating are too small because of competition, it may choose to invest elsewhere and customers may suffer as a result. Allocative efficiency may be jeopardized because investment could decline below desirable levels. To offset this problem, careful consideration needs to be given to the treatment of property rights. To ensure that new services are sufficiently developed in some network industries, a system of patents may be required and consideration will need to be given to intellectual property rights.

6.5.8 **Two-way interconnection**

The analysis above has been conducted implicitly assuming that interconnection is one-way. As discussed in Section 3.4 above, however, networks like telecoms feature two-way interconnection, and recent research has shown that under certain assumptions a competitive network industry with an industry structure like case (v) (facilities-based competition) may yield monopoly outcomes. In particular, where the services sold by competing firms are sufficiently differentiated, prices faced by customers are linear, and consumption patterns are in some sense symmetric (that is, 'isotropic' – see Part 2 of this Report) there is a greater chance of monopoly pricing.

If two-way interconnection is a feature of a competitive network industry and conditions prevail such that it facilitates tacit collusion, oversight of interconnection terms will be necessary even in phase 3. Two-way interconnection may mean therefore that these industries will be subject to more regulation than is typically the case in most other competitive industries. It is possible, however, that interconnection markets in industries like telecoms will become increasingly competitive and the significance of bottlenecks will therefore diminish.

6.6 **Regulating competition**

Ideally liberalization is aimed at establishing effective competition in some or all parts of a network industry. This is the feature of phase 3. When competition becomes effective, which it is becoming in some parts of some of the industries (for example, passenger air services and business telecoms), the emphasis of regulation shifts towards policing competition. Given the nature of network industries, and in particular their vertical structures, it is likely that vertical restraints will be a focus of regulatory activity.[14] Other issues of concern will relate to mergers and alliances, other possible restrictive practices, price discrimination (for example, undue discrimination), etc. These issues surface in many other competitive industries, but to date the scarcity of effective competition in the European network industries means that the focus of concern is still centred on monopoly abuse and emerging competition problems in phase 2.

6.7 Universal service

As already discussed, some network industries provide goods with 'merit good' characteristics.[15] A merit good is one where the state makes a judgement that certain goods are 'good' and their consumption should be encouraged. It should be emphasized that this is different from arguments related to externalities and public goods, as merit goods reflect a situation where public judgement differs from private evaluation. Household *access* to domestic water, sewerage and electricity are merit goods, and many argue that customer access to basic voice telephony services (that is, a link from a domicile to a telephone exchange) is also a merit good.[16] In practice, the application of the merit-good concept to network industries is primarily concerned with consumer access rights.[17] Merit-good arguments are used to justify public service objectives like universal service, the notion that wherever feasible, every individual in society should have access rights to basic needs, including the services provided by many network industries. In other words, universal service provides a safety net, ensuring that people who may otherwise miss out get access to basic needs. In Europe, this is usually cast as 'social cohesion'.

The discussion above focused entirely on efficiency and ignored, implicitly, other objectives like universal service. It was argued that efficiency is attained when the prices of network services reflect, or more precisely equal, underlying incremental costs. For many network services, however, efficient prices may result in some customers facing relatively high prices. This is especially likely for those living in remote areas with low population densities, as scale economies may be limited, and for those households on relatively low incomes, and in areas with geographically special conditions. Where the state views certain network services as merit goods and seeks to promote universal service, this may result in policies that lead to departures from efficiency. For example, a price ceiling may be placed on subscription charges, which may result in prices lying below cost for some consumers, so as to encourage more individuals to subscribe to a network.

6.7.1 Competition and universal service

Before examining public policy with regard to universal service, it is worth addressing briefly whether an unregulated competitive network industry can facilitate universal service. Assume for simplicity that universal service comprises access to a basic service, for example, it may mean an individual has a telephone line. It may be profitable for an individual firm in a network industry to set relatively low subscription charges (that is, to subsidize connection) to stimulate participation, and set relatively high usage charges to recoup fixed costs. Intertemporal cross-subsidization of this kind is feasible because firms in network industries typically use two-part tariffs where customers pay a fixed charge to access services (the subscription charge) and a separate usage charge related to the consumption of services.[18] The rapid growth in subscriber numbers on mobile telephony networks in Europe has, in many countries, been due in part to this form of pricing. Of course, competition will also provide greater variety and will put downward pressure on prices thereby stimulating greater participation. Thus, competition significantly contributes towards universal service.

Although competition may yield universal service, market failures may undermine the attainment of universal service as well as efficiency. Where competition is ineffective and firms have market power, as is the case during phase 1 and for much of phase 2, industry output will lie below that in a more competitive setting. Market power can therefore act against universal service because firms will tend to set excessively high prices, leading to lower subscriber numbers.

Another market failure that works against universal service and efficiency arises in the presence of network externalities. For example, where an individual is deterred from joining a network because of a relatively high subscription charge (which need not lie above cost), existing network subscribers may be denied positive club externalities. It may be the case that the additional benefits existing subscribers would receive if the 'marginal' customer were to join the network exceed the losses the firm would incur if it were to reduce its subscription charge to attract the customer. A profit-maximizing firm is unlikely to derive sufficient extra profits from the club externality generated, and therefore has little incentive to lower its subscription charge.

6.7.2 The costs of universal service

Universal service is only a problem when competition alone fails to meet the goals set by policy-makers. In the network industries, there are three broad categories of cost associated with universal service:

- uneconomic areas;
- uneconomic customers;
- uneconomic services.

Uneconomic areas tend to be remote regions, mountainous areas and areas where population density is low. The costs associated with serving such areas would far exceed the revenues that could possibly be generated. Needless to say, in Europe there are many areas that are uneconomic for firms in network industries. Uneconomic customers are those households on low incomes, such as the unemployed and a significant proportion of the elderly population. Of course, those residing in uneconomic areas are uneconomic customers, but it does not follow that an uneconomic customer resides in an uneconomic area. Many deprived inner-city regions within 'economic' areas contain substantial pockets of uneconomic customers. Uneconomic services are those services that make a loss overall. In telecoms, the provision of public call-boxes at a national level usually entails making a loss.

Universal service will be cast by a policy-maker in terms of these three categories. A policy-maker may state that all areas should be served, or that all customers should have 'affordable access' to services or that network firms should provide certain uneconomic services (for example, services for the disabled). Universal service necessarily imposes additional costs on to network firms, and it is clear that regulation is needed to attain universal service objectives. Although competition can help in attaining universal service, the existence of uneconomic areas, customers and services means that regulation is needed.

6.7.3 **Regulation, universal service and monopoly**

In phase 1, regulation is focused on constraining the prices set by a monopolist. The nature of this regulation is directed towards promoting efficiency. As regulation means curbing monopoly excess, it tends to favour universal service through lower prices. The design of price regulation may also take account of network externalities and therefore benefit universal service. Although policy aimed at efficiency may help universal service, there will inevitably be a trade-off between efficiency and universal service.

This is seen in its starkest terms in relation to Ramsey pricing. As demand for subscription is likely to be less price sensitive than usage demand, Ramsey principles imply it would be more efficient for the burden of cost recovery to be placed largely on the fixed charge. Efficiency would be achieved if a firm recovered *all* its fixed costs through fixed charges and set its usage charges equal to incremental costs. Ramsey pricing is therefore likely to lead to relatively high subscription charges which works against universal service.

The ideal way to achieve efficiency *and* universal service is to have separate policy instruments targeting each objective. Policy instruments directed towards efficiency have already been discussed. Ideally, the tax and benefit system should be used to achieve universal service. Lump-sum transfers to a monopolist and certain consumers, although typically not used in practice, could be used to meet universal service objectives. In practice, universal service costs in phase 1 are funded through cross-subsidization, which is an implicit tax on customers and works reasonably well when there is a monopolist providing services and the good in question is not easily stored. In the postal services industry, monopoly providers usually set geographically uniform prices, which implies that individuals who are largely making use of local deliveries tend to subsidize the costs of users who make disproportionate amounts of long-distance deliveries.

6.7.4 Liberalization and universal service

Distorting prices away from underlying costs via cross-subsidization to fund universal service results in unbalanced tariffs and may lead to inefficiency. Under monopoly, however, it is relatively straightforward to transfer funds from one group of customers to another. In telecoms, for many years this was achieved by setting high usage charges on long-distance and international calls, services that are used more by businesses and high-income households.

Liberalization and the entry of new firms into an industry in phase 2 can have a dramatic impact on universal service. On the one hand, new firms entering a formerly monopolized market will provide greater variety and will put downward pressure on prices. These effects are desirable and complement universal service objectives. On the other hand, if entrants are not burdened with universal service obligations but the incumbent former monopolist is, the entrants are in a position to 'cherry-pick' (or to 'cream-skim'). In other words, entrants will be able to undercut the prices set by the incumbent in those markets serving higher value customers.

Cream-skimming will therefore undermine an incumbent's ability to fund universal service objectives through cross-subsidization. Furthermore, where an incumbent's prices lie above costs required to meet universal service, it may stimulate inefficient entry. For example, an entrant may over-invest in facilities that bypass the incumbent's network. Liberalization means that the traditional method of funding universal service is not sustainable, and attempts to maintain cross-subsidization may result in inefficient entry.

Because liberalization makes it difficult to achieve universal service objectives through traditional means, alternative methods have been proposed. The most radical proposal is to rely on competition to deliver universal service. This is only likely to work in those industries where the real cost of services is declining significantly. Although technological change is tending to lower costs in most of the network industries studied in this Report, relying on the market is probably only feasible in parts of the telecoms industry. Even in this industry, however, the benchmark used to define universal service is becoming more complex and costly (see Part 2).

6.7.5 Meeting social objectives under competition

Assuming that policy-makers are unlikely to rely solely upon the market to meet universal service in increasingly competitive environments, some regulatory intervention will be required. A variety of methods have been proposed for the funding of universal service, but in practice four schemes have been adopted.

- The adoption of an industry-wide universal service fund to support the provision of universal service (largely borne by the incumbent in phase 2).
- Spreading the burden of universal service more evenly across entrants and an incumbent.
- Through a levy added onto the price charged for interconnection to the network providing universal service (usually operated by the incumbent).
- Competitive tendering of the rights to provide loss-making services and receive public subsidies.

The first scheme has been adopted in a number of liberalized telecoms markets. The issue here that is likely to generate controversy is the estimated cost of the incumbent's universal service. Chapter 11 in Part 2 of the Report outlines the methodology for computing the cost of universal service that has been proposed by the Commission in telecoms. In short, the methodology measures opportunity costs: the cost of universal service as the difference between operating costs with and without universal service obligations, less the difference in revenues with and without universal service obligations. The presence of significant common costs and the way in which these are allocated across services and customers makes this a difficult task in practice. Furthermore, hypothesizing how much extra revenue is generated because of additional customers is not easily measured. Nevertheless, in the telecoms industry, estimates have been made of universal service costs in a number of countries.[19]

The problem with the first approach is that it acts to reinforce the position of the incumbent, by making it a different, and arguably, a special player in the industry. Although the funding of universal service is shared across some or all of the firms in the industry, usually according to some measure of market share, its implementation is undertaken by the incumbent. Should an incumbent ever encounter financial difficulties, its privileged position in the market as a universal service provider may safeguard it from closure. Providing universal service may, therefore, result in managerial slack. Another difficulty may also arise because in making the incumbent seem 'special', it could provide conditions that increase the chance for regulatory capture. Certainly, by making the incumbent responsible for implementing universal service, there will be more interaction between the regulator and managers within the firm.

Further problems with this approach are connected with the allocation of universal service costs across the firms in the industry. First, the firms in the industry have to be identified. This is a relatively straightforward task when firms require individual operating licences, but where firms can operate under general authorizations, as is increasingly the case in telecoms, this may be more difficult. Second, where the number of firms is changing and increasing in an industry, the costs of implementing the funding scheme rise. Third, defining what constitutes a firm's market share is particularly difficult where firms provide very different services over a common network. It would appear that universal service funds are likely to be manageable in relatively stable industries with well-defined services, which is not a characteristic feature exhibited by many of the network industries that are being liberalized.

The second scheme certainly overcomes the asymmetry problem of the first scheme. In practice, a scheme of this kind has been implemented in the liberalized UK gas industry. New gas suppliers were permitted to enter the downstream part of the industry as long as they offer to sell in areas that have a 'balanced' socio-economic mix. This approach clearly has incentive problems: why should an entrant devote marketing resources to loss-making customers once it has entered the market? In reality, this scheme is no different to the market approach mentioned above.

The third scheme works by taxing all firms using the incumbent's essential facilities, including the separated components of the incumbent's business. This works through an adjustment made to access charges. This approach is less desirable than those above because it forces access charges to lie above cost. Faced with distorted access charges, entrants will, at the margin, invest a greater amount in their own infrastructure in an attempt to bypass the relatively expensive facilities provided by the incumbent. Such bypass is undesirable because it unnecessarily duplicates parts of the incumbent's facilities. A further problem with this approach is related to entry deterrence and foreclosure. By adding a levy onto access charges, an incumbent is in a position to increase its rivals' costs. Although accounting separation may overcome this obstacle, only structural separation provides the necessary safeguards against foreclosure.

The fourth scheme relies upon *ex ante* competition to fund universal service. This is achieved by holding auctions for the rights to provide services and receive public subsidy. This scheme was implemented in the railway industry in the United Kingdom. Prospective passenger train operators were invited to submit bids that included the amount of subsidy needed to provide various loss-making services. Successful bidders were usually those requiring the lowest subsidy to operate services. For this auction scheme to work successfully, there need to be well-defined markets. In the case of railway franchises, this is relatively straightforward. Where markets can be defined along territorial lines, it may also be feasible to auction off high-cost loss-making areas, often found in rural areas. Auction schemes in some of the industries may, however, suffer from small numbers of participants.

6.7.6 Universal service and the EC Treaty

> Without prejudice to Articles 77, 90 and 92, and given the place occupied by services of general economic interest in the shared values of the Union as well as their role in promoting social and territorial cohesion, the Community and the Member States, each within their respective powers and within the scope of application of this Treaty, shall take care that such services operate on the basis of principles and conditions which enable them to fulfil their missions.[20]

The EC Treaty explicitly allows the Member States to grant special rights and obligations to particular undertakings under Article 90(1), but any measure taken has to comply with the rules on competition, in particular, Articles 85 and 86. Article 90(2) is more specific about monopolies and services of general economic interest. These activities will have to comply with competition rules, but only in so far as the competition rules do not prevent the undertakings concerned from performing the tasks that have been assigned to them. Finally, Article 90(3) entrusts the Commission with the implementation of these rules, possibly using directives and decisions.

The provisions of Article 90 thus establish two important references. First, the legitimacy of regulation by Member States and the legitimacy of the general economic interest motivation for regulation are explicitly recognized. Second, the primacy of competition rules is established in principle. Article 90 also opens the door to a difficult exercise without providing any guidance, however; indeed, if it recognizes that general economic interest may trump the application of competition rules in cases of conflict, it falls short of providing any insight about the principles that should be followed in the evaluation of particular conflicts.

Inevitably, conflict has arisen and matters have been dealt with by the ECJ. An important decision in this field was taken in the Corbeau case.[21] Mr Paul Corbeau, from Liège, provided rapid (24-hour) mail delivery within the Liège area. He was brought to a Belgian court on the grounds that he interfered with the monopoly of the Belgian Post Office. The Belgian court submitted the case to the ECJ. The ECJ admitted that the Post Office was entrusted with a service of general economic interest, but also observed that some services provided by the Post Office could be open to competition, as long as they were separated from the services of general interest. The rapid mail delivery would presumably fall into such a category. The ECJ also insisted, however, that such services could be open to competition only if this would not compromise the 'economic equilibrium of the service of general economic interest performed by the holder of the exclusive right'. Finally, the Court decided that 'it is for the national court to consider whether the services at issue in the dispute meet those criteria'.

This decision suggests, therefore, that the undertaking providing services of general economic interest could finance those from profitable operations in other activities. In turn, competition for these other activities could be restricted in order to make sure that cross-subsidies were sufficient to cover the cost of the services of general interest. The evaluation of this balance is however left to national courts.

This decision is a matter of concern for at least three reasons:

1. The decision does not provide any precise working definition of what constitutes a service of general economic interest and what could constitute a separate service (for which competition could be introduced). What the judgement says is that mailing is a service of general economic interest because it consists 'in the obligation to collect, carry and distribute mail on behalf of all users throughout the territory of the Member State concerned, at uniform tariffs and on similar quality conditions, irrespective of the specific situations or the degree of economic profitability of each individual operation'. This justification, which might suggest rather perversely that some degree of statutory price discrimination is a sufficient condition for a service to qualify as one of general economic interest, is hardly useful.

2. The Court suggests that cross-subsidization is a sensible way of financing the services of general economic interest and one which could be enforced in court. This is of course highly debatable. Alternative ways of financing these services (as discussed above) might create fewer distortions.

3. The delegation to national authorities to evaluate which services can be opened up to competition without jeopardizing the public interest is a recipe for maximum legal diversity across industries and Member States.

In the current situation, incumbents and other third parties might have an incentive to challenge domestic regulatory provisions in court, attempting thereby to reduce the scope of services opened to competition. This is not an issue, however, where the scope of universal services is defined in a directive. For this reason, the Commission has striven to deal more explicitly with universal service through directives. For example, the Postal Directive (see Section 5.12 above) places some boundaries on universal service.

Notes

1 See Cabral and Riordan (1989) on regulatory opportunism.

2 'Reinforcing political union and preparing for enlargement – Commission opinion for the Intergovernmental Conference', COM (96) 90 Final, 28 February 1996. The Commission has also published a Communication re-affirming its principles regarding services of general economic interest,

see 'Services of general interest in Europe' (96/C 281/03) OJ C 281, 26 September 1996, p. 3.

3 The issues of regulatory capture and credibility are discussed further in Chapter 7 below.

4 What constitutes a 'fair' rate of return may be controversial in practice because of disagreements about risk assessments. Furthermore, difficulties are likely to be encountered over the way common costs are allocated between the assets employed in competitive and monopoly sectors.

5 Mayer and Vickers (1996) p. 17.

6 This is an instance of what economists call 'the general theory of the second best'.

7 Interconnection and access is also discussed in Part 2.

8 If the entrant's good is complementary to that of the incumbent, the incumbent may have an incentive to encourage entry.

9 The ECPR was first put forward by Willig (1979), especially pages 137–48, and applied to the case of the rail freight industry in the United States by Baumol (1983). Hence it is also known as the Baumol-Willig rule. On Baumol-Willig see also Baumol and Sidak (1994(a)) and (1994(b)) especially Chapter 7); Kahn and Taylor (1994); and Laffont and Tirole (1994), especially Section 9.

10 For a detailed analysis, see Laffont and Tirole (1994) and (1998).

11 A super-elasticity accounts for cross-price effects as well as own price effects.

12 This is because the super-elasticity term *SRT* can be decomposed into two components: one representing the opportunity cost of providing access adjusted by the displacement ratio, and the other the standard own-price Ramsey elasticity. See also Laffont and Tirole (1998), Chapter 2.

13 For a discussion, see Brown and Sibley (1986), especially pages 44–51; and in the context of access pricing see Cave and Doyle (1994).

14 See Commission 'Green Paper on Vertical Restraints in EC Competition Policy' COM (96) 721 Final, 22 January 1997.

15 Musgrave (1959) coined the phrase 'merit goods'.

16 Access to voice telephony services is a merit good as it allows an individual to contact emergency services and facilitates participation in the 'information society'.

17 Some emphasis is also placed on consumption of services, but this is usually limited because to encourage too much consumption of some network goods, such as water, may be bad for environmental reasons. To avoid confusion with access charges levied on network firms purchasing interconnection services from other network firms, the term 'subscription charges' will be used to denote customer access charges.

18 In practice, the fixed charge also comprises two-parts: a one-off connection fee and a monthly, sometimes quarterly, subscription or rental charge.

19 What is interesting is how these estimates vary and how for the UK costs were estimated to be negligible, see Chapter 11 in Part 2 below.

20 Article 7 (d) of the EC Treaty.

21 Case C-320/01 *Procureur du Roi* v. *Paul Corbeau* (1993) ECR I-2533.

7 The Tasks of Regulators and Regulatory Institutions

The design of regulatory institutions focuses on two fundamental issues, governance and incentives:

- Regulatory governance refers to structures incorporating legislative, executive and judicial institutions, and the mechanisms used to constrain regulatory discretion and to resolve disputes in relation to these constraints.[1]
- Regulatory incentives are the rules overseeing matters such as pricing, cross-subsidization, interconnection, etc.

The effectiveness of regulatory incentives has already been examined above, but it was assumed implicitly in the previous chapter that there existed a *given* governance structure. In practice, and especially in the EU, *both* regulatory governance and regulatory incentives affecting network industries are choice variables available to policy-makers.

In deciding on the *form* of regulatory institutions needed to oversee network industries across the EU and within Member States, account must be taken of what North (1990) terms the 'institutional endowment'. This comprises several elements, the most significant of which, for the purposes of this analysis, are the nature of the inter-relationships between the legislative, executive and judicial institutions. According to Levy and Spiller (1994), regulation of network industries is likely to exhibit greater credibility in countries where relationships across the institutions yield political systems that constrain executive and legislative discretion. In such an environment, firms will be able to invest and take a longer-term view without worrying excessively about regulatory opportunism.

Credibility, however, comes at the expense of flexibility, and in circumstances that may change suddenly, inefficiencies may arise if there is too much inflexibility. The trade-off between credibility and flexibility is a key concern in regulatory design, but it is clear that credibility is shaped significantly by the institutional endowment.

Within the EU, there are different institutional endowments found in different countries. This suggests that regulatory institutions and regulatory procedures are likely to vary within the EU, as indeed is the case. Diversity need not be a problem, as long as the governance structures in place share the ability to restrain arbitrary administrative actions. It does not follow, however, that if institutional endowments were identical across the EU, there should be uniformity in structures across regulatory regimes. Preferences of the populations in different Member States and regions may differ and this, to some extent, is likely to be reflected through different regulatory structures. Although it is important to bear in mind that the design of regulatory structures takes place in a wider political and social context, economic considerations relating to the way in which rules and discretion within a regulatory structure affect efficiency are crucial.

Another aspect of regulatory design that receives much attention is concerned with the *level* of regulation. As the internal market is leading to greater cross-border relationships involving network industries, regulatory institutions designed primarily with a view to promoting national interests may increasingly be unable to deal effectively with inter-jurisdictional problems.

For example, a single supra-national authority may be better able to resolve cross-border access disputes. Where there are negative inter-jurisdictional externalities, these may be eliminated (internalized) through centralization as this enables better coordination. On the other hand, because of asymmetric information, it is likely that local or national regulatory bodies are better informed about local conditions. Decentralizing governance structures may therefore reap rewards, as authorities will be closer to the agents being regulated.[2] The degree of centralization exhibited by regulatory structures is of great policy relevance in the European network industries. Many are calling for greater centralization of regulatory structures by bestowing more power within the Commission, and some are arguing for the establishment of sector-specific European regulatory authorities.

This chapter looks at all these issues. It begins by summarizing the key characteristics of regulatory tasks across the different phases of liberalization. By identifying the regulatory *tasks* required in each phase, it is possible to address more clearly the regulatory design problem. The analysis then focuses on the two important dimensions of regulatory design: the *form* and *level* of regulation. The analysis explores the inevitable trade-offs encountered when designing regulatory institutions. These basic principles of regulatory design are then applied to each phase of liberalization.

7.1 Regulatory tasks

The tasks required of economic regulation are couched in efficiency and equity terms, and depend very much on the market structures prevailing across the three phases of liberalization. In phase 1, monopolies prevail and in many cases these will also be majority owned by the state and have exclusive rights. Here, the tasks facing regulators relate to the prevention of monopoly abuse and possible restructuring of state-owned monopolies.

As scale economies become less important relative to market size and the significance of natural monopoly segments diminish, markets will gradually be opened up to competition in phase 2. In this phase, competition will be most active in the upstream and/or downstream components of an industry. There may, however, still be some natural monopoly elements chiefly in the infrastructure, which are likely to be operated by incumbent operators. Because of this, incumbent operators are likely to be dominant in access markets throughout much of phase 2, and if they are vertically integrated into downstream retail markets, they will probably remain dominant there as well. In this phase, therefore, competition and regulation must be balanced in order to produce desirable outcomes.

In phase 3, competition will have become effective in many parts of the industry. If natural monopoly segments are still found in the industry, these will be in parts of the infrastructure. In this phase, the industry and its derived regulatory framework does not have as many special characteristics. In particular, the industry structure will have been sufficiently transformed, and the 'rules of the game' will have become not unlike those of any other industry.

Throughout all three phases, regulators will also be concerned with social objectives. During phase 1, these will be met by placing obligations on monopoly operators. In phase 2, as competition unfolds and entry becomes more extensive, social obligations may be met by more firms in the market. Indeed, what the market delivers will increasingly be compatible with distributive aims. In phase 3, competition will ensure that many social objectives are met, but social obligations may still be required in some areas. Thus, over the three phases, the tasks concerning and the implications of social objectives are likely to diminish.

Accordingly, regulatory tasks shift across the three phases in terms of both scope and intensity (see Figure 2 in Chapter 1 above). In phase 1, regulation takes place with respect to all aspects of the industry's activities (prices, investments, allocation of output, social obligations, etc.), but in practice, the emphasis is on monopoly control. In phase 2, there is a mix of regulation and competition. Regulation aims at getting the detailed structure right: organizing and policing competition, and preventing monopoly abuse. It focuses on *inter alia* entry conditions, both in the provision of services and in the provision of the infrastructure, attempting to address coordination failures and unbundling. Particular constraints on competition can be imposed to meet non-economic objectives. As industries in this phase are increasingly competitive, if incumbents remain state-owned, pressures will grow for privatization.

In phase 3, competition is taking place as in any other industry with firms subject to mainly *ex post* control of their competitive behaviour, but some *ex ante* control, especially with regard to mergers and state aids, will also apply. The scope of regulation is limited to the imposition of particular constraints to meet non-economic objectives.

7.2 The form of regulation

If civil servants and the general public were perfectly informed, regulation would be straightforward. In the language of 'principal-agent' analysis, objectives could be assigned to civil servants (the agent) with maximum discretion over how the objectives are achieved, and the general public (the principal) could observe whether they do in fact pursue these objectives. Inevitably, however civil servants have imperfect information about the industry that they regulate, and the public cannot perfectly observe their actions. Because of the latter type of 'information asymmetry', it may be desirable to constrain civil servants' activities to reduce the risks of moral hazard.

Civil servants will be able to obtain information rents when they cannot be held responsible for their decisions in terms of the objectives assigned to them. So, the more that civil servants can be made accountable for their decisions, the less are the information rents. Accountability is thus an essential element of any regulatory framework.

A system of accountability is easier to implement when the tasks assigned to civil servants take the form of simple and verifiable rules. It is also stronger when *ex post* verification is undertaken by an independent third party (auditing) rather than by an institution closely related to the agent (which might have the incentive to connive with civil servants in covering up deviations). An independent third party could come from the media, consumer groups, political bodies, etc. The German approach to implementing competition policy sets a good example here, where the Bundeskartellamt, the German competition regulator, is periodically reviewed by an independent agency, the Monopolkommission.

It is likely that the main opportunities civil servants have for obtaining rents are associated with taking a favourable view towards the firms being regulated. This is the phenomenon known as *regulatory capture* (though there are other forms of capture like bureaucratic capture, where civil servants may capture the regulated industry to meet their own objectives, which may not accord with those of the principal, see below).[3] Two particular aspects of the tasks assigned to civil servants seem to warrant attention since they involve a trade-off between the quality of the regulation and the potential for industry capture.

First, there is a trade-off between on the one hand, the degree of precision in the implementation of regulation, and on the other hand, the scope for capture. Implementation of regulation through precise rules (which in practice means regulation via licensing) can in principle, be easily monitored. As discussed in Chapter 4, however, precise rules are likely to be inflexible and therefore unable to cover all contingencies. In contrast, the implementation of regulation through general rules (usually via general competition rules without detailed licence conditions or in the absence of licences), leaves a great deal of discretionary decision-making to civil servants and allows greater flexibility. As a result, regulation can be adapted to the peculiarities of a given situation. It is, however, difficult and costly to evaluate discretionary decisions *ex ante* and accordingly, the scope for capture is enlarged. The balance between rules and discretion will thus depend in part on the benefits of flexibility and the cost of capture. Capture problems need not increase when regulatory discretion increases, as long as there is sufficient transparency of regulatory procedures and adequate accountability. Again there is a trade-off, in this case involving regulatory resources.

Second, there is a trade-off between the degree of specialization in regulatory decisions and the scope for capture. If civil servants accumulate important industry-specific knowledge, their understanding of the industry and hence the quality of their decisions can be expected to improve. The industry specificity of the civil servants' human capital also implies, however, that their main alternative employment opportunities are in the industry that they regulate or closely related to it (for example, management consultancy). Civil servants may, therefore, have an incentive to accommodate the firms that they regulate in order to ensure adequate future opportunities – the practice of 'revolving doors'. The revolving doors phenomenon can be offset through clauses written into labour contracts that may constrain future employment opportunities, but this requires compensating remuneration for regulatory officials.

Another important trade-off affecting the form of regulation is closely related to the capture-precision trade-off above. Where rules are made very precise and governance structures constrain discretion, regulators will be able to commit more credibly to policy. Regulatory commitment is of vital importance to network industries because of the scale and duration of investments.[4] Commitment can help to lower regulatory risks, thereby favourably affecting the cost of capital and overcoming difficulties related to stranded costs. The price of commitment is inflexibility. This is not a problem if network industries operate in stable environments. In reality, however, these industries are operating in a climate of change. Indeed, liberalization itself is a major structural change. Thus, a trade-off needs to be made between flexibility which raises the prospect for regulatory opportunism, and regulatory commitment.

7.3 The level of regulation

The appropriate geographical scope of regulation depends on the extent to which decisions by national authorities fail to internalize important external effects across jurisdictions. At the same time, however, local civil servants may be better informed about the specifics of regulatory problems, not simply because of more efficient observation, but also because the firms being regulated may have a stronger incentive to reveal information to local authorities. Local authorities are better placed than central authorities to commit to not using this information against firms' interests, but whether this brings about desirable outcomes is debatable. Furthermore, when decisions are taken at the local level, regulatory authorities face stronger incentives to compete against one another. As discussed in Section 4.9 above, such competition may be far from perfect and can lead to a 'prisoner's dilemma' inefficiency.

Overall, there is a presumption in favour of decentralized regulation because of informational asymmetries, but this can be overturned in the presence of important external effects – the spirit of the principle of subsidiarity. In practice, centralized and decentralized regulatory structures are both substitutes and complements. Thus regulation will involve *both* centralized and decentralized authorities – so-called two-tier regulation – and it is the balance between these two that matters for policy.[5] The upper tier will usually be occupied by central regulatory authorities focusing on framework issues and general principles, while the lower tier is occupied by local regulators, which are better placed to deal with detail.

With two-tier regulation, there is a danger that jurisdictions will overlap and duplication and inconsistency, and possibly conflict, will arise. To overcome such problems, in October 1997, the Commission adopted a notice on cooperation between national competition authorities and the Commission in handling cases falling within the scope of Articles 85 and 86.[6] The Notice is aimed at ensuring that where a case falls within the scope of Community law, the enforcement of the Community rules will be the responsibility of just one competition authority. 'The Commission will be able to concentrate on cases with a real Community interest, while the national authorities, with their more thorough knowledge of domestic markets, will be able to take more appropriate decisions at that level.'[7]

The upper tier of regulation in Europe, executed through the Commission, has progressively acquired significant powers in the field of competition policy, largely to counter inter-jurisdictional externalities. This raises the question of whether this justifies a further extension of its powers. In this context, two policy issues arise.

- Should the Commission exercise greater control over each liberalized network industry in the EU?
- If the Commission were to exercise greater control, would objectives be better achieved through establishing a European regulatory authority to deal with anti-competitive behaviour in each industry?

Majone (1996) argues that there are net benefits from establishing EU-wide regulatory authorities, and Vogel (1995) claims that EU regulatory policy has had a significant positive impact in the field of environmental regulation, largely by promoting harmonization and coordination. On other hand, federal-level regulation in countries like the United States and Australia has not always met with success, particularly as it can lead to disruptive tensions, and hence inefficiencies, between the central and local regulatory authorities.[8]

Box 20 Industry views on a European regulatory authority

In 1997, NERA and Denton Hall published *Issues associated with the creation of a European Regulatory Authority for telecommunications* (European Commission, 1997), a detailed survey of fifty organizations active in the telecoms market. For many of the organizations surveyed, a reinforcement of regulatory activity at a European level, or even the creation of an ERA for telecoms, appeared to be a key element in meeting concerns in the newly liberalized market. No single regulatory model or approach emerged from the discussions, however. The table below shows the number of participants from the survey, in percentage terms, in favour (✓) against (✗) and with no comment/no preference (–) on the involvement of a ERA in a number of different areas.

Area of regulatory activity	✓ (%)	✗ (%)	– (%)
Interconnection	64	22	14
Implementation and enforcement of EC directives	48	30	22
Numbering	44	28	28
Licences	42	32	26
Allocation and management of radio frequencies	34	40	26
Ownership and competition regulation	30	42	28
Universal service obligations	26	26	48
Standards	24	56	20
Number portability	24	26	50
Price regulation	18	30	52
Consumer protection	14	32	54

Box 17 on p. 72 discusses a Price Waterhouse survey of executives in the gas industry. In this survey, views were also elicited as to whether the European Commission should take a leading role in the implementation of the proposed Gas Directive. Views were split with 50% saying it should and 48% opposed. Incumbent gas companies were much more opposed to the Commission taking an active role, with 56% wanting no active participation. This contrasted with the views of entrants where 67% expressed their wish for the Commission to take on a more active role. The survey indicated that the incumbent operators favoured self-regulation over greater Commission-led regulation.

In Box 20 on the previous page, some industry views are presented on centralized regulation through a European regulatory authority (ERA). Not surprisingly where inter-jurisdictional externalities are greatest (for example, in the area of interconnection across national boundaries), there is much demand for centralized regulation. In the gas industry, demand for centralized regulation was stronger among entrants and potential entrants than incumbents. This may reflect a view among entrants that national regulatory authorities are prone to capture, to some extent, by incumbents. This view may prevail because incumbents are likely to have a close working relationship with national regulators. Hence it would appear that entrants are favourably disposed to centralized regulation in areas where their interests are diametrically opposite to those of incumbents. Where interests are more closely aligned, then the views of incumbents and entrants about the level of regulation are also likely to be close.

7.4 The scope, form and level of regulation across phases

This section offers a *normative* account of the appropriate regulatory structures in each phase of liberalization. It is first assumed that a given industry is locked into one phase, that is, a static account is given. Having done this, an assessment is made of the dynamic implications as an industry shifts from phase 1 through to phase 2 and possibly into phase 3.

7.4.1 Phase 1

For the broad and detailed regulation of national or regional monopolies required in phase 1, flexibility and local knowledge would seem to be particularly important features for the regulatory institution. Since the incumbent is particularly powerful in this phase, however, the risks of capture are large. This explains in part why governments have often found it preferable to regulate industries through 'hierarchies' rather than through arm's length regulation – in other words, by keeping monopolies under public ownership.

Arguably, hierarchies allow for more powerful incentive mechanisms – and accordingly, might allow for detailed and specialized regulation while substituting industry capture by (presumably more limited) bureaucratic capture. It is unclear, however, what has been the performance of this arrangement *ex post* – given that bureaucratic capture should not be underestimated.

In terms of the level of regulation, the importance of scale economies as well as the need for standards and interoperability might provide a strong argument in favour of a centralized EU-level agency in phase 1. It may very well be that for those industries in phase 1, it would be more efficient to have EU-wide publicly-owned monopolies rather than a collection of national monopolies.

In addition, there may be scope for an EU regulatory framework given the geographical dimension of networks and the likelihood that national jurisdictions may not have adequate incentives. For example, to the extent that national authorities take account of the welfare of domestic final consumers and not that of foreign final consumers, and to the extent that travel on national networks by foreigners is more intense around borders, there will tend to be under-investment in the areas around national borders.

Similarly, to the extent that networks around borders can be seen as a reduction in trade barriers, uncoordinated national governments may be caught in the 'prisoner's dilemma' game, where insufficient bilateral liberalization takes place and hence there is insufficient network development around borders. The geography of networks in Europe certainly lends some support to the presumption that these effects may be significant. This may suggest that there is scope for EU-level coordination on the geographical extension of networks in border areas, as envisaged by the TENs projects.

7.4.2 **Phase 2**

In phase 2, there is no doubt that the regulation of entry conditions (both in the provision of services and access to infrastructure) and the general structural policy that regulation entails require important industry knowledge and significant discretion in order to adapt regulation quickly as experience accumulates. At the same time, the power of incumbent firms (the former monopolies) is usually significant and their incentives to try and affect regulation are very strong: depending on the details of the regulation, they stand to lose or to gain a great deal. This combination of circumstances is highly unfavourable: it suggests that an institutional framework that is potentially prone to capture is highly valuable, but it is precisely when capture should be taken most seriously.

Given the cost associated with inflexible regulation as well as the considerable value of industry-specific knowledge, it is desirable to develop an industry-specific institutional framework in which civil servants have a fair amount of discretion. To prevent regulatory capture in this context, the framework should be associated with strong mechanisms of accountability, which may include a periodic review of the regulatory agency by an independent board of experts.

At the same time, there may be scope for limited regulatory coordination at EU level over the two areas discussed in phase 1 (standards and interoperability; and internalizing inter-jurisdictional externalities) and with respect to the coordination of licensing. It is interesting to note that a common licensing system exists in the airline industry in Europe where competition has benefited as a consequence, whereas in telecoms, licences remain nationally defined and as yet these are not mutually recognized.

There is clearly a presumption in favour of national regulation to deal with detailed domestic issues because of informational advantages. There is, however, a coordination role for central authorities – so two-tier regulation should be in place with a centralized upper tier overseeing general principles designed to bring about consistency and a lower national tier implementing the general principles.

7.4.3 Phase 3

For network industries in phase 3, the regulatory framework should be much less complicated. For the most part, the only regulatory tool is competition policy, and this can be undertaken by an independent agency with considerable discretion. Regulatory capture is less of a risk in this context because of the dispersion of interests: all the regulated firms face the same coordination problem. Whether policy should be implemented under national competition rules or Commission rules can be determined in the usual way, as in other industries. Self-regulation should also take place to deal with coordination and standards issues, and consumer interests should be protected through credible consumer associations.

7.4.4 Dynamic institutional design

In sum, regulation in the three phases should look like this:

- **Phase 1**: EC Treaty (with exemptions) + centralized EU + industry–specific regulation + public ownership.

- **Phase 2** : EC Treaty (no exemptions) + centralized EU + national regulation + industry-specific regulation + accountability/independence.
- **Phase 3** : EC Treaty (no exemptions) + national regulation + self regulation.

It is clear from this framework that institutional design must be dynamic in nature, as illustrated in Figure 7 overleaf. This implies that the creation of new national regulatory bodies in phase 2 is desirable, but as a network industry structure matures, it might be equally desirable to abolish some regulatory agencies. In Figure 7, it can be seen that industry-specific regulation and centralized EU regulation does not feature in phase 3, meaning that these institutions and regulatory tasks are abolished. In practice, this can be achieved through 'sunset clauses'. For example, the application of price-cap regulation in practice extends over a finite horizon and at the end of each period, an industry-specific regulator assesses whether there is a need to withdraw price regulation.

It is important to ensure that the performance of new and existing regulatory authorities is not only periodically assessed and evaluated – the issue of accountability – but that the possibility of abolishing a regulatory authority through explicit 'sunset clauses' is recognized. If institutions become entrenched this could delay progress to more effective competition. Regulatory entrenchment is more likely the more heavy-handed is regulation, as shown in Figure 8 overleaf. If regulation is too light-handed, however, effective competition may also be delayed because of legal uncertainty. This is illustrated in Figure 9 on p. 140.

Notes

1 This is what Williamson calls 'contractual governance institutions', Williamson (1985), p.35.
2 See Caillaud *et al.* (1996).
3 See Laffont and Tirole (1994), Chapter 15, and references therein.
4 See Sappington (1994).
5 See Doyle (1996).
6 Commission notice on cooperation between national competition authorities and the Commission handling cases falling within the scope of Articles 85 and 86 of the EC Treaty, OJ C 313, 15 October 1997.
7 European Community Competition Policy Report XXVIIth 1997, Brussels 1998, p. 15.
8 See Sidak and Spulber (1997) for a detailed discussion on regulatory structures in US network industries.

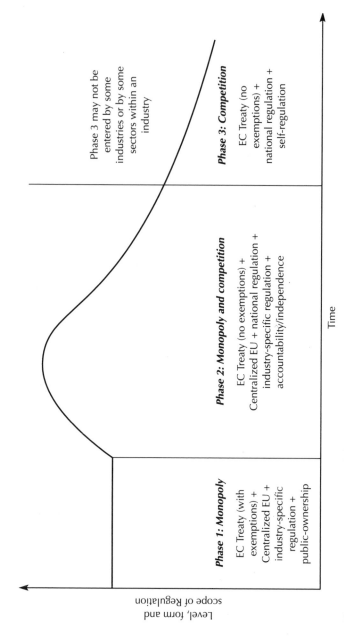

Figure 7 Dynamic institutional design

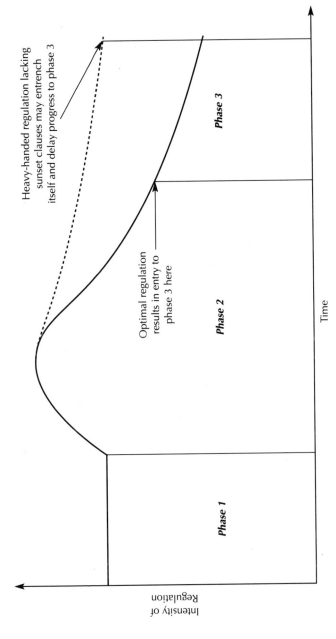

Figure 8 Heavy-handed regulation – accounting for regulatory entrenchment

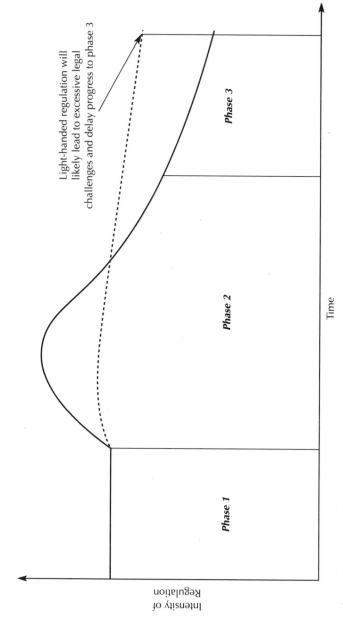

Light-handed regulation will likely lead to excessive legal challenges and delay progress to phase 3

Phase 1

Phase 2

Phase 3

Intensity of Regulation

Time

Figure 9 Dynamic institutional design – problem of light-handed regulation

PART 2: Telecommunications in Europe

Chris Doyle
Jordi Gual
Lars Hultkrantz
Leonard Waverman

8 Telecommunications: Changing Market Boundaries

As Part 1 of this Report has shown, the traditional vertically-integrated monopoly provision of network industries across Europe is being challenged by changing patterns of ownership, changing market structure, changing technology and changing regulatory policy. Nowhere is this more evident than in telecoms, where new technology, privatization and liberalization, waves of takeovers, mergers and alliances, and a process of 'convergence' with the broadcasting and information technology sectors are leading to dramatic changes in the basic economics of the industry.

Changes in the telecoms industry are creating numerous opportunities as well as considerable uncertainty. The latter makes the conflicting priorities outlined in Part 1 of this Report far more difficult to resolve from a regulatory point of view. Before focusing directly on these policy issues, however, it is worthwhile examining the basic changes in technology that are driving much of the change.

8.1 The impact of technological change

Technological change has altered the traditional structure of the telecoms industry along both vertical and horizontal dimensions. Originally, there was a single telecoms technology: the copper wire pair to the house and a hierarchy of switches, which provided voice telephony and related data services such as faxes. A typical residential subscriber would have a line connection to a local switch (called the local loop), transmission facilities (for the carriage of calls over longer distances) and trunk switches (for routing calls nationally or internationally). No other means of offering voice telephony existed, nor could the copper wire pair technology be used for other services.

Nowadays, there are alternative ways of providing voice telephony: the mobile phone is the most obvious, but there are other technologies using cable and satellite. New services like the Internet may even eclipse traditional voice telephony. Furthermore, other services can now be provided over copper wire pairs, such as video. What was once monopoly provision of a specific set of vertically related voice telephony services is now the competitive industry offerings of a changing mix of products.

The term 'convergence' is often used to describe the degree to which telecoms, audio-visual markets and information provision are evolving in common ways. Convergence in essence means that the defined market of 'telecoms services' is being eroded.[1] No longer is it possible to define narrowly how a simple voice call is transmitted, to define the services that a copper wire pair can deliver, or to define, say, the essential differences between a telephone network and a cable TV network. This blurring of market boundaries has profound implications for the structure of 'traditional' telecoms, its pricing, service diversity and regulation. In particular, it has altered the precept that telecoms is a natural monopoly requiring a single vertically-integrated provider.

Before the technological revolution, economies of scope and scale were considered to be high and so competition tended to be suppressed. Vertical integration too was favoured since again costs would be lower. Regulation and control over the resulting monopoly was designed for this one technology/one product world. Across Europe (and much of the rest of the world), the predominant issues prior to the 1980s were how to control and encourage efficiency in public/private national monopoly telecoms firms – the centre-piece of regulation in phase 1. For much of the 1970s and early 1980s, however, in most European countries outside Scandinavia and, latterly, the United Kingdom, telephone operators were inefficient with long lead-times to order a standard telephone.

Technological changes resulting partly from the semi-conductor revolution lowered the costs for long-distance transmission and switching, but not so much for the delivery of calls to the house over the local loop. Such asymmetric cost decreases plus the policy of promoting a telephone in every home led to prices becoming increasingly unrelated to costs, with fixed charges (connection and rental charges) and some local call services priced below cost, and long-distance and international call charges priced above cost. These resulting 'rate imbalances' continue to be a critical feature of telecoms in most countries. They are an obstacle to competition since competitors may be attracted into the long-distance calling market, especially international services, but will not want to provide local loops to residential customers at prices below costs.

8.2 Defining the industry

What are the technological constraints that define the telecoms market's boundaries? In other words, what are the limitations, first on new suppliers of telephony and second, on telecoms firms providing other audio-visual services?

Besides any regulatory controls, telecoms operators are constrained in their ability to offer TV services by the amount of information that can be delivered in a short interval along a copper wire pair. A 2400-baud modem limits the rate of speed of a traditional voice call to 2400 bits of information per second. A broadcast TV picture is sent at one million bits per second (1 Mb). So at 2400 baud, a TV picture that takes one second over the air would take 30 minutes over a copper wire pair.

New technology called Asynchronous Transfer Mode (ATM) however, allows 1.5 Mbs of information to be sent over the traditional telecoms firm's facilities. As a result, the copper wire pair could allow a movie, a fax, a voice call and meter reading to be carried simultaneously. Asynchronous digital subscriber line technology similarly facilitates the delivery of video through copper wires. Using these technologies, the traditional telecoms firm can become a 'multi-media' provider.

At the same time, the cable TV industry, which has traditionally been a one-way distribution system of TV signals, is now in the telecoms business, providing a two-way communications system. It too can branch out into 'multi-media': a TV set connected to a cable TV or satellite provider and an internet browser allows the user to send electronic mail, get stock quotes, make an airline reservation or 'chat' with friends.

Tables A-2 and A-3 in Appendix 2 provide some basic information on cable TV networks across Europe and how they interact with the telecoms industry. The number of cable subscribers ranges from zero in Italy and Greece to 15.8 million in Germany. Four countries do not allow the incumbent operator to own cable infrastructure (Austria, Belgium, Italy and Luxembourg), five do not allow the incumbent to provide video services, and eleven do not allow cable TV providers to offer telephone services. The incumbent's share of cable subscribers ranges from over 90% in Finland, Germany and Portugal to 7% in the United Kingdom.

Another converging technology is the personal computer connected to the Internet via a telephone line. These can now download and play video clips, as well as offering Internet telephony: without a traditional telephone instrument, the computer can dial, connect and allow two-way conversations via speakers and microphones on the computer (see Box 21).

Box 21 Internet telephony

The Internet sends information in a very different way to voice telephony over telephone lines. A traditional voice call from telephone A to telephone B involves a circuit being opened and held open for the duration of the call between A and B.

Internet traffic is broken up into 'packages'. The packages are given the final destination address and sent out across the network, taking different paths, depending on congestion and arriving at the destination often in a different order than they were sent. At the destination, the packages are re-grouped in order and delivered. This system, called the TC/ICP protocol, is a revolutionary way of delivering information. The Internet is rapidly altering the type, duration and direction of calling and creating new issues for regulators.

Through Internet service provision, the world of electronic commerce is burgeoning. Electronic commerce is where business transactions involve electronic interaction rather than by physical exchanges or direct physical contact. Although strictly speaking this is not new, other developments have occurred in recent times, most notably the growth in computer networks (Internet, Intranets and Extranets) and the emergence of the World Wide Web ('the web'), that have led to a dramatic rise in the scale of electronic commerce. In short, these developments have and are revolutionizing the way in which business is conducted. Today any company or individual connected to a computer network via a telecoms network can transact globally at a relatively low cost. Producers and customers therefore benefit from global choice – a purchase can be made from all potential suppliers of a required service irrespective of geographical location. The only boundaries constraining electronic commerce are those found in computer and telecoms networks. As most important computer and telecommunications networks in use today are global in scope, this means business can be conducted on a global scale.

It is becoming increasingly difficult to define the telecoms industry, not just because of the amalgamation of service markets. Other network industries, such as energy and railway companies, are also taking the role of information network builders and operators, for example, Banverket and Stockholm Energis in Sweden, Energis in the United Kingdom, Autostrada in Italy, and Hermes (railroads) across Europe. As mentioned in Part 1, Nortel and Norweb are conducting trials in the United Kingdom on the use of electric wires to deliver telephony to the home. Cable TV companies provide telephony in the United Kingdom and elsewhere. Broadcasting companies are also entering the markets, building two-way webcasting networks (in Sweden, Teracom).

8.3 Mobile telephony

Initially, because of high costs, mobile telephony was targeted at business users and others with a relatively inelastic demand. Now, prices for handsets, monthly service and calling are falling rapidly. Orange, a mobile operator in the United Kingdom, charges less for international calls on a callback basis than does BT. In Denmark, a mobile operator is offering call charges below the charges set by fixed operators. There are now more than 50 million mobile subscribers in Europe and the number doubled in 1997 alone. Table 6 overleaf provides details for most European countries.

The market for mobile telephony more than doubled in Belgium, France and Spain between 1996 and 1997, as Figure A-1 shows in Appendix 3. Even in the Nordic countries where penetration rates are approaching 40%, the pace of growth remains high. Since 1996, most of the expansion in mobile telephony has been on the back of digital cellular telephony. The first generation analogue systems were developed as national specific systems, but the digital GSM system (on 900 and 1800 MHz frequencies) developed in Europe during the 1980s in a concerted standardization action, is now the *de facto* world-wide standard.

Table 6 *Telecoms in The Member States*

Country	Per capita telecom revenue[1] (annual) (ECU)	Fixed long distance % (Incumbent's market share)	Mobile phones % (Incumbent's market share)	Cellular penetration rates (%)	Interconnection prices relative to best price (%)	Number probability	Price of local call (3 mins) (ECU)	Price of long distance call (3 mins) (ECU)	Bi-monthly connection fee (ECU)
Austria	393	100	75	14.3	+226	No	0.25	0.96	69.38
Belgium	399	100	50	13.1	+14	n.a.	0.15	0.49	33.11
Denmark	498	96	50	25.0	—	No	0.15	0.23	22.97
Finland	350	42	66	40.0	+0.8	Some	0.12	0.18	24.38
France	411	100	36	10.1	—	Yes	0.11	0.52	20.56
Germany	445	100	52	9.9	—	Yes	0.12	0.91	24.88
Greece	212	100	—	7.3	n.o.	No	0.04	n.a.	6.57
Ireland	438	100	72	11.3	+600	No	0.15	0.58	29.16
Italy	329	100	71	16.2	+54	No	0.08	0.71	18.92
Luxembourg	505	100	100	15.1	n.o.	No	0.12	n.a.	22.02
Netherlands	454	100	60	9.9	—	No	0.13	0.31	24.42
Portugal	258	100	50	11.5	+25	No	0.07	1.00	21.36
Spain	269	100	64	11.0	+51	No	0.08	1.02	17.22
Sweden	523	88	52	28.0	+14	No	0.09	0.22	24.10
United Kingdom	350	78	36	14.1	—	Yes	0.18	0.36	26.63

n.o. = not operational, n.a. = not available

[1] The average per capita telecom revenue is 376.

Source: European Commission (1998), *Third Report on the Implementation of the Telecommunications Regulatory Package*, 25 February 1998

The improvements in quality on mobile telephony systems means that mobile operators are increasingly in competition with the traditional wired systems. Furthermore, the mobile telephony industry is converging with fixed and data networks, so-called fixed-mobile integration (FMI). New intelligent mobile handsets (dual-mode handsets) can be used on both fixed and mobile networks automatically and developments like WAP (wireless application protocol) are bringing Internet technology to mobile phone systems allowing the use of interactive information services. SFR in France and Telenor in Norway are already piloting new navigation-based mobile phone systems using a mobile version of the hypertext mark-up language developed by Unwired Planet in collaboration with the European manufacturers Ericsson and Nokia, among others.

Unlike in fixed telephony there is extensive competition in the mobile sector with services being provided by two networks or more in most EU countries. For example, there are at least three competing networks in Denmark, France, Germany, Italy, Norway, Spain, Sweden and the United Kingdom. Despite the presence of rivalry, prices are relatively high for some services.

8.4 Policies for a changing industry

In response to the technological revolution, across Europe the telecoms industry is being liberalized. As from 1 January 1998 competition in telecommunications services has been fully liberalized in most of Europe. This means: new entrants are challenging incumbent telecoms firms and demanding interconnection; the introduction of new telecoms regulators; and the establishment of new rules and regulations governing firm behaviour.

In particular, the changes are also bringing about a series of mergers and alliances within the telecoms and related industries. The opening up of Europe's national markets to new competition is also bringing about new partnerships between telecoms firms. Increasingly, national telecoms firms are joining international alliances in an attempt to exploit economies of scale. These may lead to greater concentration and possible abuse of monopoly power, which in turn requires regulatory intervention. It is, however, important to recognize the need to be cautious about the degree of regulation required. Attempts to guard against a small wrong today could bias the future industry structure in unforeseen and serious ways tomorrow. This issue, the first conflicting priority of Part 1 of this Report, is especially important in telecoms.

One important decision that is made in each country and at the EU level is the degree to which the speed of competitive entry is important. This determines whether entrants are allowed to use the incumbent telecoms firm's facilities to encourage quick entry – the third conflicting priority. An important question is if entrants resell the incumbent's facilities, will they have the incentive to build their own networks? If there are few incentives for construction of new infrastructure, then the longer term will see little facilities entry. Thus, the form and time pattern of competition matters. Moreover, it is regulation that affects the decision by firms of how and when to enter. Regulation and competition are inexorably intertwined.

Another important question relates to convergence with the TV industry. In most EU countries, the bulk of TV regulation is handled by a different regulator than the one that oversees telecoms (see Tables 7 and 8 in Chapter 9).[2] This is potentially worrying since symmetric or at least consistent rules are required as these two infrastructure providers enter each other's markets. It is unlikely to be in society's interests to have one of several competing infrastructure providers gain competitive advantage simply because of a differing or relatively lax regulation regime.

Many of the other important issues arising from the changes in the telecoms industry have been examined in general terms in Part 1, for example, the form of regulation, interconnection rules between the incumbent operator and entrants, what prices should be controlled and how, etc. Some are particularly important in telecoms, such as universal service obligations on the incumbent to firms, rules governing the migration of customers to entrants, and the type and location of interconnection on the incumbent's network. And some are specific to telecoms, such as number portability, dialling parity, equal access, and carrier pre-selection. Many of these issues are considered in the following chapters.

Notes

1 In December 1997 the Commission published a Green Paper 'On the Convergence of the Telecommunications, Media and Information Technology Sectors, and the Implications for Regulation: Towards an Information Society Approach', COM(97) 623. Convergence is discussed in Chapter 10, Section 10.3.
2 Elements of the delivery infrastructure, in particular the digital TV infrastructure, which make use of traditional telecoms infrastructure are typically regulated by telecoms regulators.

9 Telecoms Development and European Policy

The changes in the telecoms industry – part technology-driven, part policy-induced – mean that a variety of policy-makers are involved in the way the industry operates. EU Member States are, however, at different stages of telecoms development in terms both of infrastructure and of regulation and liberalization. How do infrastructures vary, what has been the spread of other infrastructures (such as cable and wireless) and what are service differences across the EU? How do regulatory institutions differ? What is, and should be, the role of the European Commission relative to individual countries?

9.1 Liberalization

The Community has developed a regulatory framework for telecoms that provides for open and competitive markets from 1 January 1998, with transition periods for certain Member States. The Community market of 190 million fixed telephone lines presents opportunities for market entry into one of the fastest growing sectors of the economy. The market for telecommunications services in Europe has been growing at a rate of about 8% per annum (in nominal terms) since 1990. Current telecommunications investment in the Community is running at about ECU 40 billion per year.

Although Europe's market is large, it is far from homogeneous. EU countries can be divided into several broad categories by the level of telephone penetration and use, by the degree of privatization and liberalization, and by pricing patterns. Tables A-1–A-4 in Appendix 2 provides data on some basic characteristics of the telecoms sector in each country. There are major differences in:

- the pace of liberalization and degree of competition;
- ownership;
- infrastructure;
- prices and costs;
- regulation.

9.1.1 The pace of liberalization and degree of competition

Box 22 summarizes where countries are today on the liberalization range. In February 1998, the Commission published its 'Third Report on the Implementation of the Telecommunications Regulatory Package'. Greece was singled out as the country least meeting the Commission's requirements. While Greece does not have to open its fixed links voice network until January 2001, it has not liberalized other services nor has it put in place the required legislation to regulate. Next on the Commission's list was Italy which had yet to provide a licence for any fixed link competitor to Telecom Italia. Importantly, most countries other than the United Kingdom, Germany and the Scandinavian countries had not put all Commission requirements into national law by February 1998.

Despite liberalization, as Figure A–2 in Appendix 3 indicates, aside from Finland, which has had a system of competition for decades, the incumbent operator is dominant in the long distance market and has nearly 100% of the local access market in most countries. Even in the United Kingdom where competition began in the mid-1980s, BT is still dominant and handles around 78% of national calls.

Box 22 European paths to liberalization

1. **Competitive prior to Commission Directives**: Denmark, Finland, Sweden and the United Kingdom.
2. **Competitive prior to January 1998**: Netherlands.
3. **Meeting Commission timetable**: France and Germany.
4. **Delayed meeting of 1 January 1998 timetable:**[2] Austria, Belgium, Ireland, Italy and Spain.
5. **On different tracks, meeting Commission timetable later**: Greece, Luxembourg and Portugal.

The picture is quite different in mobile markets: competition is present in all but one country. The incumbent fixed line operator, however, has more than 50% of the market share in nine countries. Whether competition is sufficiently effective in the mobile sector is questionable.

9.1.2 Ownership

While there has been considerable discussion of selling Europe's publicly owned telephone operators to the private sector, the majority of shares are still held in state hands. Of the incumbent monopoly or former monopoly telecoms operators, four are still 100% owned by the state: those in Austria, Finland (Telecom Finland only), Norway and Sweden. Minority private ownership exists in five companies: France Telecom (75% state owned), Deutsche Telecom (74% state owned), OTE (Greece, 82% state owned), the Luxembourg operator and Telecom Eireann (Ireland, 80% state owned). Of course, some shareholders are themselves publicly owned: for example, one of Telecom Eireann's major shareholders is Telia of Sweden, which is itself 100% state owned.[3] Only three incumbent companies have so far been completely privatized: Finnet, which always was privately owned, British Telecom (BT) and Telefonica[4]. Telecom Italia has largely been privatized as the state only holds 9.45% of shares.

What does the continued public presence mean? Is it necessarily bad? The Scandinavian countries stand out in terms of the number of telephones, fixed and mobile, per capita, but even across these countries, there is no consistent pattern of privatization and liberalization. Telia of Sweden is 100% state owned, but faces much competition from many other landline and cellular systems. Finland, which has high quality telecoms services, has 64 licensed local fixed link operators, 10 networked long distance competitors, 3 GSM 900 licences and 33 GSM 1800 systems, while Telecom Finland is state owned. Tele Denmark is 52% state owned and faces open competition in landlines and mobile and the tariffs in Denmark are among the lowest in Europe.

The fact that private ownership of the incumbent operator is, however, not the prevailing arrangement across Europe is important for competition for several reasons:

1. State-owned enterprises do not have the same objectives as privately held firms. Lower profitability in state-owned enterprises can be attributed by management to meeting public policy objectives.
2. State-owned enterprises do not typically have the same accounting or reporting requirements as firms listed on stock exchanges.

3. State-owned firms are immune from the threat of take-over.
4. The availability of state aid to state-owned enterprises might be at lower cost than the private market would permit.

For these and other reasons, private sector competitors might consider the playing field uneven when competing with state-owned enterprises. (This relates to conflicting priority 5 in Part 1.) Hence, entry and competition might not be as rigorous as if these operators were privatized. In the EU, these issues fall clearly within the scope of the controls of state aid undertaken by the Commission following Article 92 of the EC Treaty.

9.1.3 Infrastructure

Since developments in infrastructure and competition have proceeded at different rates across countries, the spread and the degree of sophistication of networks differs. Table A-1 in Appendix 2 indicates how the basic home telephone varied across the EU between 1985 and 1995. Even in 1995, there was substantial variation across the EU in basic telephony, with Sweden's penetration rate 80% above that in Portugal.

Table A-2 in Appendix 2 shows the differences in digitalization of switches across countries as well as the amount of fibre optic cable per square kilometre and Internet hosts per capita. Competition is made more difficult the lower the degree of digitalization since non-digital switches cannot be easily configured for competitors. France, Luxembourg and the Netherlands have 100% digital switches while Germany, Greece and Spain lag the rest of the EU (1995 data).[5] Clearly, per capita income is not a good indicator of the advancement of the network since Germany is the richest economy in Europe and Greece one of the poorest.

9.1.4 Prices and costs

The prices of communication services vary widely across Europe as Tables A-4 and A-5 in Appendix 2 indicate. Many of these differences relate to different philosophies on how to pay for the fixed costs of the telecoms network. The division of costs between fixed monthly fees and usage is an important factor affecting competition. The more that the true costs of connecting people to the system are levied on calling, the more problems there are for competition: firms will enter calling markets because of high prices but not the access market because prices are below cost.

Generalizations on prices are difficult, though prices in Scandinavia tend to be lower than the average in Europe. Yet Scandinavia has difficult terrain and a low population density in many areas so low prices in Scandinavia are not necessarily due to low costs of infrastructure or operations. In general, Scandinavian countries also have the most economically efficient structure of prices, with the proportion of revenues from fixed charges (monthly fees) being the largest.

As the previous discussions showed, networks differ significantly across Europe. Hence, costs differ. In addition, the basic characteristics of countries, which partially determine costs, also differ. In simple terms, it is easier to roll out infrastructure over flat, small, densely populated countries. Studies show that a halving of the average length of the local loop reduces monthly costs appreciably. Similarly, doubling density, *ceteris paribus*, reduces local costs of access by significant amounts.

These differences have an important impact on the ability of the Commission to regulate by setting common principles. For example, when are interconnection rates set by individual countries acceptable? Could countries wishing not to encourage competition, set interconnection rates 'too high'? The Commission's Interconnection Directive 97/33/EC (Article 7(2)) states that 'charges for interconnection shall follow the principles of transparency and cost orientation'.

The Interconnection Directive also established *benchmarking* and the Commission has published a recommendation on interconnection.[6] In the Recommendation 'best current practice' for interconnection charges are given and it is stated 'where charges lie outside the ranges of "current best practice" charges, national regulatory authorities use their rights under Article 7(2) of the Directive 97/33/EC to request full justification of the proposed charges, and if appropriate, to require retrospective changes to interconnection charges'. Current best practice relates to peak rate interconnect charges in the three lowest cost Member States.

For local call termination charges, at September 1997 current best practice was defined by Denmark, France and the United Kingdom. For metropolitan call termination charges, it was defined by France, Spain and the United Kingdom. For national call termination, it was set by Denmark, Netherlands and the United Kingdom. The United Kingdom and the Netherlands are relatively small, dense and flat and the question remains as to whether this benchmark approach is reasonable for other European countries with more dispersed populations or higher costs.

The benchmarking of rates based simply on the lowest interconnection charge at a certain date is not very sophisticated. An examination of rates without some understanding of key differences in density, size and geography is too simplified a procedure.

9.1.5 Regulation

The various NRAs of the 15 countries of the EU for telecoms and broadcasting are listed in Table 7, pp. 159–61. The Commission has established stringent criteria for the telecoms NRAs, notably that they must be independent and transparent in their decision-making. These are crucial steps and without such principles, competition would likely not occur, especially when the incumbent is state owned. The range of decision-making powers given to regulators varies markedly across Europe, however, as Table 8 indicates (see pp. 162–72).

Table 8 reveals that in a number of countries, notably France, Italy and Spain, important decisions such as the setting of many retail prices are reserved for the government, not the regulator. This is undesirable and should be changed: prices in a competitive market should reflect supply and demand not political decisions. If there are social and public policy elements to be introduced into prices, these should be addressed objectively and transparently.

Similarly, there are differences across Europe in how licences are distributed, and in the process of establishing number portability. It is important that regulators across Europe are given a consistent set of attributes and powers, and that government objectives are spelled out clearly in legislation or directives to NRAs.

9.3 The role of the Commission

Given all the above differences, the role of the Commission is crucial to the path of telecoms development in Europe. The Commission both initiates liberalization (new competition) and seeks to harmonize conditions (through what it terms Open Network Provision (ONP)) in newly liberalized markets. Harmonization is particularly important in view of the internal market principles. While several countries were on paths of liberalization prior to its intervention, most of the push for competition in telecoms has come from the Commission. ONP is based on promoting open and efficient access to networks through measures on interconnection, leased lines, cost-oriented tariffs, standards, etc. Current telecoms strategy may be summarized in five broad components:

1 Liberalization: the introduction of competition in public networks and voice telephony, with the implementation of the Full Competition Directive, as of 1 January 1998.

2 Harmonization: the establishment of a set of directives guaranteeing that the process of liberalization will be effective (directives on licensing, interconnection and universal service). These directives purport to guarantee that the liberalization process will be fair, respecting principles such as non-discrimination and access to networks on the basis of cost-oriented tariffs.

3 The Commission wants a combination of general competition policy and sector-specific rules as policy instruments to guarantee the effective introduction of network service competition. This is implemented through guidelines, for example, the interconnection recommendation. Given the key role played by the large national operators in the industry, the Commission favours a strategy of strong (asymmetric) regulatory intervention, following to a certain extent the experience of countries like the United Kingdom, where entrants were somewhat favoured. For example, competitive telecoms firms were exempted from universal service obligations if they were below a certain market share, and cable operators were allowed to offer telephony but BT was prevented from offering broadcasting.[7]

4 The promotion of the separation of having separate legal entities if there is common ownership of cable TV and telecoms networks. This position has been recently established in the Cable Review.[8]

5 Universal service is defined as basic telephony services, at this point. The Commission has limited the time frame during which incumbent operators can charge for access deficits. Universal service is discussed in detail in Chapter 11 below.

The relationship between the Commission and the NRAs is discussed further in Chapter 12 below.

Table 7 European national regulatory authorities in telecoms and broadcasting, December 1997

Member State	Telecoms	Broadcasting
		NRAs
Austria	The Federal Ministry of Science & Transport The Telecom – Control GmbH The Telecom Control Commission	The Federal Chancellery The Authority on Regional Radio and Cable Broadcasting The Federal Ministry of Science & Transport The Commission for the Application of Broadcasting Law The Commission for the Application of the Law on Regional Broadcasting
Belgium	The Federal Ministry of Communication The Institute for Postal Services and Telecommunications (BIPT)	The Ministries of the three language Communities The Conseil supérieur de l'Audiovisuel (CSA) (French Community) The Media Council (Flemish Community)
Denmark	The Ministry of Research & Information Technology The National Telecom Agency (NTA)	The Ministry of Culture The Ministry of Research The Satellite and Cable Board The Local Radio and Television Boards The Local Radio and Television Committees The Radio and Television Advertising Boards The National Telecom Agency
Finland	The Ministry of Transport & Communications (MTC) The Telecommunications Administration Centre (TAC)	The Council of State The Ministry of Transport & Communications The Telecommunications Administration Center (TAC) The Ministry of Education and Culture The Ministry of Commerce & Industry

Table 7 continued

Member State	NRAs	
	Telecoms	Broadcasting
France	The Ministry of Post and Telecommunications The Autorité de Régulation des Télécommunications (ART)	The Prime Minister The Conseil supérieur de l'Audiovisuel (CSA) The Conseil supérieur de la Télématique Regional Authorities
Germany	The Federal Ministry for Post & Telecommunications (BMPT) The Ministry for Economic Affairs (as of January 1998) The Regulatory Council The Independent Decision-Making Chambers The National Regulatory Authority (as of January 1998)	The States (Länder) The Federal Ministries
Greece	The Ministry of Transport & Communications (MTC) The National Telecommunications Commission (EET)	The Ministry of Press and Mass Media (NPMM) The National Council of Radio and Television (NCRT)
Ireland	The Ministry of Transport, Energy & Communications The Office of the Director of Telecommunications Regulation	The Minister for Arts, Heritage, Gaeltacht & the Islands
Italy	The Communications Authority (currently the Ministry of Posts & Telecommunications)	The Communications Authority (currently the Ministry of Posts & Telecommunications)
Luxembourg	The Ministry of Communications The Institut Luxembourgois des Télécommunications (ILT)	The Prime Minister The Commission on Radio Broadcasting The National Council for Programmes
The Netherlands	The Ministry for Transport, Public Works & Water Management The OPTA	The Ministry of Education, Culture & Science The Ministry for Transport, Public Works and Water Management The OPTA The Commission for the Media The National Broadcasting Organisation The Dutch Competition Authority

Member State	NRAs	
	Telecoms	*Broadcasting*
Portugal	The Ministry for Equipment, Planning and Territorial Administration The Institute of Communications (ICP)	The Council of Ministers The High Authority for the Media The Institute of Communications (ICP)
Spain	The Ministry of Development The Telecommunications Market Commission (CMT) The Autonomous Communities	The Ministry for Education and Cultural Affairs The Autonomous Communities
Sweden	The National Post and Telecoms Agency (PST)	The Radio & TV Authority The Broadcasting Commission
United Kingdom	The Secretary of State for the Department of Trade & Industry (DTI) OFTEL (Proposal that certain regulatory functions will be carried out in the future by a new regulatory body, OFCOM) The Director-General for Fair Trading (DGFT) The NFPG The Radio Communications Agency	The Independent Television Commission (ITC) (Proposal that certain regulatory functions will be carried out in the future by OFCOM), dealing with infrastructure related issues and a new ITC dealing with all content issues The Radio Communications Agency The Broadcasting Standards Commission (BSC) The Monopolies and Mergers Commission (to be replaced by new Competition Directorate) The DGFT

Source: European Commission (1998)

Table 8 Powers and functions of the national regulatory authorities in telecoms and broadcasting

Member State	Licences of infrastructure and service provision	Spectrum allocation	Interconnection	Pricing controls	Content controls	Bodies to which Appeals are lodged
Austria						
Telecoms	The Telecom Control Commission	The Telecom Control Commission	The Telecom Control Commission	The Telecom Control Commission	The Federal Ministry of Science & Transport. The Ministry of Justice	The Federal Constitutional Court and/or to the Supreme Administrative Court
Broadcasting	The Authorities on Regional Radio and Cable Broadcasting	The Federal Ministry of Science & Transport	NA	NA	The Commission for the Application of the Broadcasting Law The Broadcasting Commission for the Application of the Law on Regional Broadcasting The Ministry of Justice	The Federal Constitutional Court and/or the Supreme Administrative Court

Member State	Licences of infrastructure and service provision	Spectrum allocation	Interconnection	Pricing controls	Content controls	Bodies to which Appeals are lodged
Belgium						
Telecoms	The BIPT	The Federal Ministry of Communications The BIPT	The BIPT[1]	The Federal Ministry of Communications	NA	The Conseil d'Etat
Broadcasting	The competent body of the Community concerned	The Communities within the frequency ranges prescribed by the Federal government	NA	The Federal Ministry of Economic Affairs	The competent body of the Community concerned The Conseil supérieur de l'Audiovisuel (French Community) The Media Council (Flemish Community) The Council for Local radio (Flemish Community) The Council for Advertising and Sponsoring	

Table 8 continued

Member State	Licences of infrastructure and service provision	Spectrum allocation	Interconnection	Pricing controls	Content controls	Bodies to which Appeals are lodged
Denmark						
Telecoms	The National Telecom Agency (NTA)	The NTA	The NTA	The NTA	NA	The Telecommunications Complaints Board The Telecommunications Consumer Board
Broadcasting	The Ministry of Culture The Satellite and Cable Board (cable TV and satellite licences) The Local Radio and Television Board	The National Telecom Agency	NA	The Ministry of Culture Board	The Radio and Television Advertisement	The Ministry of Culture[2]
Finland						
Telecoms	The Ministry of Transport & Communications	The Telecommunications Administration Center (TAC)	The Ministry of Transport & Communications The TAC	NA	NA	The Supreme Administrative Court or the Ministry of Transport & Communications

Member State	Licences of infrastructure and service provision	Spectrum allocation	Interconnection	Pricing controls	Content controls	Bodies to which Appeals are lodged
Broadcasting	The Council of Ministers	The TAC	The Ministry of Transport & Communications	The Ministry of Transport & Communications	The Ministry of Transport & Communications The Information Council The National Agency for the Control of Health Products and Well-Being	The Supreme Administrative Court or the Ministry of Transport & Communications The Ombudsman
France Telecoms	The Ministry of Post & Telecommunications, upon instruction by the Autorité de Régulation des Télécommunications (ART)	The ART	The ART	The Minister and the ART[3]	The Ministry for Post & Telecommunications The Conseil Supérieur de la Télématique	The Tribunal Administratif for most ART decisions[4]

Table 8 continued

Member State	Licences of infrastructure and service provision	Spectrum allocation	Interconnection	Pricing controls	Content controls	Bodies to which Appeals are lodged
Broadcasting	The Conseil supérieur de l'Audiovisuel (CSA)	The CSA	NA	The CSA	The CSA	The Conseil d'Etat
Germany Telecoms	The Federal Ministry for Post & Telecommunications (BMPT) The NRA (as of January 1998)	The NRA (as of January 1998)	The NRA (as of January 1998)	NA	NA	The administrative courts The BMPT
Broadcasting	The States (Länder)	The States (Länder) under the general framework prescribed by the MPT	NA	NA	The States (Länder) The supervisory authorities of the broadcasters	The administrative courts

Member State	Licences of infrastructure and service provision	Spectrum allocation	Interconnection	Pricing controls	Content controls	Bodies to which Appeals are lodged
Greece						
Telecoms	The Ministry of Transport & Communications (the Ministry), further to a proposal received from the National Telecommunications Commission (EET)	The EET	The EET	The Ministry	NA	The administrative courts
Broadcasting	The National Council of Radio and Television (NCRT)	The Ministry of Transport & Communications	The EET	The NCRT	The NCRT	The administrative courts
Ireland						
Telecoms	The Ministry of Transport, Energy & Communications The Office of the Director of Telecommunications Regulations (ODRT)	The ODRT	The ODRT	The ODRT	NA	The Irish Courts The District Court against decisions of the Ministry for the High Court (Transport, Energy & Communications and ODRT)

Table 8 continued

Member State	Licences of infrastructure and service provision	Spectrum allocation	Interconnection	Pricing controls	Content controls	Bodies to which Appeals are lodged
Broadcasting	The Independent Radio and Television Commission The Minster for Communications	Telecommunications and Radio Divisions of the Department of Transport, Energy & Communications	NA	NA	The Minister for of Arts, Heritage, Gaeltacht, and the Islands	The District Court
Italy Telecoms	The Communications Authority	The Communications Authority	The Communications Authority	The Communications Authority	The Communications Authority	The administrative courts
Broadcasting	The Communications Authority	The Communications Authority	The Communications Authority	The Communications Authority	The Communications Authority	The administrative courts
Luxembourg Telecoms	The Ministry of Communications together with the Institut Luxembourgeois des Télécommunications (ILT)	The Ministry of Communications together with the ILT[5]	The ILT	The Ministry of Communications together with the ILT	The Ministry of Communications together with the ILT	The Ministry of Communications The administrative courts

Member State	Licences of infrastructure and service provision	Spectrum allocation	Interconnection	Pricing controls	Content controls	Bodies to which Appeals are lodged
Broadcasting	The Ministry of Communications The Prime Minister The Commission on Radio Broadcasting	The Ministry of Communications	NA	NA	The National Council for Programmes[6]	The administrative courts
The Netherlands						
Telecoms	The Independent Post & telecommunications Authority (OPTA)	The Ministry for Transport, Public Works & Water Management The Agency for Radio Frequencies (OPTA)	OPTA	NA	NA	The civil courts
Broadcasting	The Commission for the Media The Ministry of Education, Culture & Science[7]	The Ministry of Transport, Public Works & Water Management	OPTA (with the Competition Authority to determine access issues relating to Cable TV)	NA	The Minister of Education, Culture and Science The Commission for the Media The National Broadcasting Organization[8]	The civil courts The District Court of Rotterdam (against the decision of the Ministry of Transport)

Table 8 continued

Member State	Licences of infrastructure and service provision	Spectrum allocation	Interconnection	Pricing controls	Content controls	Bodies to which Appeals are lodged
Portugal Telecoms	The Ministry of Equipment, Planning and Territorial Administration The Portuguese Institute of Communication (ICP)	The ICP	The ICP	NA	NA	The administrative courts
Broadcasting	The Council of Ministers, after consultation of the High Authority for the Media	The ICP	NA	NA	The High Authority for the Media	The administrative courts
Spain Telecoms	The Telecommuni-cations Market Commission (CMT), except where a licence is awarded by tender	The Ministry of Development	The CMT	The Ministry of Development	NA	The administrative courts

Member State	*Licences of infrastructure and service provision*	*Spectrum allocation*	*Interconnection*	*Pricing controls*	*Content controls*	*Bodies to which Appeals are lodged*
Broadcasting	The Ministry of Development, upon conferral with regional authorities[9]	The Ministry of Development	NA	The Ministry of Development until 1 January 1998	NA	The administrative courts
Sweden						
Telecoms	The National Post and Telecoms Agency (PTS)	The PTS	The PTS	The PTS	NA	The general administrative courts
Broadcasting	The Radio & Television Authority	The PST	NA	NA	The Broadcasting Commission The Chancellor of Justice/Attorney General	The general administrative courts The Administrative Court of Appeal (against decision of the Broadcasting Commission)

Table 8 continued

Member States	Licences of infrastructure and service provision	Spectrum allocation	Interconnection	Pricing controls	Content controls	Bodies to which Appeals are lodged
United Kingdom						
Telecoms	The Secretary of State for Trade & Industry (DTI) in consultation with OFTEL	The Radio Communications Agency	OFTEL	OFTEL	OFTEL	Limited right of appeal from OFTEL Orders to the High Court Possibility of appeal to the commercial courts
Broadcasting	The Independent Television Commission (ITC)	The Secretary of State of Trade & Industry The ITC The Radio-communications Agency	NA	NA (BSC)	The Broadcasting Standards Commission High Court	Right of appeal from the ITC decisions, generally before the

1. The BIPT in theory plays an advisory role by either: (i) approving an interconnection settlement *inter partes*; or (ii) by advising the Minister to impose a negotiating framework on the parties involved. Neither has occurred to date.
2. For sponsorship issues, it is the Radio/TV channels who deal with any complaints.
3. The minister is responsible for retail tariffs for basic voice services which are 'not subject to competition', but the ART has the power to give and to have published its (non-binding) views on the matter.
4. Interconnection dispute resolution. The latter are subject to an appeal to the Cour d'Appeal de Paris (civil court).
5. In the near future, the Institute will assist the Ministry in granting frequencies.
6. The national Council for Programmes advises the government on content of radio and TV programmes.
7. For terrestrial TV: (i) the Minister of Education, Culture and Science grants service licences for the public national broadcasting organizations; and (ii) the Media Commission awards air-time licences for the seven major broadcasting companies.
8. The National Broadcasting Organization is responsible for prescribing the content of public broadcasting organizations. The Dutch Competition Authority has already reviewed the possibility of applying ONP rules to cable TV operators as regards their programming.
9. The CMT has competence to interpret cable TV licence provisions.

Source: European Commission (1998)

Notes

1 See 'Commissions Recommendation on Interconnection in a liberalized telecommunications market, Part 1 – Interconnection Pricing', adopted 8 January 1998, C (98) 50.
2 Note that Spain has a derogation until November 1998, Belgium is late in transposing most EU requirements into national law and Italy missed the 1 January 1998 deadline for licensing a second fixed line operator.
3 All Figures as at end 1997, see the 'Third Report on the Implementation of the Telecommunications Regulatory Package', European Commission COM (98) 80, February 1998.
4 The Spanish government retains a 0.1% holding of shares in Telefonica.
5 Yet Luxembourg claimed it was not ready for full liberalization on 1 January 1998 and competition was delayed until July 1998.
6 Commission Recommendation on Interconnection in a liberalized telecommunications market, Part 1 – Interconnections Pricing', adopted 8 January 1998, C (98) 50.
7 Note, however, that the United Kingdom's reluctant to offer equal access is not a position favoured by the Commission.
8 See also the Draft Directive amending Directive 90/388/EC, OJ C 71, 7 March 1998, p.3.

10 The Key Policy Issues

10.1 Towards competition

The changing technological landscape in the telecoms industry poses a formidable regulatory challenge since development of the markets may be heavily influenced by public policy. The central challenge is the first conflicting priority of Part 1 of this Report: balancing short- and long-term objectives. Clearly, short-term considerations must be taken into account, but it is vital to get it right in the long term, to ensure that the system provides proper incentives to invest and innovate.

No matter what differences there are in their policies, all EU countries and regulators have the same goal: an up-to-date, innovative and low cost infrastructure. This ambition may be achieved in two ways. One focuses on short-run prices and costs and is likely to be derailed well before the objective is met. The alternative focuses on long-run allocative efficiency, ensuring a system that rewards innovation and low costs in the long run.

Three major regulatory issues will determine the overall evolution of market structures in the telecoms industry and related industries of the 'information society':

1. The conditions of access to key components (essential facilities) of the information society. This includes issues such as access to the final customer and access to key content. Access to the home is potentially one of the key bottlenecks in the telecoms market, but there is debate as to its exact meaning (for example, does it refer to the complete local loop or only to 'call termination'?)[1] Conditions of access are also important in the growing digital pay-TV market where set-top boxes (so-called conditional access systems) share some features of the local loop with respect to digital broadcast.

Defining the narrowness or breadth of these key components is a crucial decision.[2]

2. The conditions of interconnection and interoperability between different networks. As shown in Part 1 of this Report, the growth of products, services and markets in network industries is in part dependent on the exploitation of network externalities. The examples are numerous and range from mobile telephony to alternative browsing and publishing products for the Internet. The exploitation of these externalities is promoted by the adoption of standards and/or conditions that allow interconnection of operations across networks.

3. The conditions of ownership of alternative technological platforms, network infrastructures and essential facilities. Some ownership arrangements may lead to situations of abuse of dominant position and the potential elimination of competition in downstream or upstream segments of the market.

The potential magnitude of the network externalities provides a framework that may be conducive to fairly non-competitive market structures. Indeed, leading firms owning proprietary standards or key scarce resources enjoy tremendous advantages, which could also lead to market dominance.

At the same time, restricting this dominant position by providing wider access to the incumbent's assets or forbidding the simultaneous ownership of alternative platforms and networks is a complex policy. It may appear appropriate to achieve a fast introduction of the new service in the short term, but such a policy would surely provide the wrong signal from a *dynamic* perspective, possibly eliminating the incentives for the incumbent to invest in new technologies and/or delivery channels, and forgoing the potential gains of providing new services by the joint exploitation of different technologies.

Striking the balance between these two forces is particularly difficult at the current stage of technological uncertainty, since policy choices may not only favour specific business strategies, but more generally promote the development of specific technological platforms. Something like this has occurred in countries where the constraints imposed on cable companies (in terms of coverage, number and nature of licenses, and conditions for unbundling) may have placed them at a disadvantage relative to their satellite or terrestrial competitors.

Box 23 The benefits of competition

By now, it is widely accepted that substantial social benefits arise when competition is introduced in telecoms markets. This is clearly perceived with final telecoms services, but perhaps less so in the provision of infrastructure. The latter has been perceived as having significant natural monopoly components, where there may be a case for avoiding the duplication of high fixed costs.

Efficiency gains are obtained because of the presence of significant increasing returns in the industry. These gains can take several forms. First, there may be some integration economies, which accrue to firms that provide both infrastructure carrier services as well as final services to customers. Second, there may be significant economies of scale and scope at the final service level.

Typically, from a social point of view, the monopoly control that could be justified by these efficiency gains would have to be balanced with the possibilities of regulating the franchise. The case for granting a monopoly franchise will diminish the more difficult it is for the regulatory body to monitor the activities of the monopolist. In other words, the worse the information of the regulator has on the cost structure of the incumbent firm, the less likely is the prospect of a correct outcome from having one firm. In vertical relations, the regulator will need very detailed information on the costs of interconnection. More generally, the regulator will require very good information on the distribution of common costs.

Trends in the industry clearly point to an increased acknowledgement of the gains from competition. First, technological evolution has diminished the efficiency gains associated with size and vertical integration. Second, informational difficulties make it very difficult for the regulator to provide a proper regulatory framework, and competition is perceived either as an adequate complement to regulation (yardstick competition) or simply as a perfectly viable substitute.

<u>10.2</u> Obstacles to effective competition

Even if competition is deemed to be a desirable objective, the legacy of monopoly and the other constraining factors listed in Chapter 1 and Chapter 9 are likely to jeopardize the introduction of effective competition. In the short run, the incumbents in Europe will control many of the facilities that are needed by new entrants to access consumers. The policy debate focuses on what structural policies can be implemented to limit this problem. Several options are available, including:

- First, some kind of divestiture or separation, whereby the provision of infrastructure and final services are undertaken either by two fully distinct organizations, or by two entities with legal or accounting separation even if common ownership is maintained. This is vertical separation with service provider competition, case (iii) in Section 2.1 (Chapter 2) above. It was the approach used in the United States with the break-up of AT&T, where the provision of local exchange carrier services was split from the provision of long distance service. No other country has followed this example.[3]
- Second, regulating the conduct of the dominant incumbent so that fair access by downstream competitors is guaranteed. Conduct regulation may take several forms. This is vertical integration with service provider competition, case (ii) in Section 2.1 (Chapter 2) above.

One possibility within this second option is to establish regulatory conditions for interconnection that guarantee non-discrimination and fair access to the network. Of course, informational deficiencies may seriously limit the effectiveness of this policy. Moreover, there is a great debate as to what 'fair' means and who should pay for the cost of altering the monopoly network to accommodate competitors. Inevitably, entrants and incumbents disagree, often quite violently.

Access conditions may be too onerous for downstream competitors if the incumbent is able to 'capture' the regulator. Access conditions will be a liability for incumbents, if the regulator uses interconnection conditions to strengthen the competitive position of entrants.

An alternative form of conduct regulation imposes on the incumbent the provision of highly unbundled infrastructure services. Interconnection and access to the network may technically be provided at several feasible points. The regulator can promote market entry by imposing high unbundling requirements, which allow entrants to start providing services with little upfront investment.

There is a major difference if interconnection is provided at the local loop. This allows an entrant to use its own switch, bypassing the incumbent's switch. Unbundling of the local loop imposes on the incumbent the probability that entrants will pick desirable parts of its network, leaving other parts. This is especially true if the regulator

Box 24 Problems in Germany

In early January 1998, without the approval of the German NRA for telecoms, Deutsche Telekom (DT) announced a fee of DM 28.80 to customers who switched to competitors. DG IV independently asked DT for details. In March, the NRA rejected the charges.

In January 1998, the President of the German Federal Cartel Office criticised the NRA for allowing DT to overcharge for local calls. The Commissioner for EU Telecommunications sided with the German regulator.

In January 1998, the NRA halved DT's announced interconnection rates.

DT announced a fee of DM 49 for customers wishing to change to another telecoms supplier while keeping their own number (number portability). On 17 April, the NRA ruled this illegal.

DT submitted a plan on 7 April to charge customers a sliding fee — DM 49 in 1998, DM 35 in 1999, and DM 20 in 2000 – if they transferred to another long-distance carrier. DG IV and the NRA announced they were investigating.

imposes low prices on these network elements. Clearly, there is a high probability of regulatory error if there are numerous unbundled elements, each of which has to be priced. In general, unbundling should be treated with caution.

- A third possibility is to allow free entry in the provision of infrastructure of integrated services. This is facilities-based competition, case (v) in Section 2.1 (Chapter 2) above.

The difficulty with this third alternative is that, in practice, it is not clear the extent to which new entry into fixed telephony will take place, given the significant upfront costs faced by infrastructure providers in telecoms markets. If, however, the market is truly evolving or converging, then telephony is not of great concern since competition for telecoms firms will come from cable TV, satellites, wireless services and perhaps over electric wires.

Typically, new entrants in fixed telephony will focus on the development of infrastructure for specific metropolitan high-profit market segments. This is what has happened in the United States and the

United Kingdom with the appearance of competitive local exchange carriers such as MFS (now owned by Worldcom), Colt and Energis. These firms typically build out from high-density central business districts, targeting high-volume business users.

In fact, whether new entry in fixed wire-line takes place in infrastructure will depend on expected post-entry conditions, and the regulator can dramatically influence the outcomes. For example, entry has been fostered in wireless telephony in some European markets by granting entrants a period of duopoly or other forms of limited competition. Indeed, this was the policy pursued between 1984 and 1991 in the United Kingdom for the liberalization of fixed telephony.

Alternatively, regulatory conditions of the post-entry market may discourage would-be competitors. It has been argued that excessive unbundling requirements are limiting investment by US cable firms in upgrading their cable networks.

The difficulties of 'de novo' entry in infrastructure imply that the most likely entrants in the fixed telephony market are operators involved in closely related markets and there are examples of energy

Box 25 Problems in France

Early on, the French telecoms regulator (ART) announced that France was to be ahead of Commission directives requiring that customers can pre-select alternative long distance providers by 2000. The ART announced call-by-call pre-selection.

National operators (those with national infrastructure roll-out, 17 points of presence, 40% of traffic carried on its own network within five years) could request a single digit prefix. There were seven digits available and the ART probably considered that seven national operators would be many. France Telecom received the number 8, Cegetal received 7, and Bouygues received 9 – all French companies.

In fact, many national licence requests were received. On 13 February 1998, the ART issued the last two digits: Tele2 got 4 and Espirit got 6. A loser in that final round, Paris-based firm AXS Telecom sued in the Supreme Court, claiming that the selection process was discriminatory. The court agreed and stayed the final distribution of the two last numbers. Espirit then sued all the other operators that had received licences in previous rounds including Cegetal, Bouygues and France Telecom.

companies entering telecoms markets. This raises the issue of the potential impact of asymmetric regulation across infrastructures.

In summary, telecoms services can be increasingly provided on a variety of technological platforms – fixed and mobile networks, cable, the internet – and these developments are questioning the relevance of the concept of bottlenecks.[4] Regulation can, however, easily produce significant asymmetries and generate an uneven playing field. At the same time, alternative networks benefit from integration and the question of horizontal control over competing facilities becomes of paramount importance, particularly with regard to the interaction between telecoms and cable, and between cable and satellite.

Box 26 The US approach

The current US approach to these problems, as established by the 1996 Telecommunications Act, has created a regulatory framework that is, to some observers, preventing fast infrastructure investment in the local telecoms loop by potential entrants. This outcome is the result of two key features of the Act (see Harris and Kraft, 1997):

1. The excessive unbundling requirements imposed by the new regulation, which may facilitate excessive (and inefficient) entry.
2. The conditions of entry in long-distance and local markets imposed respectively on local exchange carriers and long-distance companies. Similarly, local exchange carriers can engage in competition with cable by providing video services, even if cable companies must await the permission of state regulators to enter local telecoms markets. These conditions are paralysing the liberalization of both markets and maintaining the status quo. At most, they are leading to some non-facilities-based entry in local markets.

10.3 Competition policy for converging industries

The convergence of the telecoms, media and information technology sectors has triggered a reorganization of all three industries with an increased number of mergers, acquisitions, alliances and joint ventures that cut across conventional industry definitions (see Table 9). This poses serious problems for competition policy since the economics of the industry and the inherited dominance of former telecoms monopolies may favour 'excessive' concentration. At the same time, concentration and increased size could help innovation by lowering risk. So, once again, there are conflicting priorities between competition today and promoting innovation and competition tomorrow.

Table 9 Mergers, alliances and covergence

Horizontal mergers

Rationale	*Examples*
Increasing market power/gaining minimum efficient scale	Vebacom-Urbana, Systemtechnik, Cable and Wireless Communications, Demon-Cityscape
High cost of new digital technologies	Canal Plus-Nethold
Uncertain demand for new services	Multimediabetriebgesellschaft (Kirch, Bertelsmann, etc.)
Internationalization	Global One, UUNet-Unipalm Pipex
Opportunities arising from regulatory reform	MFS-Worldcom, MCI, Telenet Flanders, NYNEX-Bell Atlantic

Source: European Commission (1997)

Vertical mergers

Rationale	*Examples*
Uncertainty of demand	Hughes Olivetti Telecoms (DirecPC), @Home
Market positioning and access to new skills	Bertelsmann-AOL, BBC Worldwide-ICL, STET-IBM
Gaining control of channels to the customer	BT-BSkyB, Disney-ABC-Capital Cities
Moving into higher margin areas of the 'value chain'	Microsoft Network-NBC, (MSNBC internet new channel)
Stave off competition from companies in related markets	US West-Time Warner, Oracle-Sun-Netscape (network computer)

Source: European Commission (1997)

Determining the general principles that should inform competition policy is particularly complex in this area because of the difficulty of defining the market, and assessing the contribution of agreements to the availability of new services and products or to the promotion of innovation and technical progress. On the other hand, since some of the key players are the incumbents, which still dominate large parts of domestic telecoms markets, the risks of agreements restricting competition or reinforcing the dominance of the market are clear.

EU policy has been based on the application of Articles 85 and 86 of the EC Treaty and on the use of the Merger Regulation.

The use of Article 85 controlling agreements in the telecoms sector has been relatively limited to alliances and cross-media ventures.[5] The Commission has, however, indicated that agreements such as those for roaming (where mobile telephones can be used across borders) or access will be monitored to ensure that they do not serve as a means of price coordination, market sharing, exclusion of third parties, or lead to the exchange of commercially sensitive information.[6]

Article 86 controls the abuse of a dominant position and also has not been frequently used in cases examining the telecoms sector. Nonetheless, in its review of strategic alliances, the Commission examines the dominant position of participant companies, taking account of their relevant geographic and product markets in order to prevent potential limitations of competition.

The Commission has outlined in its Notice on access that dominance from an Article 86 perspective means: 'A market share of over 50% ... although other factors will be considered'(para. 63).[7]

In general, competition policy decisions have been based on three principles:

- Allowing horizontal international agreements that facilitate the access to global services and the interoperability of companies providing complementary services. Agreements such as the originally proposed BT-MCI merger, GlobalOne and Unisource-Uniworld-AT&T have been cleared, although the Commission has ensured that the agreements did not involve clauses that could restrict competition or lead to anti-competitive practices.
- Forbidding vertical agreements that strengthen the position of the companies involved. This was the case with MSG Services, which involved the German national operator and large groups from the content production and distribution industry in Germany.

- Restricting horizontal international agreements between non-complementary dominant operators, ensuring that the alliance does not create dominance of the markets, such as in the proposed MCI-Worldcom merger or ensuring that market sharing agreements do not exist, or tying the approval of the agreement to the liberalization of the domestic market. Indeed, the agreement of Unisource and Telefonica, later dismantled, was contingent on the advancement of full liberalization in Spain.

10.4 Pricing issues

Pricing is very much at the centre of EU telecoms policy. Varying positions are taken by participants depending on the emphasis given to each of the following five concerns on how prices will evolve after the liberalization of telecoms markets:

- Fear of *too high margins* in those service markets in which competitive entry is slow or does not occur at all. Hence, some consumers, such as residential consumers mostly making local calls, would not benefit from competition.

- Fear of *too low margins* for entrants, squeezed between (low) retail usage charges and (high) fees for interconnection to the pre-existing network. By using these price pliers, incumbents may have a way to prevent telecoms markets from ever achieving effective competition.

- Fear of *too high margins* because of collusion among incumbents and (a few) entrants, possibly established in free negotiations on interconnection terms.

- Fear that some parts of the network with high costs of providing service will be closed down because of *too low margins*. This is the problem of universal service obligations.

- Fear that innovation in network facilities and services will be curtailed by *too low margins*, eroding the profitability of both investment in new technology by the incumbent and of entry by new firms that would have brought new technologies to the market.

These concerns are, of course, interrelated in various ways. If price squeezes can be effectively used by incumbents to deter entry, that would magnify the problem of pricing in monopoly market segments. On the other hand, high margins earned by the incumbent may encourage entry. High incumbent margins may also reduce the risk of failure to meet universal service obligations. All these concerns are also affected by active or passive policies that restrict or allow 'excessive' margins. A policy targeting one concern can therefore have ramifications for other concerns.

When rates are out of line with costs (for example, when residential access is priced below costs, or when long distance and especially international calling are priced above costs), entry decisions are ·distorted. Entrants are given incentives by prices and can 'cream-skim' or pick off high price customers. This has two side-effects:

1. Less 'cream' means price rises for other services, though this needs to happen if competition is to be effective. As a consequence, universal service, an important policy goal, must be financed in new ways, not in the old ways by which the vertically integrated monopolist operated (see Chapter 11 below).
2. Inefficient entry may occur as entrants observe the incumbent's prices not its costs. The fear here is that when the incumbent is unleashed, the entrant will run for regulatory cover.

Industry conduct and regulation are very much intertwined. The strategic interaction within the industry includes in most cases at least three types of actors: the incumbent former monopolies, entrant firms and regulators. To some extent, therefore, the actual behaviour of the industry reflects varying regulatory approaches in the different European countries. For example, a regulatory response to the first concern of monopolistic pricing may be a price cap on retail prices, as described in Part 1 of this Report. First used in the United Kingdom, a price-cap regime places a cap on future prices. Then the regulators usually find themselves directly controlling the price level since the level of prices tends to develop at the cap and not somewhere below it.

The price-cap formula, RPI-X, requires the regulator to specify the future productivity growth component X, but this is clearly impossible in an industry in the middle of a technological and institutional revolution.[8] The result is a non-market driven diversity in price level changes among different countries. Table 10 opposite shows a few examples of this variation.

Within the price cap, though, the incumbent firms are allowed to adjust (rebalance) the price structure. The scope for these changes, however, are also very much dependent on the design of the regula-

Table 10 Productivity offsets in price caps on fixed residential
telephony services

Country and Years	Productivity offset
Germany since 1993, mobile telephones	4.0
Sweden 1990–3	0.0
Sweden 1993–6	1.0
United Kingdom, currently, on some services	4.5
France, currently	4.5

tion. This is because extensive broad-base caps are not feasible on a more permanent basis:

1. Productivity growth varies substantially between different type of services.
2. Wide caps, which mix services that are provided on markets with and without competition, induce the incumbent to act more aggressively against newcomers than otherwise, since a price reduction on services under competition gives room under the price cap to raise prices of services not under competition.
3. Rebalancing can be used for price squeezing. Without a change in interconnection charges, the squeeze can be achieved by a reduction of variable call prices that is balanced by higher rental prices.[9]

For various reasons, therefore, general price caps are being replaced by differentiated caps or safeguard caps targeting specific services. In the United Kingdom, individual national and international analogue circuits are limited to a maximum increase of RPI +2%, and national and international digital circuits to RPI +1%. Different price caps on exchange line rentals were abolished in 1996. Hence, the changes in the price structure are constrained in various ways by regulation.

10.5 Interconnection and unbundling issues

Interventions like price caps are troublesome as they are likely to distort investment decisions. The strategic target of the Commission is therefore to strengthen competition so that telecoms markets can be regulated just by ordinary competition legislation – to encourage a move to what Part 1 of this Report describes as phase 3 regulation. To speed up the process, some countries have created incentives for *resale* of the incumbent's facilities and services.

Resale is based on the principle of unbundling, which gives a carrier the right to construct its network using parts of another carrier's network (although resale can be limited to a service (local calls) or a specific piece of infrastructure (the local loop)). This is a much wider concept than interconnection, which is the provision by a carrier of a specific service – the call termination and origination functions at its end-office local switch. While interconnection obligations can be founded on the essential facilities doctrine of competition law, unbundling and resale cannot. Unlike interconnection, resale makes market entry possible without the need for investment in a new network. Market competition created in this form is not, however, de-coupled from regulation: prices, quality of service, etc. will depend on the regulated conditions for use of the incumbent's network.

In fact, generous terms for unbundling and resale are likely to slow the development of real competition since potential entrants may choose to dispense with investments in their own networks, even if their stand-alone cost would be lower than the actual cost of the incumbent. Grieve and Levin (1998) and Waverman (1998) argue that, for this reason, the unbundling policy of the US 1996 Telecommunications Act is actually anti-competitive (see Box 27 on p. 189).

There are two key issues:

1. Whether established carriers may abuse their initial advantage to deter entry by high charges for access to their networks, in particular to the local loops.
2. Whether collusive conduct may arise in the process of agreeing on interconnection terms.

As discussed in Part 1 of this Report, the recent analytical literature on these aspects is fairly pessimistic. Armstrong (1998) and Laffont, Rey and Tirole (1998) demonstrate that an incumbent may be willing to abuse its dominant position by not accepting an interconnection agreement or by insisting on higher interconnection fees for calls terminating on its own network. To overcome such resistance, the entrant firm may have to invest in a larger network of its own than it would otherwise have wished – excessive bypass. The result may be network over-investment. On the other hand, if interconnection is mandatory, the entrant firm may instead under-invest in its own market coverage since it has to consider the strategic effect of expanding its network on the price competition response from the incumbent.

Interconnection agreements introduce an access revenue relation between the profit functions of competing firms that can be used for tacit collusion, the problem of two-way interconnection. As discussed in Part 1 this can result in higher retail prices than under a monopoly network because of the 'double marginalization' problem where firms are imposing mark-ups both on inputs and outputs.

These features of network competition are pervasive and are not just related to an initial phase of competition when new firms are entering the market. Another possibility is that a small group of firms charges other firms high interconnection charges while having low or zero mutual charges. The latter can be accomplished even with formally non-discriminatory prices by means of a 'bill and keep' system among the collaborating group.

Economides, Lopomo and Woroch (1996) analyse what reciprocal interconnection charges would imply for the competitive outcome. Reciprocity (or 'symmetrical pricing') means that the two carriers charge each other the same interconnection fee for terminating a competitor's call. The rule has been suggested as an instrument to neutralize network dominance. In a simple model, where customers first choose a network and then in a second stage decide the number of telephone calls, they find that mandated reciprocity will prevent an established carrier from deterring entrants. That is not the case in a more complex set-up, where the consumers choose the carrier/network and the number of calls in the same period.

These rather discouraging analytical results originate from the assumption that consumption patterns are 'isotropic'. This means that the fraction of the 'own' consumers' calls to the other network will equal the other network's market share. The implication of this is that flows in and out of the two networks are balanced when they charge the same retail prices, irrespective of the networks' market shares.

This is a reasonable assumption in many cases, but, as Laffont, Rey and Tirole (1998) note, and as the entry patterns in the United Kingdom and elsewhere show, an entrant's coverage is not necessarily random. The entrant has an incentive to target customers with specific calling patterns, for example, businesses or universities that usually have more incoming than outgoing calls. The interconnection surplus from these customers will then reduce the deficit generated by 'usual' customers. Haring and Rohlfs (1997) suggest that such conduct could actually be used to design a regulatory system for local telecoms competition that avoids excessive and heavy-handed price regulation.

With the development of the Internet, a growing variety of services *only* having incoming traffic services have emerged that substantially change the scope for strategies by entrants to balance a deficit in interconnection traffic arising from usual telephony. Isaksson (1998) analyses local loop competition under the assumption that an entrant jointly provides internet access and thus relaxes the isotropic consumption assumption. As suggested by Haring and Rohlfs, required regulation combines pricing flexibility with mandatory reciprocity. Pricing flexibility means that the incumbent is allowed to determine the access charge on its own. The entrant decides its targeting level of customers demanding Internet access.

The analysis shows that, at least under some simplifying assumptions, the equilibrium strategy for the incumbent is to choose an interconnection fee that equals the cost of terminating the call in its own network, that is, it does not use market power to mark-up access to its network. If it did, it creates possibilities for the competing entrant to make arbitrage profits from interconnection. If the entrant's cost of terminating a call is less than the incumbent's, the latter would find it profitable to reduce the fee below its (marginal) cost and accept a net outflow of calls to the entrant's network.

This possibility of using Internet-access traffic for this purpose depends on the way internet service providers (ISP) get access to their customers. In the United States, ISPs are connected to local loops in the same way as long distance carriers. They then have to lease a specific customer's local loop from the local exchange carrier. In Sweden and the United Kingdom, customers call ISPs in the same way they call someone in another network.

In the US case, the ISP pays the interconnection fee to the local exchange carrier, while in the Swedish case, the customers' local exchange carrier has to pay the ISP the same fee. Exploitation of the Internet-access service to balance the deficit from ordinary telephony for entrants suggests that the latter system is used. The Swedish experience (see the case of Tele2 in Box 27) shows that a rather small competitor can indeed challenge the incumbent and force the interconnection fees down, if it succeeds in targeting customers demanding Internet access.

Although this suggests that it may be possible to avoid excessive regulation of interconnection prices, this mechanism still requires several types of intervention. The carriers must be obliged to interconnect with each other, and the interconnection charge should be reciprocal. The incumbent should not have the possibility to discrimi-

Box 27 The case of Tele2

In 1995, the entrant firm Tele2 began 'targeting' customers who *only* had terminating traffic to Internet access modem-pools.[10] Tele2 invested in modem-pools in almost all local telephony regions in Sweden. This aimed at getting the incumbent Telia's customers to call these modem-pools, or more precisely, to get Telia's customers to spend more time in Tele2's network than vice versa. This strategy eventually became so successful that Tele2 earned an interconnection fee surplus against Telia in 1996.[11]

An important reason for this achievement is the large difference between time spent on telephone calls and on surfing the Internet. The average telephone call in Sweden is 3–6 minutes while the average internet session is about 30–40 minutes. Telia had not anticipated the households' huge interest in Internet access, and paid Tele2 over MSEK 200 in interconnection fees in less than one year before they launched their own Internet-access service on a broad front.

Telia's second counter-move was to impose extra per-call fees on calls terminating in competing networks. This was, however, not accepted by Sweden's NRA, so Telia had little choice but to offer Tele2 lowered interconnection fees. Telia offered Tele2 a 'bill and keep' contract, where the carriers skip the interconnection payment when a customer calls someone in the competing carrier's network. The contract gave the entrant the opportunity to use Telia's network for free. In doing that, however, the entrant lost the revenues from the internet access service at the same time.

From Tele2's point of view, the 'bill and keep' deal has several merits. Since the company not only relies on Internet-access service, but also is the largest provider of national telephony besides Telia, the revenue 'loss' from the Internet-access service could be compensated by higher profits from national telephony. The 'bill and keep' contract will be valid as long as the difference between the companies' claim on each other is modest. Therefore, according to Tele2, the carrier has no intention to enter the market for local calls, via indirect connected customers, since this could lead to large interconnection deficits. Thus, it will be important for Tele2 to continue the targeting of Internet-access subscribers as long as their market share in usual telephony continues to grow.

continued

Box 27 continued

The other companies in the market were taken by surprise by the 'bill and keep' arrangement, since many of them had specialized in getting customers with a lot of incoming calls from Telia's customers. The competitors now fear that these revenues from interconnection fees will vanish since Telia, according to the Telecommunications Act, has to offer all competitors interconnection on equal terms. One of these companies was Telenordia. After observing Tele2's successful strategy, Telenordia also entered the market for Internet access. Not being as strong as Tele2 on national telephony, however, it could not benefit as much from lowered interconnection fees as Tele2. It therefore turned down an offer by Telia to lower interconnection fees by 50%. After seven months of negotiations and mediation by the supervising authority, the companies finally reached an agreement in May 1997, but the terms have not become public. The *standard* intercon-

---

nate between the monopoly territory (where the entrant is not represented) and the competitive territory, otherwise it could still abuse its power by insisting on a high interconnection fee and a high retail price for off-net calls (calls originating in the competitive territory terminating in the monopoly zones).

Interconnection agreements between carriers often cover more issues than just access charges. The carriers often need to agree about technical standards, what quality to provide, etc. It may, therefore, be unrealistic to allow the incumbent to decide interconnection conditions on its own. The implication therefore would be to give the established carrier a large degree of individual discretion over the interconnection charge, but not to give a free hand.

10.6 European interconnection policy

Most EU countries have now enacted rules to regulate interconnection, typically following the guidance of the Commission's Interconnection Directive. Table 11 summarizes the key issues.

Table 11 Telecoms Interconnection (IC) Issues

Member State	Are IC agreements subject to express regulation or individual negotiation?	Are there special rules for 'dominant' operators or industry-wide rules?	Are there specific network locations where IC must take place?	Is there unbundled access to internal network functions?	Is there a preferred pricing formula for IC charges?	Are there rules on collocation?
Austria	Agreements are subject to individual negotiation by the parties. The Telecommunications Law of 1997 and a draft Decree contain specific rules on interconnection, however.	There are special rules for 'dominant' operators.	No	No, but the Ministry of Science & Transport must define by Decree a minimum range of unbundled network elements.	No	No
Belgium	Agreements are individually negotiated. A future Royal Decree, scheduled to apply as from	Currently covered only under general competition rules. A future Royal Decree,	To be agreed by contract.	Provided in the reference offer of the incumbent TO, but unlikely to be mandated.	There is a preferred pricing formula in the IC offer of the incumbent TO.	No

Table 11 Continued

Member State	Are IC agreements subject to express regulation or individual negotiation?	Are there special rules for 'dominant' operators or industry-wide rules?	Are there specific network locations where IC must take place?	Is there unbundled access to internal network functions?	Is there a preferred pricing formula for IC charges?	Are there rules on collocation?
Belgium cont.	1 January 1998, will set forth the general terms of negotiation.	to apply as from 1 January 1998, will impose obligations on dominant telecoms operators.				
Denmark	Individual negotiations, subject to specific principles found in the Act on Competitive Conditions and IC in the	There are special rules for 'dominant' operators. In practice, however, an expansive view is taken of 'relevant markets' (which	No	No	Yes. From 1999, the pricing formula will be long-run average incremental costs (LRAIC).	Yes

Member State	Are IC agreements subject to express regulation or individual negotiation?	Are there special rules for 'dominant' operators or industry-wide rules?	Are there specific network locations where IC must take place?	Is there unbundled access to internal network functions?	Is there a preferred pricing formula for IC charges?	Are there rules on collocation?
		Telecommunications Sector of 12 June 1996, as amended on 10 June 1997. means that dominance is less likely).				
Finland	Agreements are subject to individual negotiations, subject to specific rules.	Yes. A very broad view is taken of which parties have 'significant market power' (currently over 50%).	No. Unbundling, however, is mandated down to the level of the local loop.	Yes, if reasonable.	TOs with significant market power must formulate a basis for calculating interconnection charges. The Ministry has announced its intention to follow the LRAIC pricing formula.	No

Table 11 Continued

Member State	Are IC agreements subject to express regulation or individual negotiation?	Are there special rules for 'dominant' operators or industry-wide rules?	Are there specific network locations where IC must take place?	Is there unbundled access to internal network functions?	Is there a preferred pricing formula for IC charges?	Are there rules on collocation?
France	Agreements are subject to individual negotiation by the parties. France Telecom's agreement has been approved by the regulatory authorities. A Decree on interconnection has been adopted.	'Dominant' operators have additional interconnection obligations.	Yes. It must occur down to the level of a local switch if technically feasible. France Telecom's agreement also contains rules on the network location where interconnection must take place.	Yes	There exists a three-tiered pricing test: (i) negotiations between ART and France Telecom regarding what constitutes legitimate 'historical' costs (as of 1998); (ii) LRAIC cost model from 1999; (iii) comparative models with other countries if previous options are unsuccessful.	Yes. In the terms specified in Decree on interconnection as interpreted by Avis Nos 97–9. Virtual collocation is available. France Telecom's offer agreement also contains rules on collocation.

Member State	Are IC agreements subject to express regulation or individual negotiation?	Are there special rules for 'dominant' operators or industry-wide rules?	Are there specific network locations where IC must take place?	Is there unbundled access to internal network functions?	Is there a preferred pricing formula for IC charges?	Are there rules on collocation?
Germany	Individual negotiation, subject to specific rules and regulatory review.	Yes. There are special obligations placed on 'dominant' operators.	No, subject to principle of non-discrimination. Interconnection should in principle be offered wherever sought unless not technically feasible. Unbundling occurs down to the level of access to the local loop.	Yes, provided the unbundling is: (i) necessary; (ii) technically possible; (iii) no objective reasons for refusal on the basis of compliance with essential requirements; (iv) operator uses same functions internally.	Oriented towards LRAIC in the long term.	Mandated for dominant carriers. Virtual collocation is available.
Greece	Individual negotiation, but subject to general	With the exception of domestic competition	No	No	No, but interconnection charges must be 'cost-based'.	No

Table 11 Continued

Member State	Are IC agreements subject to express regulation or individual negotiation?	Are there special rules for 'dominant' operators or industry-wide rules?	Are there specific network locations where IC must take place?	Is there unbundled access to internal network functions?	Is there a preferred pricing formula for IC charges?	Are there rules on collocation?
Greece cont.	principles set out in the law and 'interconnection guidelines'.	rules, industry-wide rules apply thus far (or at least to those parties with exclusive rights).				
Ireland	Primarily a matter for agreement between the parties. The NRA will only intervene in circumstances where the parties have failed to	With the exception of competition rules as they apply to dominant companies, general rules can be deduced from	No	No	No. The general understanding is that prices should reflect costs.	No

Member State	Are IC agreements subject to express regulation or individual negotiation?	Are there special rules for 'dominant' operators or industry-wide rules?	Are there specific network locations where IC must take place?	Is there unbundled access to internal network functions?	Is there a preferred pricing formula for IC charges?	Are there rules on collocation?
Ireland cont.	reach agreement.	ONP principles as they apply to companies with special or exclusive rights.				
Italy	Thus far, individual negotiations, subject to potential regulatory intervention. The Decree implementing the Full Competition Directive entered into force and regulates IC issues.	Yes. 'Dominant' operators have specific obligations.	No	No, but there is a general obligation to offer interconnection in a sufficiently unbundled form.	LRAIC-based costing approach will be introduced (however, pricing principles in the law are very general in nature).	No

Table 11 Continued

Member State	Are IC agreements subject to express regulation or individual negotiation?	Are there special rules for 'dominant' operators or industry-wide rules?	Are there specific network locations where IC must take place?	Is there unbundled access to internal network functions?	Is there a preferred pricing formula for IC charges?	Are there rules on collocation?
Luxembourg		The 1997 Telecoms Law contains general rules on interconnection. The development of a specific regulatory framework for IC is in its preliminary stages.	Yes, in the future.	No. The 1997 Telecom Law provides that a Decree will be adopted establishing the point in the network at which interconnection will take place.	No	No	No
The Netherlands		Subject to individual negotiations. Since 1 July 1997, disputes	The current telecommunications law only contains general rules	No, but the 'interconnection guidelines' require TOs with significant	No	No. The 'interconnection guidelines' do not take a definitive	Collocation, if feasible, should be allowed by the 'dominant' operator.

Member State	Are IC agreements subject to express regulation or individual negotiation?	Are there special rules for 'dominant' operators or industry-wide rules?	Are there specific network locations where IC must take place?	Is there unbundled access to internal network functions?	Is there a preferred pricing formula for IC charges?	Are there rules on collocation?
The Netherlands cont.	are to be resolved by OPTA, the new independent regulator, which is already in operation. Interconnection guidelines were adopted in May 1997.	for the 'dominant' operator. The draft Telecoms Act contains special rules for operators with 'significant market power'.	market power to offer interconnection at the level of number exchanges (if reasonable).		position in this respect.	
Portugal	Subject to individual agreement between operators, with intervention of the NRA where agreement cannot be reached.	Thus far, there are only industry-wide rules.	No	No	No. Practice relies on a historical costs model.	No

Table 11 Continued

Member State	Are IC agreements subject to express regulation or individual negotiation?	Are there special rules for 'dominant' operators or industry-wide rules?	Are there specific network locations where IC must take place?	Is there unbundled access to internal network functions?	Is there a preferred pricing formula for IC charges?	Are there rules on collocation?
Spain	Subject to individual negotiations, subject to specific rules in the law (Ministerial Order of 18 March 1997).	There are special rules for 'dominant' operators.	Yes	No	No. General principle of cost-orientation of charges, but not per a specific formula.	No
Sweden	Subject to individual negotiation, with the NRA being able to intervene where agreement is not forthcoming.	Yes	No, subject to negotiation. Operators with significant market power. 'Dominant' TOs must, however, meet	No	Yes. Cost-based orientation tending to lean towards LRAIC formula. This principle extends expressly to mobile	No

Member State	*Are IC agreements subject to express regulation or individual negotiation?*	*Are there special rules for 'dominant' operators or industry-wide rules?*	*Are there specific network locations where IC must take place?*	*Is there unbundled access to internal network functions?*	*Is there a preferred pricing formula for IC charges?*	*Are there rules on collocation?*
Sweden cont.			all reasonable demands for interconnection with their own networks.		operators, as well as fixed-line operators, since 1 July 1997.	
United Kingdom	Subject to individual negotiation with the possibility of regulatory review.	The interconnection obligation is imposed on all operators, but licence conditions for dominant operators are more restrictive.	No. Interconnection must be at a point allowing consumers to choose carrier and allowing carrier to choose how message is routed throughout system (i.e., at a point in the network hierarchy below the regional switch).	No	Yes, cost-based, with a preference for a LRAIC model.	No. Where there is an in-site or in-building location, BT will provide access. BT will not provide access to its own ducts or other facilities where this would jeopardize its network integrity.

10.7 Cross-border issues

The Commission has rightly concerned itself with the discriminatory pricing of calls across national borders relative to the prices of calls wholly within borders. Table 12 shows an advertisement in the *International Herald Tribune* of 8 April 1998 containing prices for a company, Maxtel. In each case, it is cheaper to call the United States from the five European countries than to call the neighbouring European country.

Originally, the European countries used a collective system called TEUREM (Trans-European and Mediterranean Basin) to set principles for the settlement of traffic that crossed national borders. Since calls between two countries involved two operators, a mechanism was needed for reimbursing the operator who received more calls than were returned. The Commission felt that this system had components that kept cross-border prices high and TEUREM was disbanded in 1996. A call crossing a border, however, still faces higher prices than equidistant calls within a country even though costs are nearly the same. The Commission has recently announced an investigation into this issue.

Another cross-country issue is roaming: the agreement between two mobile operators where a telephone issued in country A can be used in country B. The telephone owner from country A can continue to receive calls when in country B, but these are charged as international calls from A to B, and these prices are not low. The country A telephone owner can also call within B and pay B country charges plus a roaming fee. Unlike calling from A to B, calling in B on an A telephone does involve extra costs. The system must be able to track the mobile telephones in the other country. Still, the roaming charges are high and these bilateral agreements may leave room for excess pricing.

Table 12 Pricing across borders

From	To the United States	To the United Kingdom	To Germany
France	19¢	21¢	25¢
Germany	16¢	18¢	22¢
Switzerland	19¢	21¢	25¢
United Kingdom	12¢	14¢	18¢
Netherlands	16¢	18¢	22¢
Hong Kong	25¢	27¢	31¢

With both these issues, NRAs have little authority since the call involves another jurisdiction. It would therefore seem natural that the Commission is the appropriate authority to end these unduly discriminatory practices.

Notes

1 See Harris and Kraft (1997), p. 107.
2 For a detailed discussion, see OCED (1997c), p. 31, or European Commission (1997), p. 28.
3 Although Ireland has recently divested Telecom Eireann of its cable TV division.
4 See Harris and Kraft (1994), p. 104.
5 A 1985 case involved the UK's newly privatized BT, in which the Commission overruled a decision of the UK government that prohibited a 'refiling' service (where messages from one country can be resent in another). The Italian government disputed the decision, but their claim was dismissed by the European Court of Justice. The Court confirmed that the competition rules apply to the telecoms operators.
6 Waverman and Sirel (1997).
7 Notice on the application of the competition rules to access agreements in the telecommunications sector: framework, relevant markets and principles, finally adopted 31 March 1998, European Commission, Brussels.
8 Also, there is, as often is the case, a conflict between a competition policy and a public utility regulation approach to this. From the first perspective, it is not indisputable that government authorities should make this kind of commercial information public.
9 Unfortunately, such a change of price schemes is also what is recommended by an analysis of efficient retail pricing (Ramsey pricing) when no account is taken of the indirect effects on market competition through the price squeeze. Grout (1996) calculates efficient rental charges to be 208% (Ireland) to 364% (France) of current (1994) levels in seven selected EU countries, while efficient international varible prices are just 30% (Finland) to 52% (Italy) of current levels.
10 For a fuller account, see Isaksson (1998).
11 Notice that most of Tele2's customers are indirectly connected through Telia's network. This implies that the carrier has to lease both the originating and the terminating trunk from Telia. Nethertheless, the Internet traffic exceeded Tele2's demand for access.

11 The Social Impact of Telecommunications

The telecoms industry tends to be perceived by policy-makers as a key high-technology activity, with wide and profound effects on several areas of social and economic life. To many observers, the magnitude and nature of those effects justify some sort of government intervention in the industry. This chapter discusses the range of social impacts that are usually considered, and assesses the rationale for policy intervention. A key issue at the heart of the social debate on telecoms is the concept of universal service. This has been discussed in general terms in Chapters 4 and 6 above. Here, the theoretical rationale for such a concept and the practical implications with regard to EU telecoms policy are reviewed in detail.

11.1 Rationales for policy intervention in telecoms

There is no question that the revolution in telecoms, particularly in combination with advances in computing and audio-visual technologies, is provoking profound social changes. The digital revolution is rapidly bringing down the costs of storing, transmitting and manipulating information across the world. Its deep and widespread impact is illustrated by the range of services and activities that are directly and indirectly affected by the revolution. Box 28 lists the most directly affected services.[1]

The real issue, though, is why should the government intervene in the face of such developments? Is the free interplay of market forces leading to an economic or technological outcome that policy-makers find inappropriate? And what is really meant by inappropriate?

Following the standard welfare economics tradition discussed in Part 1 of this Report, intervention by the government may be justified

Box 28 Services and the impact of the information economy

- Communication services
- Information services
- Entertainment services
- Access to other services provided at distance
  - Social education
  - Health
  - Other security
  - Shopping
  - Banking
  - Metering

either by equity concerns or on the basis of efficiency criteria. Equity issues will be relevant if the new technologies do not favour a group of citizens about which policy-makers particularly care. Efficiency concerns arise if telecoms technologies spread insufficiently or inappropriately relative to what would be optimal from the point of view of society.

11.2 Efficiency concerns

The main efficiency concerns that may justify action emerge from the existence of network externalities. These arise when there is a divergence between the private and social benefits obtained from adding one more user to the network.

Since telecoms networks provide interaction possibilities between all users, a new subscriber/user benefits from (and is willing to pay for) access to the set of current users, but at the same time is providing new communication possibilities to the installed base of users of the network. These social gains are not taken into account by the individual user when deciding on joining the network, and this wedge between private and social incentives will lead to underdevelopment of the network compared with what should be socially appropriate.

Market failure for this reason may have been a significant problem at a time when market penetration of telephony was low. Today, it applies, if at all, to specific categories of people, such as students, and to new services like third generation (UMTS) digital mobile services. The nature of the externality already indicates the type of intervention that is probably most appropriate: if there is insufficient connection to the network, policies aimed at lowering connection charges rather than lowering the usage fee should be favoured.

More important given the current state of development of communication networks is the fact that the presence of network externalities also has implications for market structure and the willingness of network firms to interconnect and adhere to common standards. By adopting to a common standard, each firm gets access to a larger market. In addition, because of the network externalities, the quality of the network services improves. On the other hand, compatible standards and interconnection sharpen competition between firms. Using idiosyncratic technology, firms may instead gain monopoly power even though their services are less valuable to consumers.

Economides and Flyer (1997) analyse this trade-off and find that in many cases, full compatibility cannot be expected to be an equilibrium outcome of oligopolistic competition between firms, and that the equilibria that emerge are often very asymmetric in firms' profits and outputs. They conclude that in markets with strong network externalities, dominance by one or a few firms may be an inherent characteristic of market equilibrium. In such circumstances, efficiency concerns suggest the need for competition policy, interconnection rules and standardization, though they do not justify arguments for subsidization or any other form of manipulation of demand.

11.3 Equity concerns

Government intervention on distributional grounds may take place if the development of telecoms markets hurts groups of citizens perceived to be special by policy-makers. The damage to these groups may arise in several forms:

1. Some potential users may be denied access to services, for example, on the basis of location.
2. Access may be very costly and hence, in practice, unavailable to low income user-groups.
3. Pricing policies by service suppliers may discriminate against low-use subscribers and, as a consequence, prevent their connection to the network.

Does the exclusion of certain user groups from some telecoms services justify public intervention? After all, access and use of many market services is costly when determined through market forces, and may not be affordable to certain households given their budget and preferences. Indeed, sometimes, goods and services are not even available in certain areas, as suppliers choose not to deliver the goods there given the costs and willingness to pay of potential consumers.

Moreover, it should be borne in mind that in the absence of efficiency reasons for intervention – any public action that, on equity grounds, modifies pricing policies determined in the marketplace and thus redistributes purchasing power across individuals – has an equivalent intervention through the tax system with potentially less negative effects on overall welfare since it will not distort prices.

What all this means is that telecoms services must have features that make them essential services. Given the previous discussion, what 'essential' means is either that they cannot be 'too expensive' so that a significant part of the population is excluded from access; or that they have unique characteristics that cannot be substituted (that is, in-kind transfers cannot be equivalent to the provision of a direct income transfer).

Telecoms services will be considered essential to the extent that they are perceived as a citizen's right, such as, for example, general education. Of course, the difficulty with such an approach is that it is difficult to a draw a clear line separating essential from non-essential services. For example, in Box 28, should security and information services be included and, if so, at what level of quality?

In practice, both efficiency and equity considerations will play a significant role in shaping the social interventions of governments in telecoms markets. The previous discussion sets the stage for the analysis of the universal service debate. This is the policy tool that focuses the controversies on the social impact of telecoms.

11.4 Defining universal service

The theoretical rationales for policy intervention in telecoms lead to a definition of universal service that comprises:

- the right to connect to the telecoms network;
- connection at a price that does not exclude significant consumer groups;

- non-distorted use rates, which therefore cannot be used to discourage connection;
- a set of facilities and a level of service that guarantee access to basic communications of standard quality.

The concept of prices for both connection and use that guarantee access (given other relative prices and income) should not, in principle, be controversial. The definition of basic communications and standard quality is, however, less clear-cut. Given the changing nature of the services available through the telecoms networks, what is considered as basic communication capabilities is evolving and highly debatable: is, for example, access to electronic mail with a 14,400-baud modem a basic telecoms service? As for quality, one possible way to make the concept operational is to consider the cost implications of poor quality. Alternatively, a minimum quality standard may be imposed by the regulator.

The EU defines universal service as comprising the non-discriminatory provision of an affordable voice telephony service and network access via a line supporting the use of fax and low speed data transmission.[2] The recent revision of the 1995 ONP Voice Telephony Directive, which should be implemented by EU Member States by mid-1998, confirms the principle of affordability (Article 3), establishes the obligation to ensure that all reasonable requests for connection are met (Article 5), defines the range of ancillary services considered to be part of the universal service (itemized billing, tone dialling, selective call barring, public telephones and directory and emergency services – Articles 6, 7 and 14), and sets out a framework for quality control (Article 12).[3]

Concepts such as affordable prices and reasonable requests are not explicitly defined. The directive, however, provides a clear indication that affordability should take into account national conditions and should be particularly preserved in relation to populations in high cost areas and vulnerable groups such as the elderly. To achieve these social goals, the directive acknowledges the possible use of pricing schemes such as geographical averaging, price caps and targeted tariffs, even if their implementation is only possible in a framework where there is no full competition and tariffs are still misaligned relative to costs.

The EU has, therefore, broadly followed the general principles of optimal intervention. An exception, however, is the promotion of special pricing schemes with the goal of providing support to special user groups. As previously discussed, these policies introduce new price distortions and need not be the most efficient interventions, apart from the fact that – since they are based on inherited price structures – their introduction may delay full liberalization.

On the other hand, the dynamic nature of the concept of universal service is fully recognized by the directive when it argues that the concept of universal service 'must evolve to keep pace with advances in technology, market developments and changes in user demand'. In fact, the directive already gives operators currently offering universal service the prospect of providing more advanced services (such as calling line identification, direct dialling-in and call forwarding, even if subject to its economic viability).

Once a universal service obligation is defined, its establishment and enforcement may impose a financial burden on the operators providing the services. Two controversial issues arise:

- assessing the extent of the financial burden;
- determining its financing.

11.5 The costs of universal service provision

The cost for current requirements for universal service has been studied in detail in France, Sweden and the United Kingdom. As Sweden is a long country (and sparsely populated, especially in the interior of the northern half) and usage prices are low, the results of the Swedish study are remarkable. They demonstrate that the net cost for Telia, the incumbent operator, after valuation of so-called non-financial benefits amounts to between SEK 29 million and SEK 99 million (respectively, ECU 3.3 million and ECU 14.9 million), which is regarded as a more or less negligible amount.

Similarly, in the United Kingdom, the universal service cost to BT is negligible given that the price of most access lines covers costs and that BT has advantages from being the national provider. In France, in contrast, the universal service deficit is FFr 4.5 billion or ECU 678.2 million. Of this, a large percentage is represented by the costs of residential access generally being below costs, a component of universal service which must be rebalanced by 2000.

Assessment of the net costs (costs minus revenues) of providing universal service is complex for several reasons:

1. The evaluation faces the usual difficulty of allocating to services provided under the universal service obligation, the general overhead common costs of operating the telecoms network. Moreover, on the revenue side, universal service providers might enjoy indirect benefits (in terms of access to clients and reputation) that must also be considered.

2. Second, the assessment should be based on the comparison of two alternative scenarios (provision and non-provision of universal service), with the additional complexity that in both examples, revenues and costs will depend on the regulatory framework and the prevailing market structure.

3. The net costs of universal service provision may depend also on the provision system that is chosen, for example, provision by the dominant operator, a voucher system, etc.

With regard to revenues, the burden imposed by universal service obligations depends on an assessment of the forgone outgoing and incoming calls, taking into account the possible replacement effects (some calls will be placed through public telephones anyway). In addition, a provider of universal service may also forgo future revenues, since some users currently qualifying for universal service may in the future become regular clients.

Assessment problems are even more daunting with regard to costs. As indicated above, distributing general overhead costs is a serious problem in telecoms services, where infrastructure access is provided jointly with a wide set of services. Two alternative methods of distributing common costs have been proposed:

- Total cost distribution, a method that uses reference parameters to distribute network costs across all access points.
- Long-run (avoidable) incremental costs, a method that takes account of the savings that would accrue to the operator if the capacity used to fulfil universal service obligations could be deployed in a profit-maximizing way. The emphasis in this case is in the long run, since in the short run, satisfying universal service obligations may not impose opportunity costs on the operator if there is excess capacity.

It is clear that evaluation of the effects on revenues and costs of universal service obligations will be closely affected by the existing market structure and by the regulatory constraints. The financial burden will be quite different as tariff rebalancing and competition advance in the industry. In other words, it will be crucially affected by regulatory behaviour in terms of interconnection conditions, final prices of the dominant operator and the speed of entry of new (network and service) suppliers.

Indeed, universal service costs may increase if entry takes place before tariff rebalancing, as entrants 'skim the cream' off the market. Some commentators have argued that the costs of universal service should be computed in a scenario where competition develops in the profitable market segments, so that the incumbent loses market share in those markets, with a potential negative effect on unit costs, which makes universal service provision more costly. Thus, the long-run (avoidable) incremental costs should take into account the optimal network size given the impact of a move towards full competition in both network and services.

In a related vein, it has been argued that new ways of providing universal service may alter the incentives of firms to invest in new infrastructure and potentially cut the costs of universal service provision. At least two such systems have been proposed:

- The introduction of publicly funded telephone vouchers, which allow qualifying users (targeted groups due to location and/or income) to contract universal service provision with any operator.
- The competitive auction of the right to offer services within the previously determined (high cost) geographical areas.

The EU approach to the assessment and provision of universal service was established in the Infrastructure Green Paper.[4] With regard to the costs of universal service, in accordance with the Commission's Interconnection Directive (Article 5 and Annex III), the net costs of providing the service should be computed as the difference between the net costs of operating with and without universal service obligations. Cost computations should be done following the guidelines in the directive and other recent Commission documents.[5]

The Directive does not, however, detail the key issue of how costs should be computed and, most importantly, allocated across services and groups of users. Annex V requests transparency and notification of cost procedures with regard to interconnection so that the same should apply to universal service obligations, but no unique method is established. Preferences with regard to interconnection pricing have though been established in a recent recommendation on interconnection pricing.[6]

11.6 Financing universal service

Financing universal service poses a policy problem as discussed in Section 6.7 (Part 1, Chapter 6). General welfare economics principles show that, in the absence of externalities, the most efficient financing schemes will tend to be those that do not introduce distortions within the price mechanism. This general argument does not favour special pricing schemes, which tend to favour specific groups of citizens, possibly with the exception of connection charges on the basis of the existence of network externalities.

The preferred approach promotes the approximation of retail prices to costs, and the compensation of particular users through the general tax system. This approach is also valid with regard to the possible use of surcharges on the interconnection costs as a mechanism that contributes to the financing of universal service. Such an additional charge could lead to an inefficiently low level of network access by telecoms service providers.

The most efficient financing systems are based on the establishment of a universal service fund based on tax revenues, unrelated to telecoms prices. The question is then how to determine the most appropriate tax base on which the tax should be levied. If the public financing of the universal service is founded on distributional arguments, there seems to be no reason why the funds should not be obtained from general taxation, as with other public revenue collected for redistribution purposes.

This approach is even more compelling from an efficiency perspective. If taxes are collected only on industry participants, this may hamper the development of the industry relative to others, which runs counter to the initial policy objectives. If, however, the levy affects only industry participants, its distribution between market players constitutes a powerful policy tool, which may be used to promote (or deter) entry, since there is no other efficiency argument for its distribution among competitors other than its impact on market structure.

The EU policy-framework on financing is established in the recent directives on interconnection and full competition.[7] These directives establish the following principles:

- First, only providers of public telecoms networks can be made to contribute to the funding of a universal service fund.

- Second, the sharing of costs is to be determined by an objective, non-discriminatory method, ensuring that proportionality is maintained, and that new entrants are not penalized.

Financing can be undertaken through the creation of a public fund or it can be based on the introduction of specific interconnection charges. Even if, in the latter case, the directive requests the unbundling and identification of costs, it is clear that such a provision cannot be easily justified from the point of view of the efficient deployment of infrastructure.

Notes

1 The revolution affects not only the range of services that can be provided on-line, but also other dimensions of social and economic life, for example, working conditions: home working, linkages between working teams across the world, etc.

2 The EU approach to the definition of universal service was set forward in the 1993 Communication on developing the universal service for telecommunications in a competitive enviroment (COM 93/543, 15 November 1993) and the 1994 Green Paper on the Liberalization of infrastructure and cable networks (COM 94/440, 25 October 1994; and COM 94/682, 25 January 1995). It has already been partially implemented through the ONP Voice Telephony Directive (95/62/EC, 30 December 1995). Further details on the EU perspective on this subject have been presented in Communication on Universal Service for telecommunications in the perspective of a fully liberalized environment, COM/96/73 final, 13 March 1996.

3 On 5 June 1997, a common position was adopted by the Council on the revision of this Directive and it was adopted on 28 February 1998.

4 The detailed framework for costing is presented in the Interconnection Directive 97/33/EC and the Full Competition Directive 96/19/EC, itself a revision of Directive 90/388/EC.

5 Annex III and the guidelines provided for interconnection charges (Annex V).

6 See the Commission's Interconnection Pricing Recommendation of 15 October 1997 (Part 1). Part 2 will focus on accounting separation and cost accounting systems.

7 Directives 97/33/EC and 96/19/EC.

12 The Required Regulatory and Institutional Framework

12.1 Broad regulatory principles

Part 1 of this Report, notably Chapter 7, discussed the general profile of regulatory activity over time, with a movement from tight, sector-specific regulation over the dominant incumbent in a phase 1 market structure to the use of competition policy in a phase 3 market structure.

In telecoms in most countries, there are still dominant incumbent firms with monopolies or near monopolies over traditional services and some 'essential' infrastructure. Market boundaries are changing, however, in various directions and there are entrants who wish to provide services over this infrastructure, indicating that most countries are moving into a phase 2 market structure in telecoms. Yet, regulatory regimes tend to be new and mainly embedded in the past technology specific to telephony. Three main points stand out from the earlier analysis:

- First, regulation and regulators still seem to be focused on traditional voice telephony and copper wire technology. Convergence is often an afterthought, but it should be the leading issue. The analysis above shows how changing technology is upsetting traditional regulatory tools and creating significant problems of defining markets and assessing what degree of infrastructure competition should occur.

In a few countries (e.g. Italy), one national regulator examines all aspects of the information economy, but in most countries, there is still divided jurisdiction (see Tables 7 and 8 above). For example, in the United Kingdom, OFTEL regulates telecoms, but the issuing of new UMTS (Universal Mobile Telephone Services) or third generation digital mobile licences is being done by the Radio Communications Agency. In TV, the new digital TV being launched now is supervised by the ITC and OFTEL, each with some supervisory authority. All these agencies are regulating the flows of information, which are increasingly involved in each other's territory.

- Second, while sector-specific regulation is at this point needed in many countries, it should be replaced as soon as is practicable with general competition policy. Outside the United Kingdom, it is still too early to tell whether this will occur.

In the United KIngdom, new legislation revising the Competition Act provides concurrent powers over some aspects of competition policy to both the regulator and the anti-trust agency. This development should be considered across the rest of the EU. Its benefits are a direct focus on competition policy, but its defects are the fracturing of authority over competition policy and the risk of entrenching the sectoral regulator through the lack of a 'sunset clause'. As the three phases of market structure make clear, regulation is a transition mechanism: it is essential therefore that regulators view themselves as temporary. Establishing an NRA with the condition that it be disbanded has not been done in any European country.

Moreover, there are already a number of areas where regulatory discretion should be replaced by market forces. For example, it seems clear that current licensing procedures should be replaced with more transparent market mechanisms wherever possible.

- Third, current Commission guidelines and directives in the telecoms sector set broad principles for each country, for example, regulators are to be independent. There is not much detail on what independence actually means, however, and such an approach leaves too much discretion to individual countries. Firmer Commission guidelines will almost certainly be required or the pace of liberalization across Europe will risk being too uneven. These guidelines should focus on ensuring that important specific elements of the competitive environment (licensing, pricing rules, etc.) are dealt with similarly. Equally important are guidelines on regulatory enforcement.

12.2 The institutional framework

This Report is concerned with the question of how to achieve a smooth transition to competition in the EU telecoms sector. Chapters 8 to 11 have documented the current position and the main policy issues to be resolved. In principle, opportunities for entrants and the pace of progress towards competition should be 'uniform' across Europe. There are and will be problems of three general types, however:

- In the market place between incumbents and entrants.
- Between national objectives and EU objectives, the ninth conflicting priority.
- Between regulatory and competition policy objectives, the sixth conflicting priority.

All three are often intertwined. For example, if a dispute in France between an entrant and the incumbent involves trade across intra-EU national boundaries and is not resolved satisfactorily in the view of one of the parties, it can be taken to the Commission, typically to DG IV. In this way, national regulatory disputes can become EU competition policy issues.

Karel Van Miert, the Competition Commissioner is recently quoted as saying:

> If there are still good reasons for complaining or something in the national market is not according to the rules, there will be no doubt that the Commission will be active. From time to time that might lead to conflict with national regulators, that cannot be excluded.[1]

Referral to EU competition policy above national sector-specific regulation, however, may lead to longer term problems of a lack of incentives to invest, an issue that relates to both the first and sixth conflicting priority. The fear is that DG IV may use Article 86 in ways that may be commendable in the pencil market, but which are not advisable in the telecoms market. In other words, the view of DG IV may be on price-cost margins today, not on the incentives to invest in the longer term. The Commission is aware of the problems, however, and has addressed them in its Notice on Access in the telecoms sector. Here the Commission seeks to define the right balance between sector specific regulation and the application of general competition rules. Herbert Ungerer of DG IV has stated in the context of refusal to grant access to telecoms facilities:

> Under Competition Law, in this case Article 86, obligations to supply resulting from a dominant position need very careful examination given the ramifications on the use of company's own investments for its own purposes and on its incentive to invest.[2]

So, relying on EU competition policy today may not be the right long-term solution to regulatory problems in the telecoms industry. Sector-specific regulation is crucial (as New Zealand's experiment with light-handed competition policy suggests), but the question is how to organize sector-specific regulation at the European level. There are several potential solutions to these conflicts. One answer is to create a new Europe-wide regulator. Another option is for NRAs to coordinate themselves and establish a EU-wide code of conduct. Finally, and this is the solution advocated by this Report, existing EU institutions can be reformed with a view to achieving a more uniform and neutral regulatory environment across Europe through strengthened two-tier regulation.

12.2.1 A European telecoms regulator

In 1999, the Commission will review EU telecoms policy, and on the agenda is likely to be the question of more centralized regulation of the sector and the possible establishment of an European Communications Commission, perhaps along lines of the FCC in the United States. As shown in Box 20 on p. 133, there is clearly some support for more centralized regulation in European telecoms. An ECC would solve the conflicts between national and EU regulators and would supplement EU competition policy where needed. In an ideal world, such a European-wide institution would have merit. In reality, however, there are four important constraints on institutional design: information, administration, transaction costs and politics. (Chapter 7 above focuses on some of these constraints.)

All these constraints would weigh heavily on an ECC. How is a European-wide regulator to gather information on incumbent telecoms firms and numerous entrants? How will the ECC share jurisdiction with NRAs since it is unlikely that domestic agencies will be disbanded? Providing jurisdiction to the ECC would require it giving guidance on local service rates in 15 countries. The US regime, where power is shared between national and state regulators, is not a successful one: disputes between the two jurisdictions are many and the history of attempting to define national versus state jurisdiction is one of disaster.[3]

An ECC would likely be large, cumbersome and costly. While it would probably entail a lower cost than the total of 15 separate NRAs, its size and distance from national capitals would add to its unwieldiness. Most importantly, it would be political and there would inevitably be tensions with national governments. Apart from the recently created European Central Bank, there is no history in the EU of independent transnational regulatory agencies. The models for the ECC are the Directorates-General themselves, which are certainly political. The Commission's decisions, be they on competition cases or state aids, are, in the end, political decisions informed by principles.

12.2.2 Self-regulation of national regulators

An alternative to a formal central authority would be greater collaboration among the NRAs. In a sense this would comprise self-regulation. This already exists in the shape of the European Committee for Telecommunications Regulatory Affairs (ECTRA), which offers a forum for regulators and administrators in Europe to discuss issues of interest and to undertake projects or studies which may lead to technical or administrative harmonization. ECTRA also has a limited yet significant scope to propagate 'decisions' requiring each of its members (now exceeding 40) who ratify those decisions to act in a specified manner. In 1994 the Member States agreed to set up and fund an office known as the European Telecommunications Office (ETO) which works exclusively on projects concerning ECTRA. The main activities include establishing a one-stop shop facility for licensing and promoting greater harmonization in areas such as numbering.

The problem with this kind of self-regulation is that it lacks the power to enforce consistency in Europe. Furthermore, some of activities lie outside the jurisdiction of the Commission and therefore accountability may not be sufficiently strong.

12.2.3 Harmonizing national regulators

Rather than highly centralized regulation through an ECC or self-regulation through an affiliation among regulators, a middle approach based on two-tier regulation is likely to be superior. This was discussed in general terms in Chapter 7 above. In practice two-tier regulation has been evident in European telecoms for nearly a decade or so. The upper tier is occupied by the Commission and lower tier comprises NRAs, telecom operators, consumer bodies, manufacturing firms and others. The key players in economic regulation are the Commission and the NRAs. In essence the Commission establishes the framework and principles and the NRAs implement policy.

In most EU countries, the Commission has been instrumental in opening up national communications markets. It has done so via its liberalization powers under Article 90 and its harmonization directives under Article 100(a). Both these powers come from the Commission's role 'ensuring that competition in the internal markets is not distorted'. In its 31 March 1998 Draft Notice on Access, the Commission notes the varying objectives and legal bases of NRAs,[4] and the Commission's present directives already impose minimal standards for regulators and for the interconnection regime. NRAs must be:

- independent;
- transparent;
- given effective resources;
- establishing a set of policies on interconnection, ONP and pricing.

These are minimal areas on which to harmonize the degree of regulation across Europe. The Commission, however, should also impose more detailed criteria for NRAs, including:

- If licences are to be issued, the actual individual licence should be issued by the regulator not the government – so as to make licensing procedures more transparent and independent of political meddling.
- If retail prices are to be determined, these should be set by the regulator not the government – an independent regulator is less likely to be swayed by short-term political considerations.
- Universal service is a valid goal, but regulators not governments should calculate the costs of universal service – so incumbents find it less easy to obstruct liberalization through political lobbying.

Moreover, it is very important that advances are made towards achieving similar degrees of enforcement by NRAs across Europe. Having 'effective resources' is not enough if the implementation of regulation is insufficient. Guaranteeing a level playing field across the EU implies not only setting minimum standards, but also ensuring that these standards are actually enforced. Thus, adequate resources and effective enforcement by regulators is required.

Similarly, as highlighted previously, clear steps should be taken towards the establishment of a broad regulatory framework that:

- encompasses all potential effective players in the industry in a comparable manner across Europe;
- promotes the entry of competitors based on the introduction of new facilities and innovative investment.

The purpose of this recommendation is not to establish uniform regulation across Europe, which would be inappropriate. Countries are at different stages and some like the United Kingdom and Finland are rapidly approaching phase 3 of market structure. Rather, these rules impose uniform requirements at various stages but do not require a warranty to regulate in a specific EU-ordained manner.

Notes

1 AFX News, 19 January 1998.

2 Speech given by Herbert Ungerer, DG IV, to the European Lawyers' Union, Luxembourg, 19 June 1998.

3 See Robert Crandall (1990) *After the Breakup*, Brookings; and Sidak and Spulber (1997).

4 *Op cit.* note 7, Chapter 10.

13 Forward-looking Policies for the European Telecoms Industry

Until recently in most EU countries, the telecoms industry was in phase 1 market structure with a publicly-owned monopoly provider of all services. This was not the end result of a competitive market struggle with the best surviving; it was government imposed. Indeed, a decade ago and even more recently in many European countries, it was illegal to use telephones not supplied by the incumbent. Consumers were told that foreign telephones might harm the network.

Today, no one takes that view seriously and consumers have benefited enormously from the diversity and low cost of a competitive equipment industry. Since 1 January 1998, most government impediments to entry into most other telecoms markets have disappeared. How quickly will other segments of the telecoms industry become competitive? It is very difficult to judge but a number of things are clear:

- First, competition does normally increase the number of offerings and quickens the rate of service introduction.
- Second, monopoly control via a dominant operator or imposed by a regulator can be very costly to society. Hausman (1997) has calculated the social losses in the United States from the regulatory delays of preventing local telecoms firms from offering voice answering services and from delaying the introduction of mobile telephony. The first delay cost society $10 billion, and the latter $100 billion.
- Third, there is enormous innovation occurring in the telecoms sector, and no one can predict the technology or the provider or who will be the lowest cost a decade from now. This innovation is powered by the semi-conductor revolution. The difference between the spread of this new technology in computing and telecoms is enormous. As an example, consider two new technologies, modems for computers and ISDN in telecoms: in the United States, 35% of homes have modems on their computers; in the United Kingdom,

the figure is 15%. Yet few homes, if any, use ISDN lines. In the United Kingdom in 1995, there were only 260,000 ISDN lines operational. In Europe in 1995, there were a total of 1.2 million ISDN lines for business and residential use, for a population of over 300 million population (see Table A-2 in Appendix 2). It is thus likely that a fully competitive regime would increase the spread of new technology in telecoms.

Yet, how is this competition to be fostered? As the above analysis has demonstrated, there are large potential pitfalls in any regulatory regime. Allowing too much discretion to the incumbent could decrease competition, while favouring entrants unduly could distort incentives for innovation and investment. There is no perfect regulatory regime and no error-free process.

The emphasis of this Report is on longer-term competition as being consistent with society's ultimate well-being. Therefore in an ideal world, a regulatory regime should embrace the following principles:

- Transparency and fairness.
- Symmetry in treatment for competitors, where symmetry is defined as 'that regime which does not prevent the low cost supplier from being the low cost provider' (Schankerman and Waverman, 1997).
- A balance between the concern for price-cost margins today and the dynamic evolution of the industry – in other words, a resolution of the first conflicting priority.
- Appropriate powers over all aspects of the sector, including all potential players.
- Minimal political interference with social goals imposed by competitively neutral transparent regimes.

13.1 Objectives

The central objective of the whole process of encouraging longer-term competition is, of course, consumer benefits. Competition allows consumers to benefit from new services, innovation and prices aligned with costs (except for any remaining universal service pricing). The movement of prices towards costs in regimes where competition is the most advanced – the United Kingdom and the United States – is not associated with numbers of subscribers leaving the network. At the same time, policies need to ensure that few are threatened by higher prices.

Entry is essential for competition to flourish. Ultimately, however, consumer benefits derive from appropriate investment and innovation. So, in the longer term, the goal is investment in an innovative infrastructure and provision of the best services. Thus, not only should entry occur, but in fixed telephony at least, what is needed is facilities-based entry. That in turn favours innovative infrastructure so that low cost long-term providers prevail. Moreover, regulation should promote entry in a competitively neutral way that leaves technological choices in the hands of the better informed market participants.

To facilitate desirable investments it is important that shareholders expect to earn a reasonable return. Thus, a balance should be struck in the short term between consumer and shareholder benefits.

13.2 The policy choices

13.2.1 Fostering innovation

The objectives of promoting entry and fostering investment and innovation require a policy framework that leads to facilities-based entry. The goal of this policy choice is to achieve sustainable entry, limiting the harmful effects of 'hit-and-run' strategies. Long-term entry based on the introduction of new facilities will both reduce the high mark-ups of incumbents – and thus benefit consumers in the short term – but also involve long-term commitments with investment in new technologies and infrastructure and provide longer-term dynamic advantages to users.

In practice, this policy choice implies a careful design of interconnection and unbundling policies. In particular, excessive unbundling requirements may not promote the entry of low cost providers into specific industry segments. Rather, it may discourage investment in facilities if the regulatory framework implies a risk of not preserving control of strategic assets in the future competitive industry.

Policies on innovation

1. Derogations from Commission timetables for implementing competition have been agreed for countries with poorer networks. It is a shame this has happened since it would have been better for those countries if they had followed the same timetable as everyone else. Liberalization has proved to be the most effective instrument for

efficient infrastructure development and upgrade. Indeed, Ireland has now opted for a shorter derogation period for this reason.

2. The convergence of technologies between telecoms and broadcasting probably requires a single approach with regard to network regulation (though it is far less clear with respect to content). There would be some merit in creating a single NRA to oversee telecoms and broadcasting, and this is an issue the Commission is likely to examine in its 1999 review of EU telecoms policy.

3. To ensure that there is facilities competition, regulators should be wary of excessive unbundling of the incumbent's facilities. To ensure that entrants can reach sustainable market penetration, it may be valuable to use resale for a limited period of say 3–5 years.[1] In addition, 'co-location', where entrants can co-locate their own switching facilities within the buildings of the incumbent, is a useful tool for encouraging competition. This question is covered in the Commission's Interconnection Directive (Article 11) and is subject to regulatory oversight by the NRAs. It too is likely to be an issue in the 1999 review.

In terms of incumbents' networks, it is important to find a compromise between policies that limit the risk to investment and policies that encourage entry. To build new facilities takes time: no entrant can wire-up major cities across a country quickly. Yet, there are advantages to a larger market presence, and minimal resale obligations allow entrants to build in some locations and rent the incumbent's facilities elsewhere. Since resale is limited in scope and time, it is not a long-term strategy for entrants but can only supplement infrastructure entry. Similarly, equal access to the local loop by entrants has been effective in North America via the policy of permitting entrants to co-locate their facilities at incumbents' exchanges.

4. ONP is of central importance. The fixing of prices for the use of an existing network, however, may be very different from setting the proper process for network evolution. Again, ONP is likely to be an issue in the 1999 review, and it is important that its use for new networks is consistent with fostering correct incentives for innovation.

Existing policies are designed for 'opening' up an incumbent's network. Once this is done, however, what follows? Given the importance of focusing on the longer term, regulation must then switch from supervising entry to encouraging investment. Unfortunately, in most regulatory regimes, the policies that go along with ONP tend to underpay for existing investments.

Regulators and entrants correctly say that prices for interconnection should be based on forward-looking costs. Yet, if entrants were forced into such an ONP regime, they might balk at investing at all.

The crucial test is whether an entrant would accept current regulatory obligations if it were deemed the incumbent. The answer is probably not at present. Yet, since the correct regulatory principle is symmetry of treatment (as defined above), and the correct objective is dynamic efficiency, a proper regulatory regime for the longer term is not asymmetric ONP regulations. Ultimately, the correct long-term regime is simply economy wide competition policy. The next step in that direction could be lighter handed regulation.

13.2.2 Preventing anti-competitive behaviour and creating incentives for entry

Even though the definition of the bottleneck is evolving rapidly with changing technology, structural policy should ensure that there is no control of essential facilities by a very limited number of competitors. In the long run, this is certainly an issue that can be left to competition policy, but at the current stage of market developments in many countries, it is important to ensure that the incumbent operators do not control the alternative means by which technology is providing access to the final customer (such as cable, mobile, boxes for digital TV, etc.).

It is very important that the regulatory framework takes a broad forward-looking view of the industry, bringing into the same regulatory umbrella the whole set of activities and agents that may compete and cooperate in a world of converging industries. Competition rules will have an increasing role to play in the industry. With some exceptions, this could be the best way to guarantee overall welfare in the long run, but the complexity of the issues and the informational resource advantages enjoyed by incumbents create an anomalous situation that requires the transitory existence of specific regulatory institutions to provide an effective counterweight to the power of incumbents.

This does not mean that competition policy has no role at the current stage of development of the market. Since specific regulatory bodies will still focus on telecoms for some time to come, it is particularly important that competition policy continues to be vigilant, with input into the regulatory process and with careful examination of horizontal mergers and vertical integration, from content origination to delivery to consumers' homes.

Policies on entry

1. Fostering competition with unbalanced rates is unwise since they provide poor investment signals and lead to inefficient entry. It is, therefore, important to rebalance rates as speedily as possible. The Commission indirectly requires rate rebalancing by 2001 through its limitations on how access deficits can be recovered.

2. To ensure fair competition, it is good policy for the NRAs and the Commission to examine the profitability of majority state-owned telecoms firms to ensure that adequate returns are being earned. Where returns are below private-sector standards, the Commission should analyse whether these low returns constitute state aid in contravention of EU regulations. As the Commission requires, NRAs must be independent of the incumbent and ownership interests, being more vigilant when the incumbent is state owned and enforcing stringent accounting and reporting to ensure that prices fully reflect costs. Predation (pricing below relevant costs) is not a major force in most industries, but state-owned enterprises do meet the theoretical criteria for when predation may be a strategy for the incumbent.

3. It makes sense to involve the national competition authority early on since the NRA for telecoms may not have adequate expertise in competition issues. For example, a sector-specific NRA may not be sufficiently aware of competition policy issues to examine tacit or overt collusion and the NRA may inadvertently increase the risk of collusion by choosing various forms of interconnection pricing.

   A strong interaction between the telecoms regulator and the national competition authority fulfils a number of objectives. First, it ensures that the former's decisions are consistent with competition policy. Second, the competition authority will develop communications sector expertise, which is crucial to the overall ambition of moving from sector-specific regulation in phases 1 and 2 market structure to broad-based competition policy controls in phase 3.

   Competition policy at the beginning of liberalization of telecoms or any former monopoly sector is not sufficient. A general competition authority has insufficient expertise or abilities to examine complex interconnection issues. A mandatory non-discriminatory interconnection regime and/or an industry-wide technical standard regime is required. Sector-specific regulation is needed at the beginning of liberalization, though not at its end.

4. The move towards open auction mechanisms to allocate new licences/spectrum is to be welcomed since it allows a more effective use of signals. This does not necessarily mean that spectrum should be auctioned for the highest prices: the regulator can establish criteria and multiple objectives, not simply price, but must use a transparent market mechanism to compare the bids.

13.2.3 Ensuring that services are widely distributed across society

Old notions of universal service obligations should be discarded in the new era of telecoms. The evidence shows that rising incomes, technological change and the introduction of competition have been the most effective promoters of widespread telephone access. Any political decisions that attempt to promote the use of telecoms applications (for example, access to the internet) to educational centres should therefore be undertaken as part of general education and social policy. Certainly, the telecoms industry should not finance this type of transfer.

Policies on universal service

1. Before expanding or continuing universal service subsidies, it is important to evaluate the extent to which the goals of universal service are being achieved by the markets. As part of its 1999 review of EU telecoms policy, the Commission should re-examine the financing part of its universal service policy and that part of the recommendation comprising universal service obligations on interconnection prices should be abandoned.

2. Most universal service objectives for the telecoms market correspond to education, health and other policy goals. Valid social objectives should, however, probably not be met by taxing telecoms but instead financed through general tax revenues. This is not to say that universal service is not a valid objective. Rather, promoting an efficient and innovative information infrastructure, which is open to all, is probably not a policy objective best met by taxing telecoms users: first, convergence means that taxing telecoms for internet access over cable modems is bad public policy; and second, internet access to every school is education not telecoms policy and all citizens not users should pay for that.

13.2.4 Balancing subsidiarity, diversity and the achievement of a single market

A final significant policy issue is the role of the Commission relative to that of national governments and NRAs. A central principle of the EU is subsidiarity, in essence a presumption that decisions should be taken at the most decentralized level of government possible, whether that is local, regional or national. What implications does that have for the appropriate regulation of the telecoms industry and the pursuit of long-term competition?

Policies on regulatory authority

1. Different national traditions explain the very distinct approaches adopted by different EU members to telecoms regulation. Nevertheless, it seems clear that in many countries, too much authority is still held by governments rather than NRAs. This should be discouraged and more decision-making power given to the NRAs. For example, if prices are regulated, this should be done by the NRA not the government. Similarly, all major market conditions should be examined, if required, by the NRA not the government.

2. A number of governments have not yet implemented all Commission directives related to the telecoms sector. Clearly, in order to ensure comparable treatment across the EU, they must.

3. Finally, it is important to achieve similar levels of regulatory enforcement across the EU. Lax enforcement will lead to suggestions for a European-wide regulator, an option for regulating the industry that is inappropriate in the light of the analysis above. Hence, as far as different national traditions allow, NRAs' powers and degrees of enforcement should be made more consistent across Europe. At the same time, the EU should tighten its constraints on the powers and role of NRAs. A strengthening of the current two-tier system of regulation is therefore needed.

Note

1 A similar policy has been used in Canada.

Appendix 1: Laws, Procedures and Objectives

Community laws and procedures in relation to competition

- **Legal basis:** Competition rules are set out in Articles 37 and 85–94 of the Treaty on European Union and Articles 4 and 65–7 of the European Coal and Steel Community Treaty.
- **Role of the European Parliament:** the European Parliament assesses the Commission's actions in an annual report and also issues observations on major developments in competition policy.
- **Role of the Council of Ministers:** limited to authorizing block exemptions.
- **Role of the European Commission:** oversees the application of the rules on competition (Articles 85–94), acting either on its own initiative or following complaints by Member States, companies or individuals. Since 1989, it has also been authorized to scrutinize and block large-scale mergers. Legal supervision of the Commission's actions belongs to the ECJ and the Court of First Instance which deal with actions brought against the EU's institutions over competition rules and other issues.

  With limited staff and a heavy case load, the Commission is seeking to make competition policy more effective, transparent and decentralized by encouraging the implementation of Articles 85 and 86 (cartels and dominant position) at a national level.

  DG IV is responsible for competition policy.
- **Procedures:** any agreements that may fall foul of the EC Treaty must be notified in advance to the Commission. In cases arising under Articles 85 and 86, companies may apply for a 'negative clearance', which means that after scrutiny the Commission will not take action, or for an 'exemption' which permits a restrictive agreement on the grounds that it offers substantial public benefits.

  The Commission has wide powers of investigation. Its staff can visit companies without warning to demand access to documents. It holds hearings with the companies concerned to establish the facts of the case before giving its verdict. Where anti-competitive behaviour has been established, the Commission can impose fines of up to 10% of annual turnover.

Companies may appeal against decisions to the Court of Justice, which sometimes reduces fines on appeal. EU competition law takes precedence over national law and is directly applicable in Member States.

Businesses and individuals believing themselves to be victims of infringements of competition rules can bring actions directly before national courts.

- **Community law**: adopted by the Council – or by the Parliament and Council in the framework of the co-decision procedure – may take the following forms:
  - **Regulations**: these are directly applied without the need for national measures to implement them.
  - **Directives**: these bind Member States as to the objectives to be achieved while leaving the national authorities the power to choose the form and the means to be used.
  - **Decisions**: these are binding in all their aspects upon those to whom they are addressed. A decision may be addressed to any or all Member States, to undertakings or to individuals.
  - **Recommendations and opinions**: these are not binding.

The targets and instruments of competition policy

In many instances, competition policy cases are resolved by voluntary policy changes by the countries or companies concerned. In other cases, the Commission finds in favour of the accused or it finds the case proved, and orders policy changes or imposes fines.

- **Cartels**: any collusion between groups of companies to fix prices or control production to the detriment of trade between Member States is outlawed by Article 85 of the Treaty on European Union. Certain kinds of cooperation that are judged to be positive, such as motor vehicle distribution and servicing agreements, are permitted by means of block exemption regulations.
- **Dominant position**: big firms often control very large slices of a market and can use this position to make customers pay higher prices or to squeeze out smaller competitors. Such 'abuses of a dominant position' are outlawed by Article 86 of the EC Treaty and have been applied to deal with behaviour such as unfair and preda-

tory pricing, exclusive sales agreements and discrimination on the grounds of nationality.

- **Mergers and takeovers**: in December 1989, the Council adopted the Merger Control Regulation giving the Commission the power to scrutinize mergers before they are completed to establish whether they will lead to a dominant position. It can block an agreement altogether or require companies to change it or dispose of assets so as to avoid dominant positions. The regulation applies to all mergers where the aggregate worldwide turnover of the companies involved exceeds ECU 5 billion, and ECU 250 million for the individual turnover within the EU of at least two of the companies concerned – unless each undertaking derives more than two-thirds of its EU-wide turnover within one Member State.
- **State aids**: public subsidies that threaten competition in trade between Member States are potentially in conflict with Articles 92–94 of the EC Treaty. In practice, no objections are raised to the majority of state aid cases, which are judged according to the following criteria: whether the aid promotes a development in the interests of the EU as a whole; whether the realization of a project is entirely dependent on aid being available; and whether the type and volume of aid are appropriate for the objectives. In general, permissible aids should be linked to sectoral or regional objectives.
- **Financing state undertakings**: Article 90 requires Member States to respect the competition rules in their policies for public undertakings to which they have granted special or exclusive rights. Member States must disclose their financial dealings with these undertakings and supply the necessary information when requested to do so by the Commission. Directives to strengthen competition in sectors dominated by public undertakings have been issued in the area of telecoms and air transport.

EC Treaty: 'Treaty of Amsterdam amending the Treaty on European Union, the Treaties establishing the European Communities and certain related Acts'

New article numbers, as in the Treaty of Amsterdam signed on 2 October 1997, appear in brackets after existing article number.

Principles

Article 7(d) [16]

Without prejudice to Articles 77, 90 and 92, and given the place occupied by services of general economic interest in the shared values of the Union as well as their role in promoting social and territorial cohesion, the Community and the Member States, each within their respective powers and within the scope of application of this Treaty, shall take care that such services operate on the basis of principles and conditions which enable them to fulfil their missions.

Rules on competition

Rules applying to undertakings

Article 85 [81]

1. The following shall be prohibited as incompatible with the common market: all agreements between undertakings, decisions by associations of undertakings and concerted practices which may affect trade between Member States and which have as their object or effect the prevention, restriction or distortion of competition within the common market, and in particular those which:
   (a) directly or indirectly fix purchase or selling prices or any other trading conditions;
   (b) limit or control production, markets, technical development, or investment;
   (c) share markets or sources of supply;
   (d) apply dissimilar conditions to equivalent transactions with other trading parties, thereby placing them at a competitive disadvantage;
   (e) make the conclusion of contracts subject to acceptance by the other parties of supplementary obligations, which, by their nature or according to commercial usage, have no connection with the subject of such contracts.
2. Any agreements or decisions prohibited pursuant to this Article shall be automatically void.
3. The provisions of paragraph 1 may, however, be declared inapplicable in the case of:

- any agreement or category of agreements between undertakings;
- any decision or category of decisions by associations of undertakings;
- any concerted practice or category of concerted practices;

which contributes to improving the production or distribution of goods or to promoting technical or economic progress, while allowing consumers a fair share of the resulting benefit, and which does not:

(a) impose on the undertakings concerned restrictions, which are not indispensable to the attainment of these objectives;

(b) afford such undertakings the possibility of eliminating competition in respect of a substantial part of the products in question.

Article 86 [82]

Any abuse by one or more undertakings of a dominant position within the common market or in a substantial part of it shall be prohibited as incompatible with the common market in so far as it may affect trade between Member States.

Such abuse may, in particular, consist in:

(a) directly or indirectly imposing unfair purchase or selling prices or other unfair trading conditions;

(b) limiting production, markets or technical development to the prejudice of consumers;

(c) applying dissimilar conditions to equivalent transactions with other trading parties, thereby placing them at a competitive disadvantage;

(d) making the conclusion of contracts subject to acceptance by the other parties of supplementary obligations, which, by their nature or according to commercial usage, have no connection with the subject of such contracts.

Article 90 [86]

1. In the case of public undertakings and undertakings to which Member States grant special or exclusive rights, Member States shall neither enact nor maintain in force any measure contrary to the rules contained in this Treaty, in particular to those rules provided for in Article 6 and Articles 85–94.

2. Undertakings entrusted with the operation of services of general economic interest or having the character of a revenue producing monopoly shall be subject to the rules contained in this Treaty, in particular to the rules on competition, in so far as the application of such rules does not obstruct the performance, in law or in fact, of the particular tasks assigned to them. The development of trade must not be affected to such an extent as would be contrary to the interests of the Community.

3. The Commission shall ensure the application of the provisions of this Article and shall, where necessary, address appropriate directives or decisions to Member States.

Aids granted by States

Article 92 [87]

1. Save as otherwise provided in this Treaty, any aid granted by a Member State or through State resources in any form whatsoever which distorts or threatens to distort competition by favouring certain undertakings or the production of certain goods shall, in so far as it affects trade between Member States, be incompatible with the common market.

2. The following shall be compatible with the common market:
   (a) aid having a social character, granted to individual consumers, provided that such aid is granted without discrimination related to the origin of the products concerned;
   (b) aid to make good the damage caused by natural disasters or exceptional occurrences;
   (c) aid granted to the economy of certain areas of the Federal Republic of Germany affected by the division of Germany, in so far as such aid is required in order to compensate for the economic disadvantages caused by that division.

3. The following may be considered to be compatible with the common market:
   (a) aid to promote the economic development of areas where the standard of living is abnormally low or where there is serious underemployment;
   (b) aid to promote the execution of an important project of common European interest or to remedy a serious disturbance in the economy of a Member State;

(c) aid to facilitate the development of certain economic activities or of certain economic areas, where such aid does not adversely affect trading conditions to an extent contrary to the common interest. However, the aids granted to shipbuilding as of 1 January 1957 shall, in so far as they serve only to compensate for the absence of customs protection, be progressively reduced under the same conditions as apply to the elimination of customs duties, subject to the provisions of this Treaty concerning common commercial policy towards third countries;

(d) aid to promote culture and heritage conservation where such aid does not affect trading conditions and competition in the Community to an extent that is contrary to the common interest;

(e) such other categories of aid as may be specified by decision of the Council acting by a qualified majority on a proposal from the Commission.

Article 93 [88]

1. The Commission shall, in cooperation with Member States, keep under constant review all systems of aid existing in those States. It shall propose to the latter any appropriate measures required by the progressive development or by the functioning of the common market.

2. If, after giving notice to the parties concerned to submit their comments, the Commission finds that aid granted by a State or through State resources is not compatible with the common market having regard to Article 92, or that such aid is being misused, it shall decide that the State concerned shall abolish or alter such aid within a period of time to be determined by the Commission.

   If the State concerned does not comply with this decision within the prescribed time, the Commission or any other interested State may, in derogation from the provisions of Articles 169 and 170, refer the matter to the Court of Justice direct.

   On application by a Member State, the Council may, acting unanimously, decide that aid which that State is granting or intends to grant shall be considered to be compatible with the common market, in derogation from the provisions of Article 92 or from the regulations provided for in Article 94, if such a decision is justified by exceptional circumstances. If, as regards the aid in question, the Commission has already initiated the procedure provided for in the first subparagraph of this paragraph, the fact that the

State concerned has made its application to the Council shall have the effect of suspending that procedure until the Council has made its attitude known.

If, however, the Council has not made its attitude known within three months of the said application being made, the Commission shall give its decision on the case.

3. The Commission shall be informed, in sufficient time to enable it to submit its comments, of any plans to grant or alter aid. If it considers that any such plan is not compatible with the common market having regard to Article 92, it shall without delay initiate the procedure provided for in paragraph 2. The Member State concerned shall not put its proposed measures into effect until this procedure has resulted in a final decision.

Article 94 [89]

The Council, acting by a qualified majority on a proposal from the Commission and after consulting the European Parliament, may make any appropriate regulations for the application of Articles 92 and 93 and may in particular determine the conditions in which Article 93(3) shall apply and the categories of aid exempted from this procedure.

Approximation of laws

Article 100(a) [95]

1. By way of derogation from Article 100 and save where otherwise provided in this Treaty, the following provisions shall apply for the achievement of the objectives set out in Article 7(a). The Council shall, acting in accordance with the procedure referred to in Article 189(b) and after consulting the Economic and Social Committee, adopt the measures for the approximation of the provisions laid down by law, regulation or administrative action in Member States which have as their object the establishment and functioning of the internal market.

2. Paragraph 1 shall not apply to fiscal provisions, to those relating to the free movement of persons nor to those relating to the rights and interests of employed persons.

3. The Commission, in its proposals envisaged in paragraph 1 concerning health, safety, environmental protection and consumer protection, will take as a base a high level of protection, taking account in particular of any new development based on scientific

facts. Within their respective powers, the European Parliament and the Council will also seek to achieve this objective.

4. If, after the adoption by the Council or by the Commission of a harmonization measure, a Member State deems it necessary to maintain national provisions on grounds of major needs referred to in Article 36, or relating to the protection of the environment or the working environment, it shall notify the Commission of these provisions as well as the grounds for maintaining them.

   The Commission shall confirm the provisions involved after having verified that they are not a means of arbitrary discrimination or a disguised restriction on trade between Member States.

   By way of derogation from the procedure laid down in Articles 169 and 170, the Commission or any Member State may bring the matter directly before the Court of Justice if it considers that another Member State is making improper use of the powers provided for in this Article.

5. Moreover, without prejudice to paragraph 4, if, after the adoption by the Council or by the Commission of a harmonization measure, a Member State deems it necessary to introduce national provisions based on new scientific evidence relating to the protection of the environment or the working environment on grounds of a problem specific to that Member State arising after the adoption of the harmonization measure, it shall notify the Commission of the envisaged provisions as well as the grounds for introducing them.

6. The Commission shall, within six months of the notifications as referred to in paragraphs 4 and 5, approve or reject the national provisions involved after having verified whether or not they are a means of arbitrary discrimination or a disguised restriction on trade between Member States and whether or not they shall constitute an obstacle to the functioning of the internal market.

Trans-European Networks

Article 129(b) [154]

1. To help achieve the objectives referred to in Articles 7(a) and 130(a) and to enable citizens of the Union, economic operators and regional and local communities to derive full benefit from the setting up of an area without internal frontiers, the Community shall contribute to the establishment and development of trans European networks in the areas of transport, telecoms and energy infrastructures.

2. Within the framework of a system of open and competitive markets, action by the Community shall aim at promoting the interconnection and interoperability of national networks as well as access to such networks. It shall take account in particular of the need to link island, landlocked and peripheral regions with the central regions of the Community.

Article 129(c) [155]

1. In order to achieve the objectives referred to in Article 129(b), the Community:
   - shall establish a series of guidelines covering the objectives, priorities and broad lines of measures envisaged in the sphere of trans-European networks; these guidelines shall identify projects of common interest;
   - shall implement any measures that may prove necessary to ensure the interoperability of the networks, in particular in the field of technical standardization;
   - may support projects of common interest supported by Member States, which are identified in the framework of the guidelines referred to in the first indent, particularly through feasibility studies, loan guarantees or interest-rate subsidies; the Community may also contribute, through the Cohesion Fund set up pursuant to Article 130(d), to the financing of specific projects in Member States in the area of transport infrastructure.

   The Community's activities shall take into account the potential economic viability of the projects.
2. Member States shall, in liaison with the Commission, coordinate among themselves the policies pursued at national level which may have a significant impact on the achievement of the objectives referred to in Article 129(b). The Commission may, in close cooperation with the Member State, take any useful initiative to promote such coordination.
3. The Community may decide to cooperate with third countries to promote projects of mutual interest and to ensure the interoperability of networks.

Article 129(d) [156]

The guidelines referred to in Article 129(c)(1) shall be adopted by the Council, acting in accordance with the procedure referred to in Article

189(b) and after consulting the Economic and Social Committee and the Committee of the Regions.

Guidelines and projects of common interest which relate to the territory of a Member State shall require the approval of the Member State concerned.

The Council acting in accordance with the procedure referred to in Article 189(b) and after consulting the Economic and Social Committee and the Committee of the Regions, shall adopt the other measures provided for in Article 129(c)(1).

Industry

Article 130 [157]

1. The Community and the Member States shall ensure that the conditions necessary for the competitiveness of the Community's industry exist.

   For that purpose, in accordance with a system of open and competitive markets, their action shall be aimed at:
   - speeding up the adjustment of industry to structural changes;
   - encouraging an environment favourable to initiative and to the development of undertakings throughout the Community, particularly small and medium-sized undertakings;
   - encouraging an environment favourable to cooperation between undertakings;
   - fostering better exploitation of the industrial potential of policies of innovation, research and technological development.

2. The Member States shall consult each other in liaison with the Commission and, where necessary, shall coordinate their action. The Commission may take any useful initiative to promote such coordination.

3. The Community shall contribute to the achievement of the objectives set out in paragraph 1 through the policies and activities it pursues under other provisions of this Treaty. The Council, acting unanimously on a proposal from the Commission, after consulting the European Parliament and the Economic and Social Committee, may decide on specific measures in support of action taken in the Member States to achieve the objectives set out in paragraph 1.

   This Title shall not provide a basis for the introduction by the Community of any measure which could lead to a distortion of competition.

Appendix 2: Data on the Telecoms Industry

Table A–1 Penetration rates

	Main lines per capita			Mobile phones, number	
	1985	1990	1995	1990	1995
Austria	36.1	41.8	46.6	73 700	366 919
Belgium	31.0	39.3	45.6	42 800	235 000
Denmark	49.7	56.6	61.3	148 220	822 370
Finland	44.7	53.5	55.0	258 000	1 017 596
France	41.7	49.5	56.3	287 056	1 302 400
Germany	41.9	47.4	49.5	430 000	3 750 000
Greece	31.4	39.1	49.4	0	280 000
Netherlands	40.2	46.4	51.8	79 000	462 400
Ireland	19.9	28.1	36.7	26 502*	132 183
Italy	30.5	39.4	43.4	416 000	3 863 374
Luxembourg	42.0	48.1	55.8	758	26 868
Portugal	14.0	24.1	36.1	6 461	340 845
Spain	24.3	32.4	38.5	54 700	928 955
Sweden	62.8	68.3	68.1	483 200	2 008 000
United Kingdom	37.0	44.2	50.2	1 140 000	5 670 000

* Data for Ireland are for the calendar, not fiscal, year end.

Table A–2 Some country data on European telecommunications

	Digitalization 1995	Fibre optic cable (km) 1995	Internet hosts 1997	ISDN subscribers 1995	Cable TV subscribers 1995
Austria	72.00	92 320	11.43	16 813	1 003.0
Belgium	66.00	n.a.	6.37	26 286	3 629.0
Denmark	61.00	n.a.	20.37	14 082	1 383.0
Finland	89.80	61.1	55.51	6 416	826.9
France	100.00	n.a.	4.22	n.a.	1 496.5
Germany	56.00	12.1	8.84	961 610	15 808.0
Greece	35.32	60.0	1.52	0	0.0[1]
Netherlands	100.00	n.a.	17.50	23 700	5 700.0
Ireland	79.00	14.1	7.56	2 267	476.0
Italy	75.60	21.4	2.61	49 061	0.0
Luxembourg	100.00	n.a.	8.49	1 656	170.0
Portugal	70.00	196.3	2.63	7 891	58.7
Spain	56.00	20.4	2.81	28 012	142.0
Sweden	91.00	n.a.	26.39	19 700	1 900.0
United Kingdom	87.70	10.3	10.09	260 000	1 419.9

[1] Service is yet to commence in Greece, but OTE has the exclusive rights to install cable TV infrastructure and shares the exclusive rights to service provision with national Radiotelevision S.A. (ERT, S.A.)

Table A–3 Cable TV in Europe

	Incumbent telecoms operator's provision of cable infra.	Cable companies provision of switched telephony	Incumbent telecoms operator's share of cable subscribers (%)
		services	
Austria	No	No	No	0.0
Belgium	No	No	No	0.0
Denmark	Yes	Yes	Yes	49.9
Finland	Yes	Yes	Yes	94.7
France	Yes	Yes	No	56.7
Germany	Yes	Yes	No	90 +
Greece	Yes	Yes	No	–
Netherlands	Yes	Yes	No	20.7
Ireland	Yes	Yes	No	0.0
Italy	No	No	No	–
Luxembourg	No	No	No	–
Portugal	Yes	Yes	No	98.3
Spain	n. a.	No	No	–
Sweden	Yes	Yes	Yes	61.0
United Kingdom	Yes	Yes	Yes	7.1

Table A–4 Fixed telephony: average revenue per subscriber, annual (US dollars)

	Business		Residential	
	Fixed charge	Usage charge	Fixed charge	Usage charge
Austria	222.22	1 638.41	771.52	549.30
Belgium	210.85	837.29	564.21	309.09
Denmark	214.99	464.85	449.11	180.37
Finland	211.02	316.66	421.04	144.60
France	101.36	896.48	460.82	338.58
Germany	182.53	1 075.49	562.14	352.23
Greece	147.67	913.28	554.35	380.10
Netherlands	197.57	450.10	397.47	165.32
Ireland	230.77	970.47	613.47	334.24
Italy	151.26	1 058.68	467.48	334.82
Luxembourg	n. a.	n. a.	n. a.	n. a.
Portugal	155.32	1 196.80	581.13	399.41
Spain	153.60	1 057.04	539.27	361.09
Sweden	265.77	354.67	364.30	149.83
United Kingdom	246.81	597.62	389.82	196.78

Table A–5 Mobile telephony: average revenue per subscriber, annual (US dollars)

	Fixed	*Usage*
Austria	382.86	752.94
Belgium	402.28	746.07
Denmark	109.21	426.22
Finland	143.74	491.12
France	911.11	1 113.91
Germany	323.21	875.10
Greece	n. a.	n. a.
Netherlands	295.58	815.90
Ireland	402.92	669.60
Italy	424.52	700.55
Luxembourg	595.20	894.16
Portugal	596.12	1 066.38
Spain	458.67	793.30
Sweden	148.90	664.53
United Kingdom	534.91	767.45

Appendix 3: Charts on the Telecoms Industry

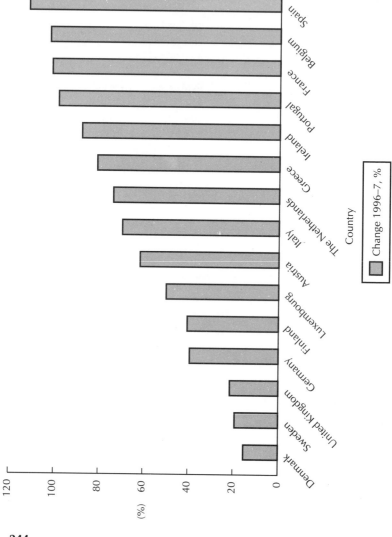

Figure A–1 Cellular growth in subscriber numbers

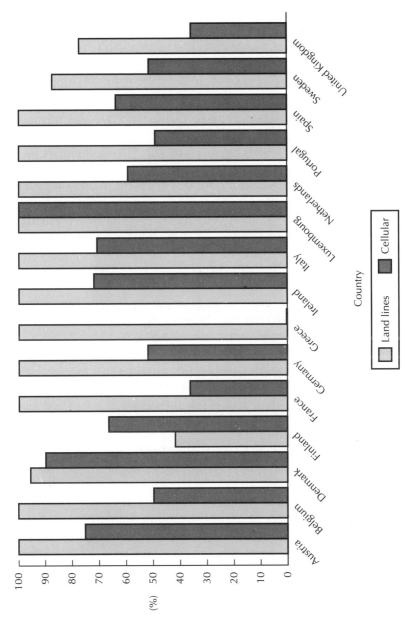

Figure A–2 Share of incumbent (%) in 1995

Bibliography

Adams, G. (1981) *The Politics of Defense Contracting – The Iron Triangle*, News Brunswick: Transaction Books.

Armstrong, M. (1998) 'Network Interconnection in Telecommunications', *Economic Journal* 108, May 1998, pp. 545–64.

Armstrong, M., S. Cowan, and J. Vickers (1994) *Regulatory Reform: Economic Analysis and British Experience*, Cambridge: MIT Press.

Armstrong, M., C. Doyle, and J. Vickers (1996) 'The Access Pricing Problem: A Synthesis', *Journal of Industrial Economics* XLIV(2), pp. 131–50.

Aschauer, D.A. (1989) 'Is Public Expenditure Productive?' *Journal of Monetary Economics* 23(2), March 1989, pp. 177–200.

Averch, H. and L.L. Johnston (1962) 'Behavior of the Firm under Regulatory Constraint', *American Economic Review* 52, pp. 1052–69.

Baumol, W. (1983) 'Some Subtle Issues in Railroad Deregulation', *International Journal of Transport Economics* 10, pp. 341–55.

Baumol, W. and J.G. Sidak (1994a) 'The Pricing of Inputs Sold to Competitors', *Yale Journal on Regulation* 11(1), pp. 171–202.

Baumol, W. and J.G. Sidak (1994b) *Toward Competition in Local Telephony*, AEI Studies in Telecommunications Deregulation, Cambridge, Mass: MIT Press.

Baumol, W., J.C. Panzar, and R.D. Willig (1982) *Contestable Markets and the Theory of Industrial Structure*, New York: Harcourt Brace, Jovanovich.

Besen, S.M. and J. Farrell (1994) 'Choosing How to Compete: Strategies and Tactics in Standardization', *Journal of Economic Perspectives* 8(2), Spring, pp. 117–31.

Brown, S.J. and D.S. Sibley (1986) *The Theory of Public Utility Pricing*, Cambridge: Cambridge University Press.

Cabral, L.M.B. and M.H. Riordan (1989) 'Incentives for Cost Reduction under Price Cap Regulation', *Journal of Regulatory Economics* 1(2), June 1989, pp. 93–102.

Caillaud, B., B. Julien and P. Picard (1996) 'National vs European Incentive Policies: Bargaining, Information and Coordination', *European Economic Review* 40, pp. 91–111.

Cave, M. and C. Doyle, (1994) 'Access Pricing in Network Utilities: Theory and Practice', *Utilities Policy* 4, (3), 181–9.

Department of Trade and Industry (1998) 'A Fair Deal for Consumers', Green Paper, March 1998, London.

Doyle, C. (1996) 'Effective Sectoral Regulation: Telecommunications in the EU', *Journal of European Public Policy* 3(4), December 1996, pp. 612–28.

Economides, N. (1996) 'Network Externalities, Complementarities, and Invitations to Enter', *European Journal of Political Economy* 12(2), September 1996, pp. 211–33..

Economides, N. and F. Flyer (1997) 'Compatibility and Market Structure for Network Goods', Stern Graduate School of Business working paper, New York University.

Economides, N., G. Lopomo, and G. Woroch (1996) 'Strategic commitments and the Principle of Reciprocity in Internconnection Pricing', Stern School of Business, New York University, downloadable from http://edgar.stern.nyu.edu/networks/.

European Commission (1997) Green Paper 'On the Convergence of the Telecommunications, Media and Information Technology Sectors, and the Implications for Regulation, Towards an information society approach', COM (97) 623, Brussels, December.

Galal, A., L. Jones, P. Tandon and I. Vogelsang (1994) *Welfare Consequences of Selling Public Enterprises: an Empirical Analysis*, Oxford: Oxford University Press.

Good, R., L.-H. Röller, and R.C. Sickles (1993) 'U.S. Airline Deregulation: Implications for European Transport', *Economic Journal* 103, July 1993, pp. 1028–41.

Green, R.G. and D. Newbery (1992) 'Competition in the British Electricity Spot Market', *Journal of Political Economy* 100(5), pp. 929–53.

Greenstein, S. M., and P. T. Spiller (1995) 'Modern Telecommunications Infrastructure and Economic Activity: An Empirical Investigation', *Industrial and Corporate Change* 4(4), pp. 647–65.

Grieve, W. and S.L. Levin (1998) 'Telecom Competition in Canada and the US: The Tortoise and the Hare', Revised version of paper presented to the Telecommunications Policy Research Conference, Alexandria VA, September 27–9, 1997.

Grout, P.A. (1996) 'Promoting the Superhighway: Telecommunications Regulation in Europe', *Economic Policy* 22, April 1996, 109–54.

Haring, J. and J.H. Rohlfs (1997) 'Efficient Competition in Local Telecommunications without Excessive Regulation', *Information Economics and Policy* 9, pp. 119–31.

Harris, R.G. and C.J. Kraft (1997) 'Meddling through: Regulating Local Telephone Competition in the United States', *The Journal of Economic Perspectives* 11(4).

Hausman, J. (1997) 'Taxation by Telecommunications Regulation', mimeo, MIT Press.

Helm, D. and T. Jenkinson (eds.) (1998) *Competition in Regulated Industries*, Oxford: Oxford University Press.

Hulten, C.R. and R.M. Schwab (1984) 'Regional Productivity Growth in US Manufacturing: 1951–78', *American Economic Review* 74(1), March 1984, pp. 152–62.

Hulten, C.R. and R.M. Schwab (1991) 'Public Capital Formation and the Growth of Regional Manufacturing Industries', *National Tax Journal* 44(4), Part 1, December, pp. 121–34.

Isaksson, B. (1998) 'Enhanced Services, Reciprocity and Local Loop Access Charges', School of Transportation and Society, Dalarna University, Working Paper, forthcoming.

Joskow, P. (1996) 'Does Stranded Recovery Distort Competition?' *The Electricity Journal* 9, pp. 31–45.

Kahn, A. and W. Taylor (1994) 'The Pricing of Inputs Sold to Competitors: A Comment', *Yale Journal on Regulation* 11, pp. 225–40.

Krugman, P. (1990) 'Increasing Returns and Economic Geography', National Bureau of Economic Research Working Paper 3275, March.

Laffont J-J.and J. Tirole (1993) *A Theory of Incentives in Procurement and Regulation*, Cambridge, Mass: MIT Press.

Laffont J-J.and J. Tirole (1994) 'Access Pricing and Competition', *European Economic Review* 38, pp. 1673–710.

Laffont, J-J. and J. Tirole (1996) 'Creating Competition through Interconnection: Theory and Practice', *Journal of Regulatory Economics* 10(3), pp. 227–56.

Laffont, J-J., P. Rey and J. Tirole (1998), 'Network Competition: I. Overview and non-discriminatory pricing', *Rand Journal of Economics*, forthcoming.

Laffont, J-J. and J. Tirole (1998) *Competition in Telecommunications*, forthcoming MIT Press.

Levy, P.T. and B. Spiller (1994) 'The Institutional Foundations of Regulatory Commitment: A Comparative Analysis of Telecommunications Regulation', *Journal of Law, Economics and Organization* 10(2), pp. 201–46.

Lichtenberg, F.R. (1995) 'The Output Contributions of Computer Equipment and Personnel: A Firm-Level Analysis', *Economics of Innovation and New Technology* 3(3–4), pp. 201–17.

Majone, G. (ed.) (1996) *Regulating Europe*, London: Routledge.

Mayer, C. and J. Vickers (1996) 'Profit-Sharing Regulation: An Economic Appraisal', *Fiscal Studies* 17(1), pp. 1–18.

Musgrave, R.A. (1959) *The Theory of Public Finance*, New York: McGraw-Hill.

North, D.C. (1990) *Institutions, Institutional Change and Economic Performance*, Cambridge: Cambridge University Press.

OECD (1997a) *The OECD Report on Regulatory Reform, Paris*: OECD.

OECD (1997b) *Global information infrastructure – Global information society: Policy Requirements*, Committee for Information Computers and Communications Policy, Paris: OECD.

OECD (1997c) *Webcasting and Convergence: Policy Implications*, Committee for Information Computers and Communications Policy, Paris: OECD.

Privy Council (1994) *Judgement of the Lords of the Judicial Committee of the Privy Council*, 19 October.

Röller. L.-H. and L. Waverman (1998) 'Telecommunications Infrastructure and Economic Development: A Simultaneous Approach', mimeo.

Sappington, D.E.M. (1994) 'Designing Incentive Regulation', *Review of Industrial Organization* 9, pp. 245–72.

Schankerman M. and L. Waverman (1997) 'Asymmetric Regulation for Multi-media Markets', London Business School Working Paper.

Sidak, J.G. and D.F. Spulber (1997) *Deregulatory Takings and the Regulatory Contract: The Competitive Transformation of Network Industries in the United States*, Cambridge: Cambridge University Press.

Sutton, J. (1991) *Sunk Costs and Market Structure*, Cambridge, Mass.: MIT Press.

Vogel, D. (1995) *Trading Up: Consumer and Environmental Regulation in a Global Economy*, Cambridge, Mass.: Harvard University Press.

Vogelsang, I. and J. Finsinger (1979) 'A Regulatory Adjustment Process for Optimal Pricing by Multiproduct Monopoly Firms', *Bell Journal of Economics* 10, pp. 157–71.

Waverman, L. (1998) 'The Political Economy of International Telecommunications', AEI, Washington.

Waverman, L. and E. Sirel (1997) 'European Telecommunications Markets on the Verge of Full Liberalization', *The Journal of Economic Perspectives* 11 (4), Fall.

Williamson, O. (1985) *The Economic Institutions of Capitalism: Firms, Markets, and Relational Contracting*, New York: Free Press.

Willig, R. (1979) 'The Theory of Network Access Pricing' in H.M. Trebing (ed.) *Issues in Public Utility Regulation*, Michigan State University Public Utilities Papers.

Winston, C. (1993) 'Economic Deregulation: Days of Reckoning for Microeconomists', *Journal of Economic Literature* 31, pp. 1263–89.

Index

access, regulation of 103–15
  accounting approach to
    112–13
  efficient component pricing
    rule (ECPR) 106–9
  global price-caps 111–12
  Ramsey access prices 109–11
  two-way interconnection 115
  and unbundling 113–14
  vertical integration 106
  vertical separation and 105–6
access pricing
  accounting approach to 112–13
  ECPR 106–9
  of network industries 24–7
Air France: state aid to 60
air transport, liberalization of
    53–61, 77
  degree of 80
  ground handling problems 56
  market imperfections 57
  third package 54
airline computer reservation
    systems 23
alliances in telecommunications
    industry 181
Amsterdam, Treaty of 231–9
anti-competitive behaviour in
    telecommunications
    industry 225–7
Armstrong, M. 186
Aschauer, D.A. 16
Athens airport: ground handling
    problems 56

Averch, H. 97
Averich–Johnson (AJ) effect on
    prices 97

cable television
  European comparisons 241, 242
  prices of 242
  market boundaries, changes
    145–6
capital investment 19
cellular telephony see mobile
    telephony
centralized regulation 45–6
colocation as interconnection
    issue 191–201
common energy policy 72–3
common transport policy 65
community policy affecting
    network industries 53
competition 3
  American approach to 180
  benefits of 176
  community laws on 229–30
  EC treaty articles on 50
  effective, obstacles to 176–80
  facilities-based 14, 15
  in France 179
  in Germany 178
  and liberalization 4–6
  and market structure 6–8
  and monopoly in deregulation
    36–9
  policy, targets and instruments
    230–1

251